Children of Globalization

Children of Globalization is the first book-length exploration of contemporary Diasporic Coming-of-age Novels in the context of globalized and de facto multicultural societies. Diasporic Coming-of-age Novels subvert the horizon of expectations of the originating and archetypal form of the genre, the traditional *Bildungsroman*, which encompasses the works of Johann Wolfgang von Goethe, Charles Dickens, and Jane Austen, and illustrates middle-class, European, "enlightened," and overwhelmingly male protagonists who become accommodated citizens, workers, and spouses whom the readers should imitate. Conversely, Diasporic Coming-of-age Novels have manifold ways of defining youth and adulthood. The culturally-hybrid protagonists, often experiencing intersectional oppression due to their identities of race, gender, class, or sexuality, must negotiate what it means to become adults in their own families and social contexts, at times being undocumented or otherwise unable to access full citizenship, thus enabling complex and variegated formative processes that beg the questions of nationhood and belonging in increasingly globalized societies worldwide.

Ricardo Quintana-Vallejo was born in Mexico City. He holds a Ph.D. in Comparative Literature from Purdue University and has been a Lynn and Fulbright Fellow. Recent publications include "Geografía humana de la colonia Roma," "Germanness Redefined in the Poetry of Zafer Şenocak and Zehra Çirak," and, in the forthcoming book *Memory in German Romanticism*, "The Forgotten Poet in Heinrich Heine's Late Poetry." He is a postdoctoral scholar in the Centro de Estudios sobre América del Norte—CISAN at the National Autonomous University of Mexico—UNAM.

Routledge Studies in Comparative Literature

This series is our home for cutting-edge, upper-level scholarly studies and edited collections. Taking a comparative approach to literary studies, this series visits the relationship of literature and language alongside a variety of interdisciplinary and transnational topics. Titles are characterized by dynamic interventions into established subjects and innovative studies on emerging topics.

The Limits of Cosmopolitanism
Globalization and Its Discontents in Contemporary Literature
Aleksandar Stević and Philip Tsang

Romantic Legacies
Transnational and Transdisciplinary Contexts
Shun-liang Chao and John Michael Corrigan

Spanish Vampire Fiction since 1900
Blood Relations
Abigail Lee Six

Holocaust Narratives
Trauma, Memory and Identity Across Generations
Thorsten Wilhelm

Translingual Francophonie and the Limits of Translation
Ioanna Chatzidimitriou

Beyond Collective Memory
Structural Complicity and Future Freedoms in Senegalese and
South African Narratives
Cullen Goldblatt

Children of Globalization
Diasporic Coming-of-Age Novels in Germany, England, and the
United States
Ricardo Quintana-Vallejo

To learn more about this series, please visit https://www.routledge.com/
literature/series/RSCOL

Children of Globalization

Diasporic Coming-of-Age Novels in Germany, England, and the United States

Ricardo Quintana-Vallejo

Routledge
Taylor & Francis Group

NEW YORK AND LONDON

First published 2021
by Routledge
52 Vanderbilt Avenue, New York, NY 10017

and by Routledge
2 Park Square, Milton Park, Abingdon, Oxon OX14 4RN

Routledge is an imprint of the Taylor & Francis Group, an informa business

Library of Congress Cataloging-in-Publication Data
A catalog record for this title has been requested

ISBN: 978-0-367-52834-8 (hbk)
ISBN: 978-1-003-05857-1 (ebk)

Typeset in Sabon
by Taylor & Francis Books

For my diasporic family.
For my husband.
For my mother.

Contents

Acknowledgements

The heart of this book is the close readings of coming-of-age novels that grew out of my work in undergraduate and graduate research. Although I have read and loved coming-of-age novels since I was a little boy, I owe to my brilliant and patient mentors and teachers the theories of identity and ideology that systematized my worldview and shaped my critical approach to literature. I am indebted particularly to the comments, insights, and kindness of Angelica Duran. I am also indebted to the generous readers of this and earlier versions of the book, both at Purdue University and the National Autonomous University of Mexico, Al Lopez, Beate Allert, Charlie Ross, Cara Kinnally, Marcia Stephenson, Wes Bishop, Valentina Concu, Nattie Golubov, Aurora Piñeiro, Claudia Lucotti, Noemi Novell, Rocío Saucedo, Guadalupe Niembro, Raúl Bravo Aduna, and Juan Carlos Rodríguez. My deepest debt of gratitude is for my students of literature and languages whose attention, curiosity, and excitement have brightened my days and enabled me to test and re-evaluate my assumptions.

Research for this book was carried out with the support of funding from a Lynn Fellowship from the Purdue University Graduate School, a Research Grant from Fulbright-Garcia Robles, an International Student Scholarship from the Consejo Nacional de Ciencia y Tecnología, a Summer Grant from the Purdue Research Foundation, and three Promise Travel Awards from Purdue University's School of Interdisciplinary Studies.

This book would not exist without the beautiful works of the displaced, marginalized, and queer authors that have bravely and painfully bared their souls for others to read. They wrote, to paraphrase R. W. Emerson, the books that made me: Chimamanda Adichie, Gloria Anzaldúa, Reinaldo Arenas, Sandra Cisneros, John Green, E. M. Forster, Wolfgang Herrndorf, Yadé Kara, Hanif Kureishi, Madeline Miller, Toni Morrison, Viet Thanh Nguyen, Gabby Rivera, Arundhati Roy, Zadie Smith, and Ocean Vuong. Thank you for letting me stand on your shoulders and see further. Thanks to my colleagues in Purdue University. I give my love to my husband, as also to my mother, and to all those who have guided and supported me.

Introduction: Diasporic Coming-of-age Novels

Accio Harry Potter

Like many readers of my generation, I first came across the coming-of-age genre when *Harry Potter and The Philosopher's Stone* (1997) made its way to my hands in 2000.[1] I was eleven, the same age Harry was when Rubeus Hagrid stormed through the door in a far off rock at the sea with a sat-on-home-baked cake—"A large, sticky chocolate cake with Happy Birthday Harry written on it in green icing" (Rowling 1998, 48)—to set Harry's formative process in motion. The cake imprinted on Harry's memory, mine, and many of J. K. Rowling's readers across the globe. Harry's formative process in a completely new environment of magic overlapped with mine, with my desire to escape our shared histories of abuse, to conquer material and abstract evils.[2] I read it in English when I grew up in the metropolis of Mexico City. The British Isles seemed as far-off a place and as magical as Hogwarts must have been to Harry. *Harry Potter* nonetheless, addressed my questions about the world—my untheorized world—and its pains in ways that were keenly relevant to my young imagination.

Harry Potter is simply a recent entry in the genre of coming-of-age novels that have captured the hearts and minds of various generations. This always-rejuvenating genre often strives to teach readers to understand their current and past feelings, processes of becoming and belonging, and in its most traditional iteration, what it means to be a model "citizen and worker" (Buckley 1974, 18). Coming-of-age novels are relevant to young readers because they show how characters experiment with identity and inspire their journeys into adulthood. Although the protagonists' formative processes are at the forefront, readers of coming-of-age novels often affiliate with the parallel formative processes of minor characters like Ron Weasley and Hermione Granger—and even of antagonists like Draco Malfoy. Harry tries imitating different older models; he fails and tries again. His mistakes lead him to a path of self-discovery whereby he forges his own self in an ever-changing world. This is not to imply that characters are self- or subject-less before they undergo formative processes, but rather to assert that selfhood is constantly forming and becoming. Coming-of-age novels enable readers to trace this process as it is developing, sometimes, and particularly in traditional *Bildungsromane*, to a great degree of accomplishment. When presented with the choice of the social milieus available to him, Harry decides to fraternize with the aloof and noble Ron rather than the cunning and rich Draco. And, in one of the book's most famous scenes, even though the Sorting Hat sees his potential for the House of Slytherin where "cunning folk use any means / To achieve their ends," Harry actively chooses to be a Gryffindor "Where dwell the brave at heart, / Their daring, nerve, and chivalry / Set Gryffindors apart" (Rowling 1998, 94).

For generations, coming-of-age novels have elicited sympathy towards their heroes in the service of prompting readers to improve themselves. Thomas Jeffers cites Henry James's account of reading *Wilhelm Meisters Lehrjahre* (1795), the originating *Bildungsroman*, in order to illustrate this process: "each reader becomes his own Wilhelm Meister, an apprentice, a traveler on his own account" (Jeffers 2005, 9). In Jeffers's view, "Goethe has endowed Wilhelm with such intelligence, well enhanced by the people he meets, that in most cases however smart we are when we open the book, we will be ever smarter when we close it" (9).[3] Traditional *Bildungsromane* such as *Wilhelm Meister* and Charles Dickens's *David Copperfield* (1850), where protagonists become accommodated family men and model citizens, have withstood the test of time and unsurprisingly continue to populate bookshelves and syllabi worldwide.

Despite the transgenerational allure and relatability of traditional *Bildungsomane*, readers marginalized in hegemonic systems that degrade their intersecting identities of ableness, class, gender, nationality, race, religion, and sexuality, among others, can find their own formative experiences underrepresented in the initial bourgeois iteration of the *Bildungsroman*. Indeed, Sandra Cisneros has talked about the "literary void" she encountered as a young poor Latina growing up and reading in the U.S. as a driving impetus to write *The House on Mango Street* (1984). Cisneros explained that her project was to "write the stories that haven't been written;" to fill the void with the stories of "My race, my gender, my class!" (quoted in Sagel 1991). Similarly, the 1993 Nobel Prize in Literature laureate Toni Morrison describes her work, such as coming-of-age novel *The Bluest Eye* (1970), as "village literature, fiction that is reality for the village, for the tribe. Peasant literature for my people, which is necessary and legitimate" (quoted in LeClair 1981). Morrison further explains about the lack of stories like her own,

> I never asked Tolstoy to write for me, a little colored girt in Lorain, Ohio. I never asked Joyce not to mention Catholicism or the world of Dublin. Never… . It is that business of being universal, a word hopelessly stripped of meaning for me… . If I tried to write a universal novel, it would be water. Behind this question is the suggestion that to write for black people is somehow to diminish the writing. From my perspective, there are only black people.
>
> (quoted in LeClair 1981)

Cisneros and Morrison, who met with a lack of literary role models sufficiently resonant with their subjectivities and experiences, wrote disruptive coming-of-age novels in which young women like themselves were the protagonists. Both Esperanza in *The House on Mango Street* and Pecola Breedlove (and the MacTeer sisters) in *The Bluest Eye* puzzle over their marginal identities and their communities with as much care and distinction as did Goethe, Dickens, and Austen. Esperanza and Pecola employ the coming-of-age genre but subvert its most traditional horizon of expectations: instead of an ideal citizen-worker, myriad possibilities burst open as coming-of-age novels shift their focus to the formative process of young diasporic individuals. Useful in unraveling the complexities of identity, writers for and from diasporic groups have used the coming-of-age genre to reflect on their relegated positions, the expectations of their societies, and their place as adults in contemporary geographical and epistemic borderlands.

While I have touched upon the works of J. K. Rowling and Toni Morrison to introduce the coming-of-age genre, I do not analyze them further as I delve into the more specific genre of the Diasporic Coming-of-age.[4] *Harry Potter* is more akin to traditional *Bildungsromane* with an accommodated character who marries well and becomes a respected and productive member of society. The outcome in this contemporary coming-of-age novel, intersecting with the young-adult fantasy genre, takes recourse in magic as an *ex Machina* that enables Harry to become a hero. Without magic, Harry would be an abused and unnourished child perhaps unable to fulfill any sort of heroic role. And, while *The Bluest Eye* can be studied as a Diasporic Coming-of-age Novel in its own right, I instead chose five novels of Latin American diasporas in the U.S., and one of the Vietnamese diaspora, because they enable analyses of linguistic barriers and differences as key parts of the characters' formative processes.

The Categories of the Coming-of-Age Genre

The term *Bildungsroman* has been controversial and contested since its inception in the early 1800s. It is a slippery term and "hotly disputed" in what Anniken Iversen calls "definitions at war" (2009, 10). Iversen explains that, while some "Internationalist Pluralist" scholars such as Susanne Howe use the term widely and disregard the German historical context to which "it is inextricably bound," "Germanist Purist" scholars such as François Jost affirm it is a German phenomenon of the late eighteenth and early nineteenth centuries (Iversen 2009, 11). Jost's view is so restrictive that even a novel such as *David Copperfield* does not constitute a *Bildungsroman* because any novel in this genre "should not be a complete biography of the hero" but represent only "the making of the hero" (Jost 1983, 132): "The original bildungsroman is not the novel of infancy in which the protagonist is pushed on stage in a pram, nor is it the novel of early upbringing" (135).

David Copperfield begins his narration from birth, while Wilhelm Meister begins as a young man. Jost argues, "David Copperfield is not Wilhelm Meister ... The former quenches his thirst with milk, the latter with wine" (136). Conversely, International Pluralists "insist that there is a strong bildungsroman tradition outside of Germany" and "that many twentieth- and twenty-first-century authors—especially female and minority authors—have reacted against and subverted 'the traditional bildungsroman' in order to assert alternative views of subjectivity and ways of becoming an adult" (Iversen 2009, 11). Pin-chia Feng even goes as far as calling a *Bildungsroman* "any writing by an ethnic woman about the identity formation of an ethnic woman, whether fictional or autobiographical in form, chronologically or retrospectively in plot" (2000, 15).

Because *Bildungsroman* too often conveys the geographic and historical distinction of Germany in the early 1800s, I use the broader and vernacular "coming-of-age novel." The coming-of-age novel is an umbrella term that encompasses varied iterations of the genre across history and the world. All coming-of-age novels share a common emphasis on the inner lives and internal drives of their protagonists, and necessarily showcase the formative process of a young person who becomes an adult. Coming-of-age novels contain these two characteristics regardless of whether they are traditional *Bildungsromane*, the originating and most archetypal form of the genre, or Diasporic Coming-of-age Novels, the contemporary and globalized subgenre that I study in this book. Both these two subgenres show the formative processes of young people. However, traditional *Bildungsromane* illustrate middle-class, European, "enlightened," and overwhelmingly male protagonists who become accommodated citizens, workers, husbands, and fathers whom the readers should imitate. Conversely, Diasporic Coming-of-age Novels have manifold ways of defining youth and adulthood. The culturally-hybrid protagonists, often experiencing intersectional oppression due to their identities of race, gender, class, or sexuality, must negotiate what it means to become adults in their own families and social contexts, at times being undocumented or otherwise unable to access full citizenship, thus enabling complex and variegated formative processes that beg the questions of nationhood and belonging in increasingly globalized and multicultural societies worldwide.

Other languages have parallel terms that highlight different dimensions of the genre. The Spanish *novela de formación* [novel of formation] underscores the process of becoming, especially as the suffix -ción implies the action of the verb to form. The French *roman d'apprentissage*, which allows the translation as either *apprenticeship* or *learning*, implies the development of skills or a trade and underscores the matured understanding of the heroes' societies and selves. The English "coming-of-age" also emphasizes the process in the gerund and gives prominence to the social and legal "of age," the access into maturity when full legal rights and responsibilities such as voting are acquired. Even German has a recognition of

Entwicklungsroman, which shifts the prominence from *Bildung* [education], and self-formation, to any sort of development as education. The category of the *Künstlerroman* is also relevant, as many coming-of-age novels center on formative processes of artists who, through their formative processes, become the archivers of the memory and zeitgeist of their time and place, effectively encountering "for the millionth time the reality of experience" and forging, "in the smithy of [their] soul, the uncreated conscience of [their] race" (Joyce 1975, 384).

The markers of maturity that signify a character has *come of age* are specific to the represented cultures and epochs. The definition of adulthood may use legal demarcations such as becoming liable or responsible for illegal acts and crimes, being able to vote, drink alcohol, serve as a public official, and give consent for intercourse, marriage, and parenthood. They may be linked to citizenship and democratic participation in national and international forums. As such, depending on setting and epoch, only certain privileged people have been able to reach full adulthood because rights have differed across gender, class, and national origin—among many other legal categories. In traditional *Bildungsromane*, the stories mostly end when able-bodied protagonists from socioeconomically advantageous backgrounds become idealized adults. At the end, they are successful "citizen[s] and worker[s]" and have married (Buckley 1974, 18) and have thus made a "pact between the individual and the world" (Moretti 2000, 22). In contemporary Diasporic Coming-of-age Novels, markers of maturity are varied and can include, but are not limited to, diasporic characters coming to terms with their sexuality and coming out, attaining a formal education, standing up to violence, or asserting their complexity in an environment that seeks to stereotype them and flatten their identities, often by becoming masters of the hegemonic society's language (in this study, either English or German) as writers or actors.

The issues of citizenship and belonging are key to Diasporic Coming-of-age Novels because they delineate what kind of adult young protagonists can hope to become and the extent to which they can participate in society. Citizenship, as Richard Bellamy explains, "has been linked to the privileges of membership of a particular kind of political community—one in which those who enjoy a certain status are entitled to participate on an equal basis with their fellow citizens in making the collective decisions that regulate social life" (2008, 18). If a character does not have access to citizenship because of their status as refugee or how they first crossed the geographical borders of the host society, they may not be able to participate democratically as an equal to their peers. In the case of the Puerto Rican diaspora, a character might be said to be a citizen in the social context of the mainland United States but, as of 2020, does not have full federal voting rights. In such cases, one cannot equate adulthood with full democratic citizenship and, instead of a marker of maturity, participation in the nation can rather become a source of anxiety. Further, all minorities in the host society face what Lisa Marie Cacho describes as "social death," a system of white supremacy where "certain populations' very humanity is represented as something that one becomes or achieves, that one must earn because it cannot just be" (2012, 6). Protagonists from diasporic minorities must oftentimes prove not only that they have become adults, but also must assert their right to exist and have rights by "being 'properly' law-abiding," in Cacho's ironic view, a supposed "precondition for becoming American [and, thus] the prerequisite for legal recognition" (92). Xenophobic marginalization is thus a fundamental theme of Diasporic Coming-of-age novels that drastically affects the formative process of young people whose subjectivities "are refashioned as their connection to space and their civil rights are denied" (Guidotti-Hernández 2011, 8).

We can find the seeds of Diasporic Coming-of-age Novels in the history of the literary genre. They bloom into their contemporary characteristics as the result of the representation of the cultural zeitgeist of diaspora and multiculturalism. Unlike any branch of the coming-of-age novel before it, Diasporic Coming-of-age Novels intricately portray experiences of migration in an ever-increasingly cosmopolitan world where people from multiple backgrounds interact and influence each other, blurring strict definitions of nationhood and citizenship. As one of the approximately 255 million migrants worldwide (United Nations 2016) writing in a foreign language that splits my own tongue, I find the experiences of the protagonists in these novels to be closer to my own and bear more significance than any other form of narrative.[5]

The precursors of the first *Bildungsromane* were "Proto-*Bildungsromane*," German medieval texts that display characteristics of the coming-of-age genre but rely too-heavily on *Schicksal* [destiny] as a plot device and an overwhelming force that compels characters to develop. Wolfram von Eschenbach's thirteenth-century poem *Parizival* and Gottfried von Straßburg's coeval *Die Geschichte der Liebe von Tristan und Isolde* are two such examples. However, Goethe was the first to write a protagonist with stronger inward than outward concerns; in Jeffers's terms, Wilhelm Meister was the first protagonist to fix his "attention ever more burningly, and resignedly, on the self" (2005, 3). In traditional *Bildungsomane* the heroes' purpose was no longer to kill dragons or save kingdoms from curses, but plainly to grow up and fit in. The formative process became the driver of plot; the ultimate objective of the male bourgeois protagonist was to become a financially successful family man and serve as role model to primarily young readers—and secondarily to the guardians, parents, and overseers of those young readers. In Diasporic Coming-of-age Novels, the protagonists' purpose has become to understand their identities in nuanced terms and develop markers of maturity that often differ from hegemonic ideas of adulthood within historically situated settings of displacement or diaspora.

One may argue that the genre itself came of age internationally with authors such as England's Charles Dickens and France's Gustav Flaubert who transported it to their social contexts but retained the genre's classical structure and its didactic purpose of providing examples for readers. Dicken's *David Copperfield* (1850) and *Great Expectations* (1861) and Flaubert's *L'Éducation sentimentale* [Sentimental Education] (1869) embody mostly idyllic conclusions that depict the moral and social goals of their generations. Though critical of industrial practices in the case of the former and of impermeable class structures in the latter, these *Bildungsromane* eventually enabled their heroes, David, Pip, and Frédéric, to attain a commendable social and economic role: David becomes a respected writer and journalist, Pip becomes a gentleman in London, and Frédéric is, at the end, a member of the middle class.

According to Miguel Salmerón, the *Bildungsroman* represents the hero's formation from the beginning up to a determined degree of perfection. He adds that, through this representation, the protagonist's coming-of-age motivates the coming-of-age of readers (2002, 46–47). This didactic purpose becomes more apparent in the case of eighteenth-century readers. According to Ian Watt, novels were a luxury attainable only by "a small portion of the labouring classes who were technically literate" (2001, 40). The aristocracy had little interest in novels because they did not deem them "established and respectable forms of literature and scholarship" (42). Thus, the *Bildungsroman* was one of the genres of the novel produced and consumed by the bourgeoisie: unsurprisingly, early *Bildungsromane* depicted young white males whose final accommodations represented the values and practices of the middle class.

In terms of the intimately-related matter of plot to characters, Salmerón argues that all the events form a "causal mosaic" that describe, in great detail, the hero's upbringing. Both the central theme and the plot of the novel are built upon the *Bildung*, a term "conceived by the Weimar classicists" to refer to an "individual's cultivation" (Jeffers 2005, 35). We can identify the causal mosaic in Jerome Buckley's archetypal plot, in which the succession of events leads to the "degree of perfection":

> A sensitive child grows up in the provinces, where his lively imagination is frustrated by his neighbors'—and often by his family's—social prejudices and intellectual obtuseness. School and private reading stimulate his hopes for a different life away from home, and so he goes to the metropolis, where his transformative education begins. He has at least two love affairs, one good and one bad, which help him revalue his values. He makes some accommodation, as citizen and worker, with the industrial urban world, and after a time he perhaps revisits his old home to show folks how much he has grown.
>
> (Buckley 1974, 18)

Traditional *Bildungsromane* depict the consolidation of a society's values embodied in the hero and they map a society's hierarchies of achievement and definitions of adulthood. Jeffers explains: "in the event-racked revolutionary years of the late eighteenth century, the emergence of the hero's character increasingly mirrored the emergence—socially, economically, politically, ideationally—of the world around him" (Jeffers 2005, 2). As well, they often map a physical space that, unlike the archetypal plot process, often begins and ends in urban settings.

The emergences of the heroes' worlds are in part cartographical as these novels create the cities in readers' imaginations. Readers of Dickens are familiar with his depiction of industrial London, its factories and cruelties. The hungry orphan of *Oliver Twist* (1838) and child laborer in *David Copperfield* made their way into other vernaculars and places during Dicken's lifetime, as the author himself authorized their translation into the French (Morarasu 2007, 97) and U.S. readers famously awaited the serial sections of Dickens's works, drawing London on to the European map and on to the international imaginary. The early depictions of space planted the seed for the intricate cartographies of cities common in Diasporic Coming-of-age Novels such as Piri Thomas's violent and racially-segregated New York in *Down These Mean Streets* (1961) and Hanif Kureishi's 1970s punk and sexually-liberated London in *The Buddha of Suburbia* (1991).

The traditional plot ends immediately after the formative process concludes. However, there are many instances of non-traditional coming-of-age novels where the process remains open at the end.[6] The heroes' incomplete formative processes and by extension variations of the traditional plot correlate with large social conditions like diaspora and war. Incomplete formative processes occur in many non-traditional *Bildungsromane* written during or shortly after World War I. In E. M. Forster's *Maurice* (written 1913–1914, published posthumously 1971), the formative process of a homosexual man culminates in the titular character's unexpected renouncement of his social standing in England in order to go into exile with his lover Alec Scudder. *Maurice* follows many of the steps in the traditional plot, but the protagonist's relationship with a poor man leads him to ponder and ultimately reject his position as a gentleman in society. Unlike David Copperfield's society, Maurice's thwarts his ability to achieve "a degree of perfection." In James Joyce's *A Portrait of the Artist as a Young Man* (1916), Stephen Dedalus exiles himself from Ireland to France, in hopes of finding a place where he can become an artist and, in forging his own self, also forging the collective soul of his people. In Herman Hesse's *Demian: Die Geschichte von Emil Sinclairs Jugend* [*Demian: The Story of Emil Sinclair's Youth*] (1919), World War I interrupts Emil Sinclair's formative process, and the ending does not show a final accommodation: the narrative ends in an infirmary close to the battlefield, depicting an incomplete process. As opposed to *David Copperfield*, *Demain* does not offer a final and ideal middle-class adult because the war removes Emil from class structures and wounds his body to the point of death. Emil's wounds evidence his participation in the unavoidable disintegration of the social body amid a whole society of injured that cannot contribute to the maintenance or development of its ideal social structures.[7]

Heather Fielding is among recent scholars such as Iversen, José Santiago Fernández Vázquez, and Pin-chia Feng whose projects bring attention to coming-of-age novels from international, postcolonial, and feminist perspectives.[8] For example, shifting the key concept of accommodation to one of belonging and focusing entirely on female and minority authors, Fielding offers a model of reading so that the ending of coming-of-age novels are evaluated not by the success of the heroes as citizens and workers or the degree of perfection they achieve. In what she terms the ethnic *Bildungsroman*, novels are evaluated by the completed or failed processes of diasporic heroes' assimilation. Fielding's new term rightly recognizes that the archetypal plot does not fit with novels that involve immigration and cultural hybridity. However, Fielding's reading unfortunately defines the hero's goal in strict assimilationist terms: in "the ethnic bildungsroman or assimilation narrative ... an ethnic character 'grows' along a trajectory that culminates in his or her assimilation to the nation" (2011, 201). Her reading thus flattens, for example, the character of the protagonist of Kureishi's *The Buddha of Suburbia*, Karim Amir, so much so that he is rendered a caricature. The successful assimilation of the culturally and racially hybrid son of an Indian immigrant and a white English woman into English society of the late 1970s occurs in the entertainment business when Karim secures a job as a television actor in London where he plays a stereotypical Indian teenager whose parents own a corner store. Fielding argues that "*Buddha's* culminating moment of assimilation is its final paragraph" when "Karim has his epiphany about what it means to be British" among his family and friends as he "locates himself in three communities: 'people I loved,' 'this old city,' and the 'tiny island'" (Fielding 2011, 209–210). Fielding's reading does not acknowledge that in this final paragraph Karim feels ambivalence rather than a culminating belonging, "happy and miserable at the same time" (284), or that Kureishi points to an ominous future where Karim's hope is misplaced by setting this dinner on March 29, 1979, the day after the vote of no confidence in the government of James Callaghan.[9] The rise of conservatism is what Karim's friend Terry characterizes as England's falling apart and "the rise of the Right" (Kureishi 1991, 258).[10] Further, the ethnic *Bildungsroman* sees non-white, non-native protagonists as agents of assimilation in stable communities, thus disregarding the fact that many protagonists dwell in diasporas. In coming-of-age novels where heroes confront intersecting forms of oppression, a completed formative process becomes impossible.

The Diasporic Coming-of-age Novel

The Diasporic Coming-of-age Novel offers a broad, historically sensitive subgenre that encompasses the experience of diasporic characters in the globalized societies of the late twentieth and twenty-first centuries.

Diasporic Coming-of-age Novels focus on the internal development of culturally-hybrid subjects as they puzzle over how their identities awkwardly fit into the diasporic settings they inhabit. Part and parcel of the broadening of this set of experiences is a greater variability of the heroes' age, class, gender, and other cultural constructs than in a strictly assimilationist ethnic *Bildungsroman*. This variability in turn affects the plot process and duration. Wilhelm Meister is a young man in the opening paragraphs and Pip is a seven-year-old orphan at the opening of Dicken's *Great Expectations* (1861); these and other traditional *Bildungsromane* expand through many years as they achieve maturity. Conversely, the duration of the narrative sequence in the Diasporic Coming-of-age Novel vary to a much greater degree, as the processes of identification are many times interrupted or left open. Diasporic Coming-of-age Novels can be limited to childhood as in the cases of Rudolfo Anaya's *Bless Me, Ultima* (1972) and Sandra Cisneros's *The House on Mango Street*. They can encompass adolescence and early adulthood, as in Carlos Bulosan's *America is in the Heart* (1946), Piri Thomas's *Down These Mean Streets* (1967), and Junot Díaz's *The Brief Wondrous Life of Oscar Wao* (2007). They can portray lifetime processes, as in Reinaldo Arenas's *Antes que anochezca* [*Before Night Falls*] (1992), Julia Alvarez's *In the Time of the Butterflies* (1994), Chang-Rae Lee's *Native Speaker* (1995), Cristina Garcia's *Dreaming in Cuban* (1996), Zadie Smith's *White Teeth* (2000), Khaled Hosseini's *The Kite Runner* (2003), and Mohsin Hamid's *The Reluctant Fundamentalist* (2007). Where traditional *Bildungsromane* offered—and catered to some—readers' ideal models of imitation, the Diasporic Coming-of-age Novel empowers readers to think of identity as complex and dynamic, thus attune to the globalized world in which this genre emerged: to resist rather than show the difficulty attainment of stereotypical societal roles, in deference to nuanced portrayals.

In Diasporic Coming-of-age Novels, the representation of the heroes' social environments is key to understanding why they often cannot fit into bourgeois spaces. The heroes have experienced the often-traumatic movement of diaspora, either personally or in their families' recent histories. Although the term *diaspora* is frequently associated with the Jewish dispersion from the Kingdom of Israel during the 8th century BCE, Virinder Kalra argues that diaspora is any "forced movement, exile and a consequent sense of loss derived from an inability to return" (2005, 10). Bill Ashcroft further asserts diasporas are "voluntary or forcible movement of peoples from their homelands into new regions" (2007, 61). Diaspora can be compulsory as in the cases of peoples taken from West Africa to the Americas during the European slave trade, and the vast numbers of indentured agricultural laborers from China and India forcibly removed in the nineteenth century after "slavery was outlawed by the European powers" (61). Diaspora can be more volitional—often a painful last resource of exile driven by forces such as poverty, persecution, and discrimination or the search for asylum, education, and employment.

I use the term diaspora instead of "migration," "immigration," "exile," "expatriation," or "guest work" because it enables, first of all, the conceptualization of the coming-of-age novel as a public and communal utterance. While the other terms may refer to either individual or small geographic displacements, diaspora necessarily "suggests identification with a group, however scattered, committed to the same work of cultural retention, reproduction, and revival of a home culture in an alien, foreign, 'host'" (Ortíz 2017). In helpfully analogous terms to what Deleuze and Guattari described as "minor literature," the term diasporic "takes a collective value" and "forces each individual intrigue to connect immediately to politics. The individual concern thus becomes all the more necessary, indispensable, magnified, because a whole other story is vibrating within it" (Deleuze and Guattari 1986, 17). Further, diaspora "insists on the expansion of the temporal range of study to include at least two, often multiple, sometimes numerous, even countless, generations" (Ortíz 2017). As expected, Diasporic Coming-of-age Novels parse the relationship between the protagonists and their parents as they constitute incomplete and imperfect role models, often unable to understand the influence of the host society's culture on the young protagonists. In contrast, traditional *Bildungsromane* almost always have a mono-generational focus. Finally, as Ricardo Ortíz argues, diaspora "retains an entirely informal, unofficial, ambiguous, even improvisatory, undocumentable (and for this reason often expressive, imaginative, creative, critical) sense" that enables the nuance analyses and myriad diasporic experiences that comingle in this book.

Diaspora often implies the crossing of a geographic border. Diaspora can thus call our attention to experiences of violence not only within the host society, but also in the process of border-crossing (often depicted as parallel to the formative process; i.e. to cross is to grow up), which is the opprobrious setting of Yuri Herrera's *Señales que precederán al fin del mundo* [*Signs Preceding the End of the World*] (2009), studied in Chapter 4, and the recent coming-of-age films, Cary Joji Fukunaga's *Sin Nombre* [*Nameless*] (2009) and Diego Quemada-Díez's masterpiece *La Jaula de Oro* [*The Golden Dream*] (2013). The term diaspora often enables a profound analysis of collective movement intersected with violence, which necessarily plays a key role in the coming-of-age of the young people who experience it. It comes as no surprise that the Borderlands of Diasporic Coming-of-age Novels, in particular the U.S.-Mexico border, have been conceptualized metaphorically as "una herida abierta" [an open wound] by Gloria Anzaldúa and (2007, 25), recently, as a "no-man land" and a "big common grave" where "at the forensic institute of Pima County, Arizona, alone, more than 2,200 human remains have been registered since 2001, the majority of which are still unidentified" by Valeria Luiselli (2017, 40).

Whether focused on the lived experience of migration or subsequent-generation diasporic characters, diasporic novels invariably represent hybrid subjectivities where the displaced (and particularly their descendants) preserve some aspects from their originary culture and transform others: "The descendants of the diasporic movements generated by colonialism have developed their own distinctive cultures which both preserve and often extend and develop their originary cultures. Creolized versions of their own practices evolved, modifying (and being modified by) indigenous cultures with which they thus came into contact" (Ashcroft 2007, 62). Hybrid subjectivities regularly clash with the expectations of ideal maturity and adulthood in the host society because they do not fit into prescribed models and are met with nationalism, racism, glass ceilings, and impenetrable social hierarchies. The racism that diasporic characters experience is often akin to a "killing abstraction" whereby a xenophobic host society "creates spaces of living death and populations 'dead-to-others'" (Cacho 2012, 7).

The Global Stage

The seven chapters of *Children of Globalization: Diasporic Coming-of-age Novels in Germany, England, and the United States* are divided into three parts. Part 1, composed of Chapters 1 and 2, is predominantly historical. It addresses the German origins and early English transformations of traditional *Bildungsromane* in order to showcase the perennial malleability of the genre, the horizon of expectations of originating works, and the historic and generic context for Diasporic Coming-of-age Novels. Part 2, Chapters 3 through 5, examines six Diasporic Coming-of-age Novels with particular attention to the variability of formative processes. Diasporic Coming-of-age Novels show the ways in which the subversion of the horizon of expectations of traditional *Bildungsromane* reflects or reveals the profound changes that the societies of Germany, England, and the U.S. have undergone due to modern diasporic movements. The protagonists of these six novels begin and end in different stages of maturity and accommodations. While some reach nuanced understandings of their identities and how they fit into, resist, or even disregard narratives of nationhood, others end in opprobrious conditions unable to understand themselves or the world around them. Part 3, Chapters 6 and 7, examines recent Diasporic Coming-of-age Novels to theorize the possible futures and trends of the subgenre, in particular the hyperawareness and, at times, academic knowledge the characters display of migration and the history of their diasporic community, the explicit discussion of intersectionality as a key element of subjectivity, and the commingling of different diasporas that share vital interactions with each other.

In part 1, the focal points of Chapter 1 are the seeds, birth, and development of *Bildungsromane* in Germany. Two Proto-*Bildungsromane*, Wolfram von Eschenbach's *Parizival* and Gottfried von Straßburg's *Die Geschichte der Liebe von Tristan und Isolde* [*The Love Story of Tristan and Isolde*], illustrate the early Germanic interest for the development of the self through time. These thirteenth century Proto-*Bildungsromane* follow the heroes, Parzival and Tristan, throughout their lifetimes, starting with stories of their ancestors and conceptions. The chapter subsequently studies in Goethe's *Wilhelm Meisters Lehrjahre* [*Wilhelm Meister's Apprenticeship*] (1795) the shift from the external driving force of *Schiksal* [destiny] to the internal forces of desire, self-determination, and experimentation. The chapter then traces the development of the genre through Novalis's *Heinrich von Ofterdingen* (1800), Ludwig Tieck's *Der Runenberg* [*The Runenberg*] (1804), and Goethe's sequel *Wilhelm Meisters Wanderjahre* [*Wilhelm Meister's Journeyman Years*] (1821) in order to show that, even in these early examples of the genre, endings can deviate from the heterosexual middle-class family ideal. Readers encounter subversions to the archetypal plot from the very start.

Chapter 2 focuses on the structural and thematic transformations of traditional *Bildungsromane* in nineteenth- and twentieth-century England. The four novels showcased in this chapter attest to the diversification of readership and themes, as well as the capacity of the genre to voice marginalized experiences. The first, *Pride and Prejudice* (1813) by Jane Austen, is, alongside *Wilhelm Meister,* one of the two texts that Franco Moretti identifies as the prototypical *Bildungsromane* in his key study *The Way of the World.* It is vital to incorporate the novel's groundbreaking depiction of a female formative process and of marriage as one of the key driving forces into maturity. *Pride and Prejudice* illustrates the ideal marriage for traditional middle-class *Bildungsromane,* one socioeconomically-suitable and, significantly, based on true affection. One of the most influential *Bildungsromane,* Charles Dickens's *David Copperfield* also uses the formative process as driver of plot and evinces suitable marriage as the ultimate marker of maturity. Innovatively, it shows the main character struggle with poverty and implies the impossibility of a bourgeois adulthood for a working-class character; David is able to avoid a life of poverty because of his family connections and, eventually, fulfils the archetypal plot. This chapter studies the important structural transformation of *Great Expectations* (1861), also by Charles Dickens, which does not end with the protagonist Pip as a married man. Instead, it opens the genre to the possibility of relationships that do not culminate in marriage. Finally, in the twentieth century, E. M. Forster's *Maurice* (written in 1913–1914 and published posthumously in 1971) uses the formative process of the young gay protagonist as driver of plot but rather than an accommodation in his society, Maurice subverts the expectations of traditional *Bildungsromane* and chooses a self-imposed but hopeful exile over his privileged position of gentleman in England.

In part 2, Chapter 3 introduces the Diasporic Coming-of-age Novel in contemporary England with two of the most widely-read novels of the past few decades. Similar to Germany, post-war England saw a great influx of immigrants, in particular from the former British Empire. Randal Hansen explains: "When the British Nationality Act of 1981 was passed … multiculturalism was indisputably a part of British political and social life" (2000, 3). The themes of partial or non-belonging to the wider national community, hybridity, and marginalization emerge in the Diasporic Coming-of-age Novels. *The Buddha of Suburbia* (1990) by Hanif Kureishi follows the tumultuous coming-of-age of Karim Amir, "a funny kind of Englishman" (1991, 3), not Indian like his father but not English like his mother either. Karim's formative process showcases some of the most salient characteristics of the Diasporic Coming-of-age Novel. The story omits his childhood and adulthood, instead focusing on the transformative period of adolescence, when people often rebel against their parents' teachings, but do not yet know what they want their adulthood, professional career, and relationships to be. This culturally hybrid protagonist, in a process of self-forging, encounters contradictory expectations from the characters around him and society at large. These mixed expectations confuse him as he is unable to discern an ideal way to be an adult and citizen in a society that marginalizes his identities of race and sexuality. While different characters in Diasporic Coming-of-age Novels deal with similar crises of belonging in varied ways, Karim's particular outcome is ambivalent: A fairly successful soap-opera actor who is irremediably type-cast and who is simultaneously happy and miserable in this accommodation. *White Teeth* (2000) by Zadie Smith depicts three concurrent formative processes of second-generation teenagers from the Jamaican and Bangladeshi diasporas. The novel adds two possible outcomes for the formative processes of diasporic protagonists: on the one hand, Irie Jones disregards narratives of nationalistic identity and is thus able to find bliss and fulfilment. On the other hand, the twins Magid and Millat end up either rejecting their cultural heritage categorically or taking it to a religious fundamentalist extreme. The adolescent twins end in the non-accommodation of court-mandated community service.

Across the Atlantic the focal points of the next two chapters are Latin American diasporas in the U.S. In addition to cultural hybridity and complex identity formation, the themes that emerge include glass ceilings, poverty, segregation, and racism within U.S. cities—rather than between urban centers and provinces—and its implications for issues of belonging. The focal texts of Chapter 4 depict the Mexican diaspora, the largest one in the U.S. According to Juan Gonzales, "the Mexican diaspora is at the core of our country's Latino heritage. Not only are two of every three Latinos in the United States of Mexican origin, but only Mexicans can claim to be both early settlers on U.S. soil *and* the largest group of new arrivals" (2011, 96). Sandra Cisneros's *The House on Mango Street* (1984) uses the voice of young Esperanza to paint the portrait of her poor Latino community of Humboldt Park, Chicago. Her collective utterance is a new development in the genre of the Diasporic Coming-of-age, which often uses the formative process of a marginalized individual in order to show the oppression their community suffers. Esperanza ends her formative process as an accommodated writer and artist who never forgets her community and who returns, not in person, but with the novel itself. The protagonist of Yuri Herrera's *Señales que precederán al fin del mundo* [*Signs Preceding the End of the World*] (2015) depicts the opprobrious setting of many migrants as it follows young Makina in a perilous northward journey across the U.S.-Mexico border.

Chapter 5 focuses on two Diasporic Coming-of-age Novels of the Greater Antilles diasporas. These novels portray the political power of the genre when its objective is not only to depict the marginalization of its protagonists, but also to affect the social setting it fictionalizes. By intermingling with the narrative genres of memoir and *testimonio*, these novels push the boundaries of the genre in order to become politically effective: to protest segregation and oppose Fidel Castro's regime. *Down These Mean Streets* (1967) by Piri Thomas follows young Piri in a New York City that either considers him Black or Latino but can never reconcile his dark skin with his Puerto Rican identity. Piri's lack of introspection and internalization of misogyny and homophobia interrupt his formative process so that, at the end, the character is still immature and unable to move forward into adulthood. *Antes que anochezca* (1992) by Reinaldo Arenas uses the formative process as driver of plot in order to depict the cruelty and indignities that young homosexual Reinaldo experiences in Fidel Castro's Cuba. His self-imposed exile in Miami and then New York proves equally hopeless, as he contracts the human immunodeficiency virus (HIV) and ends his life in suicide, a terrible but real possibility in Diasporic Coming-of-age Novels where the social settings utterly crush the bodies and spirits of the characters.

In part 3, Chapter 6 travels back to Germany, the birthplace of traditional *Bildungsromane*, studying two Diasporic Coming-of-age Novels in a now overtly multicultural nation very distinct from the one that engendered the genre. The themes of cultural hybridity and the struggle with prejudice emerge in these novels as different types of outcasts come together in and around Berlin, one of the foremost multicultural megalopolises. A great influx of foreign workers during the 1950s and 1960s transformed "the Federal Republic of Germany into an immigration country" (Triadafilopoulos 2006). Consequently, "the continuing crisis of German identity since unification and the de facto settlement of Turkish and many other 'other' Germans make it imperative to rethink Germanness" (Cheesman 2007, 32). Contemporary Diasporic German Coming-of-age Novels reflect the current state of Germanness—which is one of flux and fluidity. Yadé Kara depicts this crisis of Germanness in her novel *Selam Berlin* (2003), where Hasan, a Turkish young man who leaves the Bosporus for the Spree, experiences the reunification of Germany as he attempts to find his place as an artist. The second novel, Wolfgang Herrndorf's *Tschick* (2010), follows Maik Klingenberg, a fourteen-year-old German boy from an abusive family, and Andrej Tschichatschow (Tschick), a young repatriate from Russia, as they explore Germany in a stolen car. Their formative processes support each other so that by means of their friendship and trust, they become able to reach stages of maturity.

Chapter 7 discusses the possible futures of the Diasporic Coming-of-age Novel. In taking a retrospective view of the book as a whole, this chapter enumerates the essential characteristics of the coming-of-age genre in general and of Diasporic Coming-of-age Novels in particular. Finally, it analyzes two recent Diasporic Coming-of-age Novels to parse the possibilities the genre can enable in years to come: Ocean Vuong's *On Earth We're Briefly Gorgeous* (2019) and Gabby Rivera's *Juliet Takes a Breath* (2019). These novels represent the possibility for profound analyses of the topic of diasporas as a key part of the formative processes of autodidactic and highly intelligent protagonists who understand their identities in academically complex and intersectional terms, whose experience of intermingling with varied diasporas is mundane, and who importantly are global and globalized citizens acutely aware of the effects that international historical processes have on their own formative processes and identities.

That all ten Diasporic Coming-of-age Novels have been translated, some like *White Teeth* into more than twenty languages, attests to the genre's popularity. But it is not only their linguistic translations that have made them accessible to readers worldwide, but also their inherent cultural transferability. They are able to depict common experiences of marginalization and cultural hybridity that young readers and adults are able relate to whether they are in Berlin or Mexico City, in major urban cities or small towns, all affected by globalization. Diasporic Coming-of-age Novels are an enabling resource to address contemporary diasporas and globalization, especially the questions they beg: Who am I and what is my place in the world? Individuals from diasporic communities have used them in contemporary multicultural metropolises to explore their hybrid—often messy and marginalized—identities and tell their stories. Much like a puzzle difficult to put together, these hybrid outcasts have the challenging task of figuring out who they are and how they fit in national and global frames. They weigh the expectations of their parents, their immediate communities, and the ever-changing world around them. The answers they unravel are often not definitive, satisfactory, or even appeasing, but Diasporic Coming-of-age Novels enable tentative answers that are nuanced, fill literary voids, and capture linguistic and global journeys and transformations.

Notes

1 Published in the U.S. as *Harry Potter and the Sorcerer's Stone* in 1998.
2 Rowling's book series has been translated into 80 languages, making the experience of reading it an almost ubiquitous one. A testament to globalization, the significance of Harry Potter in my own coming-of-age is shared to different degrees, regardless of immediate geography, by the over 500 million readers reported in Rowling's website Pottermore.
3 In Jeffers's view, the classical writers of the genre furthered the "Weimar classicists' case [German humanist movement of the late eighteenth century] for the cultivation of the individual," so that whole generations of educated bourgeois

men's "consciousness and conscience were, in the authentic Joycean sense, 'forged'" (2005, 4).

4 I capitalize "coming-of-age" when it is part of the phrase "Diasporic Coming-of-age Novel" in order to foreground it and make it equivalent in prominence to *Bildungsroman*, which should always be capitalized following standard German noun-capitalization rules.

5 That said, I, and many readers of my generation, enjoy earlier iterations in their own achievements—they are simply put, well worth reading.

6 Porter Abbott notes that the novel's end does not necessarily equate with closure: "When a narrative resolves a conflict, it achieves closure, and this usually comes at the end of a narrative." However, "closure does not have to come at the end of the narrative; in fact, it does not have to come at all" (2008, 56).

7 Hesse famously published *Demian* under the pseudonym Emil Sinclair, the main character of the novel. He did this because it was necessary "if the book was to be effectual in its appeal to disillusioned postwar German youth. Since his name was closely associated with prewar Impressionism, Hesse was convinced that German youth, fascinated as it was by postwar Expressionism, would not even deign to read his *Demian* let alone heed its appeal to the individual to seek self-knowledge and to attempt self-realization" (Mileck 1961, 167).

8 José Santiago Fernández Vazquez proposes that traditional *Bildungsromane* follow a colonialist logic that contrasts with the great quantity of postcolonial writers who use the genre to narrate the experiences in their nations, both during colonial and post-independence periods.

9 James Callaghan was the leader of the British Labour Party. This vote of no confidence would lead to the election of the Conservative Party's Margaret Thatcher two months later.

10 Karim's hope for a better future takes place in the context of the beginning of a conservative government led by a Prime Minister who repeatedly expressed sentiments against immigrants, especially people of color: "She thought it quite wrong that immigrants should be given council housing whereas white citizens were not... . She made clear, however, that she had 'less objection to refugees such as Rhodesians, Poles and Hungarians, since they could more easily be assimilated into British society'" (Swaine 2009).

PART I

1 The Birth of the *Bildungsroman*

Definitions and Origins of the Genre from Wolfram von Eschenbach to Johann Wolfgang von Goethe

The genre of coming-of-age novels depicts protagonists' formative processes in which readers encounter detailed experimentations with identities and the acceptance and rejection of various role models throughout a "process of identification, that inserts individuals into ideologies and ideological practices that, when they work well, are lived as though they were obvious and natural" (Weedon 2004, 6). In a process of identification, individuals internalize cultural signs, symbols, and cultural practices available in the people they imitate. Individuals are in a constant process of becoming. They ultimately internalize some of the expectations and identities that they actively chose to imitate and embody or that ideological and repressive state apparatuses impose on them.[1] The genre is ubiquitous in bookstores and syllabi worldwide, attesting to its importance. Yet, it is a relatively new form of narrative. In the original German and most traditional iteration, these novels are often called *Bildungsromane*, a term Germany's Karl Morgenstern first coined in 1820, "with specific reference to *Wilhelm Meister*" (Jeffers 2005, 49). Morgenstern explained that Johann Wolfgang von Goethe's *Wilhelm Meisters Lehrjahre* [*Wilhelm Meister's Apprenticeship*] (1795) must be called a *Bildungsroman* because the *Bildung* [formation] is the subject matter:

> *Bildungsroman* wird es heißen dürfen, erstens und vorzüglich wegen seines Stoffs, weil er des Helden Bildung in ihrem Anfang und Fortgang bis zu einer gewissen Stufe der Vollendung darstellt; zweytens aber auch, weil er gerade durch diese Darstellung des Lesers Bildung, in weiterm Umfrage als jede andere Art des Romans, fördert" [It must be called *Bildungsroman* first and foremost because of its subject matter, since it represents the formation of the hero in its beginnings and progress to a certain stage of plenitude; second as well, because through this representation, it furthers the reader's *Bildung* to a greater extent than any other kind of novel].
>
> (Morgenstern 1820, 13[2])

Almost two decades before the publication of *Wilhelm Meisters Lehrjahre*, in 1778, Johann Gottfried von Herder announced in *On the Cognition and*

Sensation of the Human Soul the need for detailed biographical sketches that could facilitate the understanding of the *Bildung und Erziehung* [formation and upbringing] of individuals in a way that had never been done before. The *Bildungsroman* emerged as the answer to the quest of self-formation, and it required of the individual, "the integrity and faithfulness to sketch *himself*, fully, as he knows and feels himself" and "enough courage to look into the deep abyss of Platonic recollection and to suppress nothing to himself, enough courage to pursue himself through his whole living structure, through his whole life, with everything that each index finger points out to him in his inner I" (Herder 2002, 197).

Jerome Buckley and others such as Franco Moretti, Miguel Salmerón, and Susanne Howe echo Morgenstern's assertion that, in addition to the edifying objective of the genre, originary and traditional *Bildungsromane* end when the protagonist has achieved a "stage of completeness" (Morgenstern 1820, 13). These theorists outline a number of steps that the archetypal plot follows. Most notably, Buckley provides an archetypal plot that follows a specific formula, cited in the introduction to this book. Many *Bildungsromane* follow this formula to a large extent. The definition of citizen and worker can sometimes vary and the industrial urban world is sometimes absent, but both the precocious imagination of the protagonist and the failed attempts at a heterosexual romantic relationship are prevalent. In traditional *Bildungsromane*, these failed attempts eventually lead to a successful marriage. Traditional *Bildungsromane* end with portraits of idealized adult role models who marry appropriately for their socioeconomic class. They are edifying, complete, heroic. In the words of François Jost, they show "the making of the hero" (Jost 1983, 132).

A new feature of traditional *Bildungsromane* was its parsing and pondering on definitions of nationhood and correct citizenship. Moretti explains that traditional *Bildungsromane* strengthen the protagonists' "sense of belonging to a wider community" and that "time must be used to find a homeland" (Moretti 2000, 19). In order to belong fully in the social whole, at the end, "the classical *Bildungsroman* must always conclude with marriages" (22). For Moretti, the institution of marriage is a "metaphor for the social contract" (22). It constitutes a "pact between the individual and the world," not antonymic to celibacy, but rather to death or disgrace (23).

Susanne Howe's definition coincides with Buckley's archetypal plot, but she underscores the process of trial and error:

> The adolescent hero of the typical "apprentice" novel sets out on his way through the world, meets with reverses usually due to his own temperament, falls in with various guides and counsellors, makes many false starts in choosing his friends, his wife, and his life work, and finally adjusts himself in some way to the demands of his time and environment by finding a sphere of action in which he may work effectively.
>
> (Howe 1930, 4)

These "false starts," engines of the plot, enable protagonists to experiment with the options around them. Through a process of trial and error, heroes may adjust their paths. Morgenstern explains that at the end of these paths, the protagonist has a "stage of completeness" (1820, 13), Buckley asserts the protagonist finds an "accommodation" (18), Howe a "sphere of action" (1930, 4), and Salmerón a "degree of perfection" (2002, 46). Regardless of the discrepancy in terminology, these theorists concur that the classical plot of the *Bildungsroman* shows fully-formed adult characters at the end, products of successful—albeit often sinuous—formative processes. Their context is a relatively stable one in contrast to the globalized world of later Diasporic Coming-of-age Novels.

Readers can find the most salient steps of the archetypal plot and marriage in Goethe's novel *Wilhelm Meisters Lehrjahre*. However, the *Lehrjahre* is far more complex than Buckley's archetypal plot would suggest and its hero finds—and ultimately belongs to—forms of social organization where marriage is not the organizing principle. Friederike Eigler asserts that the *Lehrjahre* has often been read reductively, a trend present even in the earliest of Goethe's readers: "Die systematische Reduzierung des Romans beginnt bereits bei seinen Zeitgenossen und findet in der Prägung und Fortschreibung des Gattungsbegriffs *Bildungsroman* ihren Höhepunkt" [The systematic reduction of the novel begins already with his contemporaries and finds its culmination in the coinage and continuation of the genre term *Bildungsroman*] (Eigler 1986, 94).[3] Indeed, the novel contains possibilities for social and epistemological organizations that underscore homosocial bonds and non-hegemonic family unions: the *Turmgesellschaft* [Society of the Tower] and the theater troupe are two of the most salient. Susan Gustafson argues that relationships in the *Lehrjahre* "challenge eighteenth- and early-nineteenth-century family norms" as the novel "highlights the spontaneous connections that arise when women and men, men and men, women and women, and adults and children encounter each other and discover their elective affinities" (Gustafson 2016, 67). The protagonist spends most of his attention not on pondering the institution of marriage and its conventions, but rather on the complexities of theater, performance, the life of the mise-en-scène, and the study of the self through the mirror of character embodiment. Gustafson, citing Broszeit-Rieger, goes as far as to argue that "the *Lehrjahre* seems to be rejecting the concept of family altogether" as "intact families are only found in earlier generations" (68). It is true that Wilhelm Meister has false starts with love and parenthood, which stir his formative process and eventually—though briefly—anchor him in marriage. But Goethe's narrator does not frame Wilhelm's formative process as a desire to marry or to become a model citizen for young readers to imitate. Instead, Wilhelm is mostly interested in the life of art, in travelling, in the genesis and evolution of the individual, and engaging in ontological conversations wherever he can find them. Moreover, readers may find key points of Buckley's archetypal plot in Goethe's novel only if they do not consider the sequel *Wilhelm Meisters Wanderjahre* [*Wilhelm Meister's Journeyman Years*] (1821). Many theorists of the *Bildungsroman* disregard the *Wanderjahre*, as it does not continue to uphold marriage as the fundamental social pact, a matter I address later in this chapter.

The present chapter focuses on the emergence of this first and originary iteration of the coming-of-age genre with the pioneering example of *Wilhelm Meisters Lehrjahre*, "the archetype of the European *Bildungsroman*" (Moretti 2000, v). Although the *Lehrjahre* is often read as the most traditional *Bildungsroman* (i.e. prescriptive of the archetypal plot), Wilhelm Meister's formation powerfully shows that, from the very beginning, coming-of-age novels are far more complex and intricate than the archetypal plot process and the necessity of marriage would suggest. Chapter 2 then focuses on the first structural and thematic transformation of the genre in England. These initial chapters evidence the great malleability of the genre from its emergence. *Pride and Prejudice* (1813) by Jane Austen, and *David Copperfield* (1849) by Charles Dickens built on the complex formative process of Wilhelm Meister. The formative processes of their protagonists, Elizabeth Bennet and David Copperfield, are among the seeds that over centuries in settings worldwide bloomed intro prolific branches of the coming-of-age genre. The great number of developments has rendered the term *Bildungsroman* too narrow to encompass all types of "coming-of-age novels," a capacious and vernacular term. One of the most exciting and global variations, the Diasporic Coming-of-age Novel, is the subject of Chapters 3, 4, 5, 6, and 7.

In turn, the traditional *Bildungsroman* found its seeds in "Proto-*Bildugnsromane*," long medieval narrative poems depicting the formation of children into knights and kings driven by the external factors of *Schicksal* [destiny] and duty. Goethe wrote the first novel to underscore the youthful "attributes of mobility and inner restlessness" (Moretti 2000 5), and to have stronger "inward than outward concerns" (Jeffers 2005, 3). It is the first to have a more dominant internal than external focus and drive, and to direct its "attention ever more burningly, and resignedly, on the self" (3). It is relevant to note that Goethe's keen interest in the formation of the individual is framed in a larger philosophical tradition of the eighteenth-century's ontological interrogations. A salient example is G. W. Leibniz's *The Principles of Philosophy known as Monadology* (1714), in which he explains the concept of the monad, "a simple substance" which has "no windows through which anything could come in or out" as a metaphor for the individual (Leibniz 2007, 1–2). Leibniz relevantly characterized monads as being necessarily "unlike every other," their differences being internal, "based on what each is like in its own nature rather than merely on how they relate to other things" (2). The changes in monads, like individuals in the first *Bildungsromane*, come thus primarily "from an internal force, since no external causes could ever influence its interior" (2). Equally relevant to the German context, deeply concerned with the question of the formation of the self, is Immanuel Kant's definition of the Enlightenment in his 1784 essay

"Beantwortung der Frage: Was its Aufklärung?" ["Answering the Question: What is Enlightenment?"]. Kant explains that "Aufklärung ist der Ausgang des Menschen aus seiner selbstverschuldeten Unmündigkeit" [Enlightenment is people's emergence from their own self-inflicted immaturity] (1784, 1). Kant goes on to argue that one emerges from this immaturity by bravely developing one's intellect and reason. What Kant describes in his essay is indeed a conceptualization of adulthood where brave rationality is equated with maturity. Traditional *Bildungsromane* are closely related to this definition of Enlightenment because they depict the struggles necessary in the emergence from immaturity and ultimately depict idealized and rational adult citizen-workers.

Proto-*Bildungsromane*

Two examples of Proto-*Bildungsromane* are Wolfram von Eschenbach's thirteenth-century romance *Parizival* and Gottfried von Straßburg's coeval *Die Geschichte der Liebe von Tristan und Isolde* [*The Story of Tristan and Isolde's Love*]. Both texts depict a tension between the external forces of destiny—often magic and supernatural—and the internal force of self-determination. The Proto-*Bildungsromane*'s reliance on *Schicksal* determines that part of the narrative account requires the stories of previous generations and parallel stories. In Parzival, books seven through fourteen, out of a total of sixteen, are concerned with the adventures of Gawan, a digression which is neither characteristic of traditional *Bildungsromane* nor coming-of-age novels. *Parzival*'s heterodiegetic poetic voice (i.e. the third-person narrator outside of the diegesis) begins not with the story of the titular protagonist, but with his father Gahmuret's travels. For the first two of the sixteen books, Gahrumet goes to the African kingdom Zazamanc, where he marries Queen Belacane. Their son Feirefiz wears his hybridity on his mottled skin. Gahmuret's restless spirit takes him away from Belacane and back to Europe, where he marries Queen Herzeloyde. Unable to stay in one place for long, he leaves to fight in a war where his death brings his adventures to a halt. Herzeloyde tries to prevent her son, Parzival, from following in his father's footsteps and raises him in the woods. However, the forces of destiny prove to be too strong. Young Parzival meets three knights who tell him of King Arthur. Once he hears of the world of chivalry, nothing can deter him from perusing it. As he begins his quest to become a knight, he meets his cousin Sigune, from whom he learns his true name and his lineage. Parzival has an internal drive that pushes him to become a knight and reject the quiet life his mother had planned for him. However, this drive is not something that he chooses, but rather is externally predetermined by the inheritance of the restless spirit of his father. Parzival does not puzzle over what he ought to become: his name and lineage already dictate his identity and his formative process is merely to successfully internalize it.

In the adventures of Parzival, we encounter some of the key character-istics of *Bildungsromane*. As it will often be the case in *Bildungsromane*, Parzival finds a guide in the knight Gurnemanz, who teaches him that the main duty of a knight is self-restraint and temperance, particularly when it comes to curiosity. A knight must not ask too many questions. Parzival is young and makes a mistake, or a false start in Howe's terms, when he takes this advice too literally later in the story. Parzival then fulfils one of the most crucial steps of traditional *Bildungsromane* when he marries Queen Condwiramurs. However, the marriage is not the final point of arrival as in *Bildungsromane*, but only a stop in his journey. Mirroring his father's story, he takes leave from her to continue his adventures. He becomes a knight in King Arthur's court and is tasked with the search of the Holy Grail. He is almost successful in his quest when in the fifth book he arrives at the castle of the Grail. Here, he fails to ask the Fisher King Anfortas—his uncle—about a strange wound he has or the magic of the faraway castle. When he wakes up, Parzival thinks it was all a dream. Sigune later reveals that he had been in fact in the presence of the Grail but he had failed because he had not asked the right questions. He had taken Gurnemanz's advice to not ask questions too literally, without regard for context. Parzival spends many years looking for the castle to no success, while the romance digresses and for several books focus on the adventures of Gawan. Parzival appears as a minor character in Gawan's story, but does not reclaim the focus as main character until the last two books, fifteen and sixteen.

When Parzival regains the narrative focus, the romance tells the final part of a story that only partially resembles *Bildungsromane*. Parzival's wife Condwiramurs has had two sons, Kardeiz and Loherangrin, turning Parzival into a father, but, importantly, an absent one. In the last book, Cundrie the sorceress leads Parzival back to the castle of the Grail, where he is to fulfil his destiny and replace his uncle Anfortas as king. Parzival reunites with his wife and sons. At the end, we see Parzival depicted as Lord of the Grail and father, marrying off his sons to proper Christian brides and thus reproducing the social structure.

Parzival's formative process follows several of the *Bildungsroman's* archetypal plot's points. Parzival has a precocious imagination that his mother tries to suppress. He has a false start as he attempts to secure the Grail, but tries again and eventually succeeds. He marries young and makes the same mistakes of his father, but he is always faithful and at the very end becomes a better family man. The narration meets many of the criteria of the traditional *Bildungsroman*. Indeed, in his incomplete essay on the genre (published posthumously in 1979), Mikhail Bakhtin lists *Parzival* among texts "constructed on the idea of testing a hero" and that concentrate "the whole plot on the process of the hero's education" (1986, 16, 20). However, *Parzival* is not yet a fully-formed *Bildungsroman*. The text follows Parzival through many years, but always in action, never in pondering. The poetic voice relays Parzival's fascination with chivalry and his feelings of remorse when he fails, but readers cannot access Parzival's own mind, struggles, or imagination. In contrast with traditional *Bildungsromane* where the protagonists' mental processes are plainly depicted so that readers know the motivations and struggles that drive their actions, it is difficult to ascertain what Parzival thinks of his own identity or process, as it is reported on by a different and external voice. Parzival does not evaluate the moral or practical repercussions of several paths laid before him by circumstance as one would expect in a *Bildungsroman*. Instead, he simply follows one single and predetermined one. Parzival is *destined* by name and lineage to become the Lord of the Grail. It is not that he forges his path through trial and error; his path is already set. He never truly strays from his path in order to experiment with his identity. His failures delay his objective, but do not deviate him from it. *Schicksal* is unequivocal and remains unchallenged, leaving readers with a narration that is too external to be classified a *Bildungsroman*.

In similar terms, Straßburg's coeval *Die Geschichte der Liebe von Tristan und Isolde* primarily follows the formative process of Tristan and secondarily of Isolde, two star-crossed lovers separated by fate. None of the aforementioned scholars cite this work in the *Bildungsroman* tradition because it is often studied with a focus on the love story, as a tragedy, or its implications for feudal social hierarchies. Although overlooked, *Tristan und Isolde* is also a Proto-*Bildungsroman* with a formative process at its core. Like Parzival's, Tristan's formative process is reigned by external, often magical, forces which the protagonist and his lover are unable to fend off. The love story is tragic in that the lovers try to defy the forces of fate but succumb to them, eventually paying dues for their hubris. Where self-determination is valued in the entrepreneurial spirit of eighteenth-century Bildungsromane, in *Tristan und Isolde*, defiance of destiny results in suffering and death.

Mirroring Parzival's structure, the story begins with Tristan's lineage, the knight Riwalin and Blanscheflur. Riwalin dies in battle at the hands of Morgan, a ruthless conqueror, and Blanscheflur dies of sorrow shortly after, foreshadowing the dreadful end of their son. Rual and Floräte adopt Tristan, who is instructed in letters and music, as well as hunting and the ways of knights. Such a rigid education comes with an expected outcome, a characteristic that is eventually inherited by traditional *Bildungsromane* such as *David Copperfield*, where the titular protagonist is explicitly educated to become a gentleman. As a direct result of his education, when Tristan is fourteen he is inducted into the court of King Marke of Cornwall. Much like Parzival, in the moment when his true identity is revealed to him, he becomes bound by fate to knighthood in general, and to avenge his father in particular. Tristan travels to neighboring Parmenie where he defeats Morgan. Although he has a claim to the land there, he must go back to the court of King Marke, to whom he owes his fealty.

As expected, Tristan continues to correctly fulfil his duties when he defeats Morold, brother-in-law of Gurmun, the King of Ireland. Morold had threatened King Marke's sovereignty. However, Tristan is wounded with a poison that can only be cured by Morold's sister, Queen Isolde. As he makes his way to Ireland, Tristan disguises himself as Tantris, a musician who is admitted into the court of King Gurmun and is charged with the education of young Isolde, Queen Isolde's daughter. No love develops between the young pupil and the disguised Tristan, but a mutual admiration is born. Upon his return to Cornwall, Tristan tells King Marke of young Isolde. The King becomes infatuated with this tale and tasks Tristan to bring her to become his queen. Tristan once again travels to Ireland and, conveniently, King Gurmun has offered young Isolde's hand in marriage to whomever can kill a pesky dragon. The inclusion of this mythical creature is an obstacle that precludes *Tristan und Isolde* from being a *Bildungsroman*, where magical adversaries will be replaced by societal obstacles to be fought with imagination and resourcefulness rather than a sword and shield. The problem of the dragon strikes readers as contrived precisely because Tristan's destiny is prescribed and not a consequence of his own self-forging. Tristan is successful in the task of dragon-slaying, but his identity as the killer of Morold is accidentally revealed. In a key scene where Tristan is bathing after battle, Isolde observes him first with the intention of vengeance for her uncle while Tristan is vulnerable. However, the sight of naked Tristan makes her change her mind, suggesting that their later love is born first of lust and not external forces. Although reticent, Gurmun sends Isolde with Tristan.

Before young Isolde's departure, her mother Queen Isolde gives her a love potion so that she can fall for King Marke and make her married life easier. As a magical plot device and external force, the love potion is antithetical to the internal plot engine in *Bildungsromane*. The forces of destiny are then confounded, as it is Tristan and Isolde who accidentally take the potion— thinking it wine—and fall irremediably in love with each other. On the shores of Cornwall, Isolde is no longer a maiden. The romantic union of the lovers comes in direct contrast with Isolde's union to King Marke, whom she marries, all the while meeting Tristan in secret. While the union with Tristan stems from love and desire, her marriage to Marke is the consequence of her father's offer of payment for slaying the dragon. In feudal marriage, she is property and a means to continue Marke's lineage but with Tristan, she is an agent of love. The lovers eventually escape to a magical grotto, against social mores, thus asserting an incipient freedom that much later blooms in coming-of-age novels. The lovers hide until the fanfare of king Marke's court, a symbol of their inescapable societal obligations, disturbs them. Tristan thinks to put his sword between them that night and when Marke finds them, he forgives them, as he sees them sleeping apart, divided by the sword that represents knighthood. Love fails.

Instead of a final accommodation as citizen, worker, and role model, magic-infused tragedy concludes the narrative. Tristan travels abroad again and marries a different Isolde: Isolde Weißhand, his second relationship in terms of Jerome Buckley's archetypal plot. However, instead of the "good one," this second Isolde is worse, jealous and cunning, and finally causes the protagonist's death. There is a repetition of the name which signals his refusal to let go of the original young Isolde. Towards the end, Tristan is fatally wounded in battle and knows that only the magic of young Isolde can save him. His friend Kaedin travels to Cornwall with this message: if young Isolde is willing to help Tristan, she would sail to him with white sails but if she is unwilling, Kaedin would return with black ones. Isolde Weißhand, having heard the conversation between her husband and Kaedin, tells Tristan that she sees black sails at the shores even though the sails are white. Tristan is killed by the news. And young Isolde, seeing that she is too late, dies as well.

In this story, Tristan must choose between his individual desire materialized in Isolde and his knightly destiny, embodied in King Marke. This decision is intersected by larger forms of socioeconomic and epistemological organization. The married couple represents a capitalist model in which the heterosexual family is the basic social building block; vassalage in King Marke's court represents a feudal model. While the marriage of the lovers appears as a possibility for a short time, the dominant societal feudal structure triumphs. In this sense, the destiny of the character thwarts self-determination. The decision to love despite and in opposition to vassalage leads to the eventual doom of the protagonists and their tragic ending. By contrast, the protagonists of *Pride and Prejudice* and *David Copperfield* champion a type of marriage that is not only one of "true affection," but as socially decorous as discussed in Chapter 2 (Austen 2016, 70).

The *Bildungsroman* Prototype: Wilhelm Meister

Proto-*Bildungsromane* precede the prototype of the *Bildungsroman* genre, *Wilhelm Meisters Lehrjahre*, which fixes its attention on the internal development of the self, the experimentation with identity, and the momentary assimilation into the institution of marriage. In the *Lehrjahre*, the heterodiegetic narrator intermingles with the voice of the protagonist often and throughout, enabling readers to access the protagonist's internal thoughts at length, especially what he wants to do and who he wants to become. In a monumental shift away from long narratives of knights and royalty, the narrator of this *Bildungsroman* first describes Wilhelm as a young man, a member of the middle class, son of a successful merchant. His experiences in his young adulthood with the theater spark his passion and imagination. His interest for the theater contrasts with the worldview of his parents, who want their son to follow their lead into the world of commerce. Wilhelm's mother tries to halt Wilhelm's artistic curiosity by telling him that his addiction to the theater causes unrest at home and makes his father angry. Wilhelm challenges his mother as he poses the rhetorical question: "Ist denn alles unnütz, was uns nicht unmittelbar Geld in den Beutel bringt, was uns nicht den allernächsten Besitz verschafft?" [Is it all useless that does not immediately put money in our pocket, that which does not enlarge out property?] (Goethe 1985a, 11). Wilhelm goes on to argue that they already have more than they need, using their large house as evidence of their substantial fortune. This episode evidences Wilhelm's will to resist the external forces of his parents' expectations and the path of less resistance in favor of his own interests and desire to self-forge.

The woman whom the protagonist should marry is not predetermined by the forces of destiny. There is no feudal arrangement for the continuation of lineage nor the exchange of women as payment, for example, for dragon-pest control. However, marriage is still an integral part of the story in traditional *Bildungsromane*, even if the choice of partner is more flexible and other considerations such as love and suitability gain relevance. Since no marriage is arranged for Wilhelm, he can experiment with relationships. As in all other aspects of his life, he experiences false starts in selecting his partner. Wilhelm's false start is embodied in the character of Mariane, a young actress who he thinks pure and innocent. She attracts him to the theater world but later proves to be his "bad relationship" (Buckley 1974, 8). In this very first part of the novel, Wilhelm states his love for her as though it would be enduring: "Ich liebe dieses zärtliche, gute, liebliche Geschöpf so sehr, daß mich jeder Augenblick meines Lebens verdrießt, den ich ohne sie zugebracht habe" [I love this tender, good, lovely creature so much, that I would regret all moments of my life that I did not spend with her] (Goethe 1985a, 25). On the one hand, Wilhelm feels commerce could be his path, as his parents have laid out for him. On the other hand, the theater and Mariane charm him. This internal conflict becomes particularly clear in a poem he writes, where he describes two female figures fighting for him: "Ich erinnere mich noch eines Gedichtes … in welchem die Muse der tragischen Dichtkunst und eine andere Frauengestalt, in der ich das Gewerbe personi-fiziert hatte, sich um meine werte Person recht wacker zanken" [I remember a poem in which the muse of tragic poetry and another female figure, that personified commerce, bravely quarreled for my worthy self] (Goethe 1985a, 32). The muse of art and creation is initially victorious as Wilhelm becomes fascinated with the theater and Mariane. The muse's victory is brief as Wilhelm discovers Mariane is having an affair with a rich and older lover, Norberg. Such a disillusionment with love is an entirely new characteristic of the genre, as Proto-*Bildungsromane* do not offer any room for the experimentation with relationships. It is Wilhelm's internal disappointment with Mariane rather than an external and magical force that temporarily discourages him from the life of the artist and nudges him to pursue business with his friend Werner.

The theme of self-determination is key to these first few chapters in the novel. The conflict between art and commerce certainly has external components, namely Wilhelm's parents, their expectations, and his life-long friendship with Werner. However, the conflict is predominantly internal.

Wilhelm uses the intimate means of poetry to express his anxiety to decide his path by means of the metaphors of the female figures. In contrast to Parzival's story, both paths lay before him but neither is predetermined.

Wilhelm becomes bored and restless and yearns for a creative outlet that the theater can provide. His drive for the theater is only dormant and, although he has acceded to external forces of the middle class pushing him to be a business man, he remains, in his own words, an "unordentliche[r], unruhige[r] Mensch, der ein Leben fortzusetzen wünschte, das ihm die Verhältnisse der bürgerlichen Welt nicht gestatteten" [disorganized, restless person who wishes to resume a life not allowed by the conditions of the middle-class world] (Goethe 1985a, 276). Wilhelm breaks again with the expectations of his family and friends when, in his travels, he attaches himself to a theater troupe. His access and experimentation with the world of art is made possible by both his freedom to explore and the focus on his inner self. The latter shows readers how Wilhelm is attracted to the troupe not by the prospect of art, but by a moral decision which deviates him from the path set by his parents and friends. A chance encounter that enables a life-changing moral decision is a new feature of traditional *Bildungsromane*.

A new feature of the genre emerges in Chapter 4 of Book 2 (of a total of nine books or volumes—in German, *Bände*). Wilhelm intervenes he when notices that the manager of the troupe beats Mignon, a young Italian girl. This moral decision then prompts him to join them and become a father figure to the girl. This is his first experimentation with fatherhood, a social role he will embody by the end of the novel. Unlike Proto-*Bildungsromane*, Wilhelm finds a social site where he can experiment with and ponder on the role of father.

One of the foremost examples of his internal process of self-forging driving the plot forward happens when the troupe performs for a Baron. Wilhelm meets the Baron's natural son Jarno, who introduces him to the works of William Shakespeare. Of key importance is the play *Hamlet* (1609), which Wilhelm reads, memorizes, and decides to perform. Wilhelm says he identifies with the soliloquies in the play because they show the "Kraft der Seele, Erhebung des Geistes" [power of the soul and the elevation of the spirit] (Goethe 1985a, 214). Wilhelm feels a kinship with the hero of the play, the melancholic Danish Prince, who famously struggles with the task of avenging his late father by killing his uncle, who usurped the throne and queen by means of murder. Wilhelm adopts Hamlet's melancholy and sees his own formative process mirrored in the Prince's intricate decision-making process. Both protagonists puzzle over the paths laid before them, evaluating at length what their decisions will mean for their identities, in short, to be or not. Further, both characters love the theater and use it to understand themselves and the world around them.[4] As such, the world of the theater becomes key to Wilhelm's formative process. Ellis Dye explains the interplay of identity formation in this nexus:

Wilhelm understands Hamlet correctly and discerns a true soul-mate in him, so that in enacting the part he objectifies and better understands himself. That is, a pre-existent self and a literary character so closely resemble each other as to constitute a genuine identity but an identity visible to the subject only as object. Hamlet is equivalent to a fortuitous objectification of Wilhelm's own self and can therefore serve as a vehicle of his growing self-knowledge.

(Dye 1992, 71)

Hamlet holds a "mirror up to nature" in which Wilhelm can see a formative process, much like his own, and, as an actor, play with it (Shakespeare 2012, 701). In identifying with Hamlet, Wilhelm projects his own struggle with identity on to the character's. The formative process of the subject Wilhelm and of his object Hamlet overlap so closely that pondering over one is also pondering over the other. In the sections where melancholic and pensive Wilhelm sees himself as the Danish Prince and analyzes his development, Wilhelm simultaneously examines his own. This complex juxtaposition evidences Wilhelm's sophisticated process of identification. Wilhelm does not merely forge his path through action, but scrutinizes what his actions mean for his idea of self.

As the novel progresses, Wilhelm's maturation is evidenced by his realization that the actors in the troupe have taken advantage of him for too long, spending his money and expressing no gratitude. In an episode where the troupe is attacked by bandits, the actors leave the wounded Wilhelm for dead. Wilhelm becomes again disenchanted and returns by his own volition to the path of commerce: "Ich verlasse das Theater und verbinde mich mit Männern, deren Umgang mich, in jedem Sinne, zu einer reinen und sichern Tätigkeit führen muß" [I am leaving the theater and joining men whose association leads me, in every sense, to a pure and reliable occupation] (Goethe 1985a, 514). His apprenticeship in the theater comes to an end and he finds access to the life of the aristocracy and the homosocial possibility of masonry through his noble friend Lothario. Wilhelm becomes a father when he discovers that Mariane, who is now deceased, had a son by him. His son is appropriately named Felix, Latin for happy, as Wilhelm joyfully assumes the role of not simply a father figure, but rather a father in fact.

The closing chapters of the novel do not adhere to the archetypal plot as Wilhelm and Lothario's sister Natalie grow closer together and eventually form an unconventional family unit. Because Natalie is kind and gentle to Wilhelm's (possibly biological) son Felix, he increasingly sees her as a mother. Natalie promises that if Felix survives a critical illness, she will marry Wilhelm, thus transferring the life-and-death stakes that are externally apparent in Proto-*Bildunsromane* to the inward force of affection. At the end of the story, Wilhelm, Natalie, and Felix become a family of sorts, not bound by blood but by affection, an ending that clearly contradicts Moretti's assessment of marriage as the necessary resolution of traditional

Bildungsromane. This family unit is not an idealized "pact between the individual and the world" whereby Wilhelm sacrifices his freedom for the social whole (Moretti 2000, 23), as Moretti argues, but "possibly partially biological, if Felix is Wilhelm's biological son, and is also at least partially adoptive as Natalie takes Felix into her heart [...] a family that has been drawn together by their affinities of the heart" (Gustafson 2016, 135). Moreover, as Matthias Pirholt argues, Moretti's reading disregards that Wilhelm accesses "the petty nobility," which "in opposition to high aristocracy, and represented by Natalie and her brother Lothario, is a class that lacks both influence and culture" (2009, 78). So Goethe does not celebrate marriage as an ultimate goal, but rather "is critiquing the aristocratic and civil family structures of his age" (Gustafson 2016, 69), while simultaneously "highlighting the elective affinities that draw families together based on love and connections of the heart" (69). Wilhelm gains a space in the aristocracy, but it is not as idyllic as it has been made out to be. The marriage then quickly loses all its importance in the sequel, the *Wanderjahre*, and completely disappears from the diegesis.

With *Wilhelm Meisters Lehrjahre*, readers are also provided with profound insights into the protagonist's thoughts and motivations. The story is told by a third person narrator, but Wilhelm's voice is prevalent and ubiquitous. Subsequent *Bildungsromane* such as *Pride and Prejudice* will follow this model where the narrator is omniscient but the main character's voice is conveyed clearly throughout. Other traditional *Bildungsromane* ripen into a model that is most prevalent among contemporary coming-of-age novels, the autodiegetic narrator. Wilhelm sowed the seeds as he presents in his own perspective and ponders epistemological questions on art and identity, his struggles with the expectations of the world around him, and the relationships that he develops with strangers and relatives. Readers witness the false starts Susanne Howe mentions, as Wilhelm tries his luck in the theater and fails, only to try again and eventually join the shadowy *Turmgesellschaft*, which marks the end of his apprenticeship. Wilhelm finds his son and achieves a "stage of completeness" (Morgenstern 1820, 13). Goethe's *Lehrjahre* embodies some of key plot points of the traditional *Bildungsroman* and powerfully heralds the great variability and multiple possibilities for social organization and critique in the ampler category of the "coming-of-age novel."

For Jeffers and Moretti, Wilhelm's story ends in the *Lehrjahre*. His marriage to Natalie is the "good relationship," and they perceive the novel to fit with Buckley's archetypal plot. However, if one considers *Wilhelm Meisters Wanderjahre,* the sequel Goethe published more than twenty years later, the complete story of Wilhelm Meister does not conform with the archetypal plot and does not espouse a heterosexual union as the necessary form of social organization. The *Wanderjahre* is a shorter novel full of fragments, at times epistolary, at times a succession of aphorisms. It is impossible to assert with certainty that it is still a traditional

Bildungsroman. The very first *Bildungsroman* thus inherently holds the source of the countless branches into which the coming-of-age genre blooms.

This incohesive sequel mixes genres and opens the life-paths that Wilhelm could follow. It starts with the travels of Wilhelm and Felix. They are no longer a family unit as Natalie appears only as the addressee of Wilhelm's letters, not as a character in the diegesis. In the first chapter Wilhelm and Felix meet a family that reminds Wilhelm of the gospel of Matthew, specifically the holy family's flight into Egypt. Wilhelm intriguingly describes the man of this family in terms that suggest the possibility of sensual desire: "Ein derber, tüchtiger, nicht allzu großer junger Mann, leicht geschürzt, von brauner Haut und schwarzen Haaren" [A sturdy, able, not-too-tall young man, scantily dressed, with brown skin and black hair] (Goethe 1985b, 18). The narrator asserts that Wilhelm sees this figure with *Erstaunen* [astonishment or amazement] and immediately trusts and wants to spend time with him. This conceivable homosexual desire does not culminate in anything concrete. However, the mere suggestion of a desire that does not conform to heterosexual marriage destabilizes the tenets of traditional *Bildingsromane*, which some coming-of-age novels will further subvert. As Wilhelm and Felix travel on, they encounter in the figure of Jarno, the man who initially introduced Wilhelm to the works of Shakespeare, and a further destabilization of the archetypical plot ensues. Jarno, who now calls himself Montan, has at this time renounced all forms of social life in favor of communion with nature. Montan tells Wilhelm that he finds happiness in this lonesome existence: "Die Menschen wollt' ich meiden" [I wanted to avoid people] (Goethe 1985b, 43). As such, Jarno embodies the possibility of a life path that, although unusual, can be fulfilling, and an option that did not exist in the *Lehrjahre*. In terms of the narrative genre itself, the text breaks with the traditional succession of events from childhood and into adulthood as the journey continues to unfold with many digressions and stories within the story. These embedded stories are in turn strange and incohesive, as they jump from narrative to drama and back to narrative without warning.

If studied in isolation, the original *Wilhelm Meisters Lehrjahre* embodies some of the characteristics of the traditional *Bildungsromane* and is a useful point of reference to study other *Bildungsromane* in both the German tradition and international examples that end in marriage. However, Wilhelm's sequel refigures the "degree of perfection" he had achieved at the end of the first novel as a state less complete than previously represented in *Bildungsroman* scholarship such as Jeffers's and Moretti's. Goethe's sequel wanders from the traditional *Bildungsroman*. Certainly, the complex preoccupation with identity is still present, as evidenced by two aphorisms at the end of the second part of the novel: "Wie kann man sich selbst kennenlernen? Durch Betrachten niemals, wohl aber durch Handeln. Versuche, deine Pflicht zu tun, und du weißt gleich, was an dir ist. Was aber ist deine Pflicht? Die Forderung des Tages" [How can one know oneself? Never through contemplation, but fully through action. Try to do your duty and you will immediately know who you are. But what is your duty? The demands of each day] (Goethe 1985b, 513). In these aphorisms, Goethe states that knowing oneself does not happen all at once. This particular conceptualization of a process of identification does not and cannot yield the fully-formed adult, citizen, and worker that the first novel presents. The sequel truly offers an alternative approach as it affirms that we know ourselves through the actions of every day and therefore only in the process of constant becoming.

Other Early German *Bildungsromane*

Algonside Wilhelm Meister, other *Bildungsromane* emerge during the epoch in the region. Novalis's *Heinrich von Ofterdingen* (published posthumously in 1802) and Ludwig Tieck's short novella *Der Runenberg* (1804) attest to the epoch's interest in the formation of the self as they explore and expand upon the genre and its archetypal plot. The malleability of the genre is so fundamental that even Goethe's coevals developed twists and turns that deviate from the archetypal plot. In the case of Novalis's *Heinrich von Ofterdingen*, it is impossible to assert whether it coordinates with Buckley's plot as its second part remained unfinished when the author died in the spring of 1801. Novalis stated his plan for Heinrich in a letter he wrote to Ludwig Tieck where he explained that Heinrich would have been "als Dichter verklärt" [transfigured into a poet] (quoted in Pirholt 2012, 114), but we never encounter this full-fledged poet. There is no final degree of completeness, only "proof of Heinrich's poetic talent" (114). Without an ending, and because of a strong sense of *Schicksal* embodied in the metaphor of the blue flower, *Heinrich von Ofterdingen* cannot be classified as a traditional *Bildungsroman*. However, readers find many of the genre's characteristics in it: *Heinrich* portrays a complex formative process that stresses internal struggles; shows a protagonist who is deeply concerned with matters of love, development, and identity; and, cheerfully marries the young Mathilde at the end of the first part. The first part of the novel, entitled "Die Erwartung" ["The Expectation"], "tells the story of Heinrich's experiences and education, which will eventually lead up to the transfiguration in the second part" (114). In it, the blue flower is a key symbol to understand Heinrich's formative process. Heinrich first encounters the flower in the stories of a stranger, then recalls them and dreams of far off places, adventures, all sorts of men, and strange monsters. The blue flower, which draws him near and fascinates him in his dream becomes a metaphor for travel and the exciting exploration of the world and the self. However, it could also be a manifestation of destiny since his father also dreamed of the blue flower years before. In his father's dream, the image of the flower is intermingled with that of his future wife holding a baby in her arms. The dream motivates Heinrich's father to travel to Augsburg, where he first meets Heinrich's mother. The flower seems to be an external and supernatural force that guides people's fates, but it could also be a manifestation of Heinrich's internal and unfulfilled desire to travel and begin his formative process. His father's tale of the flower prompts Heinrich's mother to set his travels in motion. She wishes him to meet new people and places, and to find "die Reize einer jungen Landsmännin" [the charms of a young countrywoman] (Novalis 1964, 49). Heinrich's travel to his mother's homeland is accompanied by merchants who recognize Heinrich's talent for poetry. After several encounters and digressions, Heinrich reaches his mother's native Augsburg and meets his maternal grandfather Schwaning. Here the gears of *Schicksal* turn as he is introduced to Klingsohr and his daughter Mathilde, in whose face Heinrich recognizes the blue flower. As destiny would have it, Heinrich falls in love with Mathilde almost immediately. She is sensitive and gentle. By the end of chapter eight, they have sworn to be inseparable forever: "Eine lange Umarmung, unzählige Küsse besiegelten den ewigen Bund des seligen Paars" [A long embrace and countless kisses sealed the eternal bond of the blessed pair] (126). Klingsohr promises to give them a marriage feast.

If the novel had ended here, we could say that the novel portrays a completed formative process and a degree of completeness. The short second part of the novel entitled "Die Erfüllung" ["The Fulfilment"] (Novalis 1964, 149), however, drifts far from the conventions of the archetypal plot. It takes place in a dream-like world in which Heinrich discusses the nature of language and poetry with the pilgrim Sylvester. Sylvester concludes that because his heart is innocent he will become a prophet and all truth will be revealed to him. The second part of the novel expands the conventions of the genre to diminish the importance of the physical self and develop the world of the mind. It is possible that Novalis would have taken the novel deeply into this dreamlike realm of poetry, which comes in direct contrast to the materiality of the first part. Such developments transcend even the strict configuration of traditional *Bildungsromane* so that *Heinrich* steps into the realm of the larger and more flexible genre of "coming-of-age novels."

Der Runenberg, published nine years after the *Lehrjahre*, features external elements of the supernatural akin to Proto-*Bildungsromane*. However, it also resembles traditional *Bildungsromane* because the internal force of self-determination is the main driver of plot. This short text maintains a balance between the magical forces that sway the meaningfully-named protagonist Christian and his will to become a family man. However, supernatural forces prove stronger at the end thus preventing the character from achieving a "stage of completeness." At the beginning of the novel we encounter young Christian alone in the woods. He has left home because he does not want to become a gardener like his father, which is to say that he wants to veer from the social practices of taking on the work of one's parents that feels so much like destiny. Christian explains, "Mein Vater war Gärtner im Schloß und hatte vor, mich ebenfalls zu seiner Beschäftigung zu erziehen" [My father was a gardener in the castle and wanted to teach me his trade]

(Tieck 1933, 272–273). However, as Christian expresses, "Mir war die Gartenarbeit zuwider" [Gardening was abhorrent to me] (273). The internal drive to choose his own profession takes him far from home. Christian has a restlessness common in *Bildungsromane*. It is an internal anxiety that often prohibits protagonists from simply surrendering to the expectations of their parents and society. And as Christian ponders on the topic of destiny, the heterodiegetic narrator informs us that Christian wants "eine fremde Umgebung zu suchen, um sich aus dem Kreise der wiederkehrenden Gewöhnlichkeit zu entfernen" [to search for an unfamiliar environment, in order to escape the loop of a repetitive routine] (270). This character representation spurs the plot. Christian goes through a process of trial and error. He wants to be a fisherman, then a tradesman, but after trying these out, he decides to keep searching. He eventually decides to be a hunter and goes into the wilderness. He suffers the hardship of hunger and solitude, but he resolves not to go back home as the will to self-forge dominates his life. Shortly after a main plot point of traditional *Bildungsromane* is fulfilled when Christian meets a stranger who becomes a mentor and teaches him how to thrive in the woods.

Der Runenberg underscores the supernatural elements of its world when, after spending some time together, the stranger leaves Christian in order to go to the Runenberg, a magical hill that has an old mine-shaft, a magical element more akin to Proto-*Bildungsromane*. Beckoned by a supernatural force, antithetical to *Bildungsromane*, Christian descends into the mine and finds a beautiful woman who seems immortal. She sings and undresses before Christian. In this dream-like setting, she gives him a tablet full of jewels that he loses and that will again become relevant towards the end of the novel. He then wakes outside of the mine feeling as if it had all been a dream, much like Parzival's first visit of his uncle, the Fisher King Anfortas. Strangely, Christian does not recognize the country and, as he wanders, he arrives at a village he had never seen before. Christian's aimless wandering contrasts with his personality in the beginning of the text where he is assertive and takes the reins of his future by deciding his profession. When the supernatural is present, Christian seems to succumb to the external forces that lure and guide him. His wandering is aimless and he stumbles on both the supernatural woman and afterwards the village by chance. His initial resolve echoes *Wilhelm Meister* but the magical and unfamiliar are more similar to the force of destiny in *Parzival*.

In an odd turn of heart, Christian decides to live with the family in the village and take up gardening. The narrator does not explain this unexpected decision which, in *Bildugnsromane*, would be pondered at length. Instead, he merely says, "daß Christian als Gärtner bei ihm einziehen solle. Dieser konnte es unternehmen, denn er hoffte, daß ihm nun die Kenntnisse und Beschäftigungen zustatten kommen würden, die er in seiner Heimat so sehr verachtet hatte" [Christian would move in with him as a gardener. This Christian could do, because he hoped that the knowledge and employments, that he had despised in his hometown, would now be useful] (Tieck 1933, 279). Christian soon marries a village girl, Elisabeth, and they have a daughter, Leonora. In the archetypal plot this would be a possible ending, as Christian states he is content. He has found an accommodation as citizen and worker. However, the story does not end here. Except for his joyous reunion with his father, the events that follow are full of misfortune and despair. It is possible that at the last moment in the narration when Christian is happy as family man and gardener, Tieck is cautioning readers of the repercussions of straying from such an ideal life.

Towards the end of the novel, a stranger stays with Christian's family for a long time. He announces that he must leave but entrusts Christian with a fortune, which Christian can keep for himself if the stranger does not come back within a year's time. This responsibility disturbs Christian's happiness and the household loses its peace. Eventually, Christian goes into the woods, where he sees the stranger approaching and fears he will have to return the money. As the figure advances, Christian sees that is not the stranger but an old hideous woman. The *Waldweib* [wood woman] turns out to be the beautiful figure from the beginning, who gives back the tablet full of jewels that Christian had lost. Christian disappears into the woods for many years. Back in the village, Christian's father dies lamenting the loss of his son and Elisabeth is forced to remarry a cruel man. Christian returns many years later announcing that he has collected many treasures, but when he empties his sack only gravel comes out. Elisabeth and Leonora are completely desolate as Christian has failed to fulfil the roles of family man, citizen, and worker. Christian, now "Der Unglückliche" [the unhappy] goes back into the woods never to be seen again (290).

Christian's is a strange formative process that interweaves supernatural forces and the struggle for self-determination. He first tries to find his own way but the supernatural interrupts his formative process. It is possible that the strangers and the *Waldweib* are all the same being, ensnaring Christian with illusory riches. Elisabeth, his family, and work are real and make Christian happy. In the archetypal plot, Christian would look at the palpable sources of his happiness and achievement and stay with Elizabeth. However, the uncanny calls to him more strongly, leading him down the path of despair. This novella shows a formative process, but rather than ending it with an accommodation, it shows a non-traditional ending in unhappiness. *Der Runenberg* can be read as a cautionary tale that depicts the agony of rejecting real contentment and an idyllic marriage in exchange for illusory treasure.

The long narratives and novels discussed demonstrate that the traditional *Bildungsroman* is a genre of the novel that, unlike other forms of narrative, focuses predominantly on a formative process. The internal forces of self-determination and the need to ponder on and experiment with one's identity are the key drivers of the plot and the main objectives of the protagonists. Rather than supernatural forces pushing them forward or a quest to fulfil a predetermined destiny, the protagonists forge their own paths through processes of trial and error. They imitate several role models, experiment with varied occupations, and make false starts. In traditional *Bildungsromane*, but not necessarily in all "coming-of-age novels," the protagonists ultimately attain a degree of completeness as citizens and often members of the middle class, but most importantly as spouses and parents. In this originary iteration, the novels guide and further the readers' own processes of identification, prompting them to improve themselves.

Bildungsroman is a term that many theorists associate exclusively with Buckley's plot, Germany, and the eighteenth century. For this reason, I use "coming-of-age novel" to encompass the myriad of variations that have come thereafter. The characteristics of the original iteration have inspired plentiful and varied coming-of-age stories through the centuries and across the globe. The focus of Chapter 2 is the structural and thematic transformations of traditional *Bildungsromane* in nineteenth- and twentieth-century England in *Pride and Prejudice, David Copperfield,* and *Great Expectations*; and *Maurice* (written in 1913–1914 and published posthumously in 1971) by E. M. Forster. The study of these four key novels in the development of the genre illustrates how coming-of-age novels continued to develop in the global stage to portray a myriad of experiences that this fluid genre enables.

Notes

1 See Althusser, Louis. *On the Reproduction of Capitalism: Ideology and Ideological State Apparatuses.* Verso, 2014.
2 Translations from German are mine unless otherwise noted.
3 Unless otherwise noted, translations from German are mine.
4 Like Wilhelm, Hamlet uses theater as a tool to understand and ponder a truth about his world. While Wilhelm uses his reflection on the theater as a way to reflect on his own identity and melancholy, Hamlet stages a pantomime and a short play, *The Murder of Gonzago,* in which a king is murdered and his throne usurped in order to present it to his uncle. He uses this play to observe his uncle's reaction and thus discover a hidden truth about his murderous ascent to the throne. Hamlet successfully uses the theater to uncover the truth about his uncle. Wilhelm finds truths about his *own* self in his reading and performance of theater. It is also relevant to note that Hamlet asserts that it is possible to better understand the world by employing the means of theater when, in Act III, Scene 2, he instructs the players on how to act, to "suit the action to the word, the word to the action" in order to achieve authenticity, and, most importantly, that the "purpose of playing" is to hold "the mirror up to nature; to show virtue her own feature, scorn her own image, and the very age and body of the time his form and pressure" (Shakespeare 2012, 701). Wilhelm takes these words to heart, and uses the play to learn from Hamlet, thus furthering his own formative process.

2 The Thematic and Structural Transformations of the Coming-of-age Novel in Nineteenth- and Twentieth-Century Britain

Jane Austen, Charles Dickens and E. M. Forster

Coming-of-age novels were first born in the German tradition of the late eighteenth century. Amid many long medieval narrative texts that depicted the formative processes of children who became heroes and knights, traditional *Bildungsromane* distinguished themselves by affording their protagonists a new freedom to explore and evaluate their identities and decide to a much larger extent who they wanted to be, their professions, their morals, and whom they would marry. Early coming-of-age novels are more accurately termed "traditional *Bildungsromane*" because they use archetypal plot points—such as the search for a mentor and the experimentation with romantic relationships doomed to fail before the right one emerges—and often culminate in marriage and the depiction of idealized adult citizens and workers. Traditional *Bildungsromane* have fundamental didactic and moralizing purposes as they imparted on young male middle-class readers the entrepreneurial spirit of self-discovery and advised them to ultimately marry and become active citizens, productive workers, and family men.

As the ever-malleable coming-of-age genre developed, it variably took on only certain elements of the archetypal plot and instead enabled the exciting emergence in the late twentieth century of "Diasporic Coming-of-age Novels," the subject of Parts II and III of this book. These are novels where culturally-hybrid, marginalized, and diasporic protagonists puzzle over their identities and marginalized places in globalized societies and cosmopolitan settings. But before this contemporary development, the coming-of-age genre travelled throughout Europe and beyond in the nineteenth century, reworking the archetypal plot and coming-of-age in international settings.

Traditional *Bildungsromane* journeyed and grew in particularly striking ways in nineteenth-century England. Many novels depict interesting generic variations, but three key novels of the nineteenth century and one of the twentieth century show the tremendous malleability of the genre, its diversification of readership and themes, and its capacity to voice marginalized experiences: *Pride and Prejudice* (1813) by Jane Austen; *David Copperfield* (1850) and *Great Expectations* (1861) by Charles Dickens; and *Maurice* (written in 1913–1914 and published posthumously in 1971) by E. M. Forster. *Pride and Prejudice* and *David Copperfield* follow all the fundamental points of the archetypal plot, especially the ending. As expected, most *Bildungsroman* scholarship accurately lists these nineteenth-century novels as classic examples of the genre. They are, therefore, the most apt examples for demonstrating that, even though they use the archetypal plot conventions, they rework and invigorate the genre. For the first time, they address an exceptionally large and diverse audience and break new ground by depicting the struggles and formative experiences of marginalized people—namely women in Austen and the working class in Dickens—who were not shown in protagonist roles in earlier *Bildungsromane*. The third novel, *Great Expectations*, subverts the tenets of the archetypal plot with its famous two-ending controversy, still hotly disputed in contemporary scholarship. The original ending thwarts all possibility of marriage and happiness; the revised one coordinates with the dogma of romantic union and happiness, but neither culminates explicitly in marriage. The fourth novel, *Maurice*, is particularly transformative, as the ending in marriage and thus the archetypal plot become impossible for Maurice Hall, a homosexual gentleman and member of the landed gentry. These last two are thus "coming-of-age" novels rather than traditional *Bildungsromane*, still with an introspective formative process as their central theme and force of plot, but no longer directed towards a family unit or the final representation of an ideal citizen and worker.

All four novels diversify the boundaries of readership and innovatively include social commentary. They also position happiness as a central theme. Their thematic and structural innovations sow the seeds that in contemporary diasporic communities bloom into Diasporic Coming-of-age Novels. Rather than offering a new direction in the scholarship of these four novels, I show how they bridge the traditional German *Bildungsromane* with the contemporary Diasporic Coming-of-age genre.

The Austenian Marriage of True Affection

The main innovation of *Pride and Prejudice* to the genre is in terms of gender. The focus on a female protagonist deeply shifted the key aspects of the genre as it gave greater importance to the analysis of oppressive societal structures and the possibilities of deciding her own path within a limited sphere of influence. The famous first line of the novel cleverly reveals this power structure by placing on men the agency of choosing a spouse and the authority afforded by property: "It is a truth universally acknowledged that a single man in possession of a good fortune must be in want of a wife" (Austen 2016, 1). While the titular character of Goethe's *Wilhelm Meisters Lehrjahre* could choose his profession and spouse with great freedom, Elizabeth Bennet's prospects are far more restricted. Nonetheless, Elizabeth ponders on her identity and place in society to such an extent that she rejects two marriage proposals suitable to her social station because she does not feel affection for the suitors—thus subverting the societal expectation that women should marry as soon as possible.

Social class is key to the coming-of-age genre since it determines the scope of career paths available to characters. While traditional *Bildungsromane* represent middle-class careers, coming-of-age novels represent a wider range of possibilities for education and employment. An abundance of Austen's scholars has attempted to classify her and her characters into a particular social class. This is due to the pervasive effort in coming-of-age scholarship to examine the often relevant overlap between the authors' biographies and their fictions. However, it is no simple task to assert whether Austen herself, or her characters, belong to a particular socioeconomic class, as scholars place her (excluding the extremes of substantial wealth and poverty) in varied points of the spectrum. A few examples serve to illustrate how ardently debated Austen's social position is in a crowded scholarly scape. Austen's contemporary Sir Walter Scott argued that she "confines herself chiefly to the middling classes of society; her most distinguished characters do not rise greatly above well-bred country gentlemen and ladies; and those which are sketched with most originality and precision, belong to a class rather below that standard" (Scott 1815, 193). In contrast, Claudia Johnson explains of the author, rather than characters, that "many readers contend that Austen was a socially confident member of the landed gentry and, with that, the ruling class" (Johnson 1988, xviii). And to contest Austen's belonging to the landed gentry, Robert Irvine asserts that Austen's father George Austen could not possibly be considered upper class since he earned a modest annual income of £200, while the income of a gentry family would have been between £1,000 and £5,000 (Irvine 2005, 2). Indeed, George Austen was "propertyless," and Jane Austen spent her "most productive years as what Barbara Pym would call a 'distressed gentlewoman'" (Johnson 1988, xviii). This description of Austen's financial realities is indeed reflected in her work, as Kathryn Sutherland describes Austen's unfinished novel *The Watsons* as "a study in the harsh economic realities of dependent women's lives" (Sutherland 2005, 15).

Because of the considerable disparity in Austen's socioeconomic taxonomy, a claim that *Pride and Prejudice* is an autobiographic working-class, or even middle-class, *Bildungsroman* would be done on shifty ground at best. Indeed, it is even difficult to assert with confidence the social position of the protagonist Elizabeth Bennet: "Her father's property consisted almost entirely in an estate of two thousand a year, which, unfortunately for his daughters, was entailed, in default of heirs male, on a distant relation; and their mother's fortune, though ample for her situation in life, could but ill supply the deficiency of his. Her father had been an attorney in Meryton, and had left her four thousand pounds" (Austen 2016, 22). Although the family's income was enough to classify them as landed gentry (Irvine 2005, 2), upon their father's death, the five Bennet sisters would be dispossessed. Their mother was decidedly middle class, her father being a lawyer. Thus, it comes as no surprise that Mrs. Bennet would be keen on marrying her daughters to rich gentlemen, as evidenced by her conversation with Mr. Bennet at the very beginning of the novel, where she is excited that Netherfield Park, a nearby property, has been occupied by the single and rich Mr. Bingley:

> "A single man of large fortune; four or five thousand a year. What a fine thing for our girls!"
>
> "How so? How can it affect them?"
>
> "My dear Mr. Bennet," replied his wife, "how can you be so tiresome! You must know that I am thinking of his marrying one of them."
>
> (Austen 2016, 2)

The depiction of life and relationships in the novel centers mostly on the landed gentry. However, there is a latent danger that the Bennet sisters could lose their social station if they are unable to find husbands. It is therefore not a novel about the experiences of the working class, but about the coming-of-age of a woman pressured to secure her position in society and livelihood through marriage. At the end of the novel, the protagonist successfully marries above her station, thus fulfilling the main objective of the archetypal plot. However, her motivations and indeed her ideas of the institution differ greatly from those of earlier and coeval *Bildungsromane* and are intimately linked to the marginalized and precarious position of women.

Franco Moretti argues that *Pride and Prejudice* is one of the first and most classic examples of *Bildungsromane* because it concludes in a mandatory "perfect marriage" that works as "a metaphor for the social contract," not contrary to celibacy but to "disgrace" (Moretti 2000, 22–23). The desire to marry, defined by mores in a very specific social class and geo-historic site (nineteenth-century England), corresponds to the ultimate objective of the archetypal plot and seems so strong it is almost supernatural. Importantly for women, marriage in Victorian England entailed a change of surname and thus a new belonging and an upheaval of one's identity. But despite this "truth universally acknowledged" and key preoccupation, the protagonist does not marry at the earliest opportunity. She instead puzzles over what the right marriage means and waits for years to become engaged to the rich gentleman from Derbyshire, Mr. Fitzwilliam Darcy.

Lending urgency and twists to the plot, the novel entertains the possibility of Elizabeth never marrying. She rejects two proposals, Mr. Collins's and the first of Darcy's, before accepting Darcy's second, only after he has proven his affection and moral integrity. The novel thus expands on the definition of the traditional *Bildungsroman*, asserting that the final degree of completion of this heroine is not marriage in itself, but the *right* kind of marriage, "to the advantage of both" (Austen 2016, 266), one that is not only socially convenient but also happy, a "marriage of true affection" like that of her parents (70). In the prototypical *Bildungsroman,* Wilhelm Meister's marriage affords him access into the aristocracy so it is in that sense also an advantageous one. The thematic innovation for Elizabeth is that in addition to the individual happiness from the fulfilment of a societal institution that cements her belonging in the landed gentry, her marriage generates a complementary and shared happiness between the spouses rooted in love between equals.

The novel begins in close connection with the archetypal plot. The arrival of Mr. Bingley, a rich man in search of a wife, sets in motion the social apparatus so elegantly described in the first line of the novel. Even though Mr. Bennet seems to appear oblivious to the need of their daughters to marry, he calls on Bingley so that his daughters can eventually meet him. Mr. Bennet understands the social setting and his important role in advancing the objective of marriage. As such, Mr. Bennet functions as a driver of plot when he successfully orchestrates a meeting. A ball takes places in the town of Meryton, where Elizabeth first meets Bingley's friend Darcy, who appears odious, representing one of Elizabeth's "bad relationships," according to the archetypal plot. But *Pride and Prejudice* develops the genre by continuing to follow not only the formative process of Elizabeth Bennet, but instead several concurrent coming-of-age stories; mainly those of the Bennet sisters. In particular, the novel follows the eldest, Jane, and the youngest, Lydia. Secondarily, several other coming-of-age stories serve as models for identification and disidentification, such as that of Elizabeth's best friend and confidante Charlotte, who marries Collins, for whom marriage is nothing but "a business" (Austen 2016, 74), in large part because she adheres to a more restricted *Bildung* convention.

The archetypal plot of traditional *Bildungsromane* indicates that protagonists experience "bad relationships" in order to experiment and eventually build the "good one." The first attempt at a relationship with Darcy fails because in harsh arrogance Darcy rejects Elizabeth in the first quarter of the novel: "he looked for a moment at Elizabeth, till catching her eye, he withdrew his own and coldly said, 'She is tolerable; but not handsome enough to tempt *me*'" (8). He later develops an attraction to her wit and charm, but he must prove his integrity and feelings later in the novel. The first possibility for marriage then does not come from Darcy, but from the relative Mr. Collins, a young clergyman expected to inherit Mr. Bennet's entailed estate. In his overconfident marriage proposal, Mr. Collins assumes Elizabeth would be overjoyed at the prospect of marriage, even implying that he is doing young Lizzy a favor. Collins tells Elizabeth:

> Thus much for my general intention in favour of matrimony; it remains to be told why my views were directed towards Longbourn instead of my own neighbourhood, where I can assure you there are many amiable young women. But the fact is, that being, as I am, to inherit this estate after the death of your honoured father (who, however, may live many

years longer), I could not satisfy myself without resolving to choose a wife from among his daughters, that the loss to them might be as little as possible, when the melancholy event takes place.

(Austen 2016, 75)

Although Mr. Collin's rationale would be sound in the most traditional *Bildungsroman*, Lizzy shows the genre developing, as she rejects him on account of his stupidity, much to the surprise of her mother Mrs. Bennet, who calls Elizabeth headstrong and foolish.

In contrast to Elizabeth's rejection, her friend Charlotte accepts Mr. Collins's subsequent marriage proposal. Like Elizabeth, Charlotte does not feel affection for Mr. Collins, but, unlike Elizabeth, who waits for a better match, Charlotte agrees to the marriage "solely from the pure and disinterested desire of an establishment" (106). This decision fits Charlotte's earlier explanation that "happiness in marriage is entirely a matter of chance" (18). At this, Elizabeth reacts with anger and later tells her sister Jane that Charlotte's marriage lacks "either merit or sense" and "in every view it is unaccountable!" (117).

This bad relationship of the protagonist, which doubles as a parallel counter-case, contributes to the genre's redefinition of *any* marriage as access to the social whole. Elizabeth is developing her idea of a correct marriage, one where the partners are socially suitable but also affectionate and equal in wit and intelligence. Through Charlotte's marriage, Elizabeth learns that marriage without love is undesirable. Despite Jane's explanation that it is advantageous to Charlotte because "she is one of a large family" and therefore has few chances a more "eligible match" in terms of respectability and fortune, Elizabeth condemns the marriage (117). She maintains that Mr. Collins is a "conceited, pompous, narrow-minded silly man" and therefore Charlotte's marriage is an affront to "principle and integrity;" supporting Charlotte's decision would be to think "selfishness is prudence, and insensibility of danger security for happiness" (117). Thus by assessing the formative processes around her, her own notion and desire becomes clearer.

On the opposite end, a marriage with love without socioeconomical merit occurs when young Lydia elopes with the trickster Wickham, thus risking disgrace for the whole Bennet family. In Lydia's reversed case, she marries for affection without thinking at all of her social station. Unlike Wilhelm Meister who only thinks, but never actually elopes, with an actress who would ruin his socioeconomic prospects, Lydia truly risks disgrace by running away with Wickham, who only agrees to marry her (and thus preserve her honor) in exchange for an annual income that, unknown to Elizabeth, Darcy provides. Innovatively for the genre, the experiences of the characters around Elizabeth inform her own process of identity formation and her opinions about the institution she will ultimately access.

Also aligned with the most salient structural characteristics of the traditional *Bildungsroman* is the prominence of the protagonist's voice in the text. Although *Pride and Prejudice,* much like *Wilhelm Meisters Lehrjahre,* has a third-person narrator, its voice often quiets down so that the protagonist can relate, in her own words, her life, opinions, and musings. As Moretti asserts of the novel, "the classical *Bildungsroman* has the reader perceive the text through the eyes of the protagonist" (2000, 56). Even though Elizabeth internalizes the opinions of others and society at large without much resistance at times, as the novel progresses, her own opinions become predominant. This process of self-forging of the inner mind is particularly apparent in two moments of the novel that plainly address the development of Elizabeth's own opinions. Both episodes involve Darcy and, while the first shows him express a condescending opinion about her mind, the second shows her assertiveness. In the first, Darcy says to Elizabeth: "I have had the pleasure of your acquaintance long enough to know that you find great enjoyment in occasionally professing opinions which in fact are not your own" (Austen 2016, 150). In the second, Elizabeth rejects Darcy's first marriage proposal asserting her own view of Darcy and of the detestable prospect of marrying him:

> In such cases as this, it is, I believe, the established mode to express a sense of obligation for the sentiments avowed, however unequally they may be returned. It is natural that obligation should be felt, and if I could feel gratitude, I would now thank you. But I cannot—I have never desired your good opinion, and you have certainly bestowed it most unwillingly. I am sorry to have occasioned pain to anyone. It has been most unconsciously done, however, and I hope will be of short duration. The feelings which, you tell me, have long prevented the acknowledgment of your regard, can have little difficulty in overcoming it after this explanation.
>
> (Austen 2016, 163)

Elizabeth begins by acknowledging what her expected answer should be; that is, showing how well she understands her station and what marriage to Darcy would mean. However, she disregards societal pressures and in an act of bold self-forging rejects him, affirming her own opinion of what her ideal internal life ought to be despite the risks to her economic well-being.

The key marker of the protagonist's maturity is not simply that she gets married to anyone that could improve her station, like Charlotte did, but rather that it is only Elizabeth, and not her family or society, who can decide whom she should marry. And, instead of simply assuming she will marry him for his station, Darcy must prove his worth by anonymously paying for Wickham's annual stipend and thus protecting the reputation of the Bennet family. In her own right, Elizabeth has asserted her own worth when she defends her family against the contempt of Darcy's aunt Lady Catherine de Bourgh who thinks Elizabeth is of too low a station to marry her nephew. Elizabeth explains she is resolved to marry him and thus, as she states, "act in that manner, which will, in my own opinion, constitute my happiness, without reference to *you*, or to any person so wholly unconnected with me" (307). In the end, they marry against the wishes of Lady Catherine and are thankful for their happiness. The novel thus ends in accordance with the archetypal plot, but it expands on the genre by introducing a multiplicity of simultaneous coming-of-age stories that shape the protagonist's formative process, depicting the hardships of women who cannot choose a profession and instead must rely on marriage to secure their income and position, and pondering on what marriage is and what the ideal marriage should be.

The Dickensian Working-Class *Bildungsroman*

The key thematic innovation of *Pride and Prejudice* in the representation of women's subjection is mirrored in importance by the depictions of the voiceless working class in Dicken's *David Copperfield*. *David Copperfield* uses the salient points of the archetypal plot and ends with the representation of the protagonists as a successful middle-class writer, but broadens the definition of traditional *Bildungsromane* as it shows the titular character struggle with poverty in the underworld of industrial London. The portrayal of the hardships of poverty and hunger during childhood are central to Dickens's adult characters and readers. This key thematic reformation has enabled frequent and sharp research from the perspective of class. Underscoring the importance of childhood for the health of the social body politic, Dickens's "fictions taught Victorian audiences that childhood traumas were crucial to the formation of the adult self and contributed to societal ruptures" (Houston 1994, 6). As Gail Houston argues, "Dickens's fiction is anchored in the belief that although class and gender are fictional constructions, real people's lives are affected in complex and coercive ways by such constructions" (xv). Houston explains that Dickens's Victorian society "expected the lower class and women in general to starve voluntarily" (xiii). This important context is powerfully represented in perhaps the best-remembered scene in all of Dicken's fiction: the hungry titular character of *Oliver Twist* (1837) reprimanded for asking "please, sir" for some more gruel (Dickens 1999, 20). This key moment in Dicken's fiction is not an isolated case, but indeed one of similar present also in *David Copperfield*, whose years-long hunger is an entirely new theme in the coming-of-age genre.

Childhood trauma is linked to poverty in *David Copperfield* when the dispossessed young David must work in London in his stepfather Edward Murdstone's wine bottling factory. His life there differs greatly from any episode in *Wilhelm Meisters Lehrjahre* or *Pride and Prejudice*, where poverty remains a threat but is not a lived experience for the main characters. David is very poor, spending any money he receives on food: "When I had money enough, I used to get half-a-pint of ready-made coffee and a slice of bread and butter. When I had none, I used to look at a venison shop in Fleet Street; or I have strolled, at such a time, as far as Covent Garden Market, and stared at the pineapples" (Dickens 1981, 189). Despite his destitution, David never steals, begs, or borrows, thus choosing not to break the societal mores and laws of Christian middle-class England. His untainted moral character later enables his reincorporation to middle-class society. In contrast, his landlord and friend Mr. Micawber goes to prison for being an insolvent debtor and years later, still buried in debt, decides to emigrate to Australia unable to align with the Christian morality of Victorian society. This contrast implies the boundaries of construction of the novel's generic aims. The possibility of becoming a criminal does occur to David, but he invokes the Christian God as protection from such a path:

> I know I do not exaggerate, unconsciously and unintentionally, the scantiness of my resources or the difficulties of my life. I know that if a shilling were given me by Mr. Quinion at any time, I spent it in a dinner or a tea. I know that I worked, from morning until night, with common men and boys, a shabby child. I know that I lounged about the streets, insufficiently and unsatisfactorily fed. I know that, but for the mercy of God, I might easily have been, for any care that was taken of me, a little robber or a little vagabond.
>
> (Dickens 1981, 193)

Although David eventually escapes poverty in industrial London and finds his way to relatives in the countryside who help him continue his process of introspection and trajectory to become a gentleman, this experience powerfully breaks with the exclusive representation of middle-class life in previous and coeval *Bildungsromane*. In depicting working-class struggle, Dickens broke open a path for the coming-of-age genre initially concerned with the middle class but nowadays widely used by people facing different and often intertwined forms of marginalization and oppression.

In addition to this thematic development, *David Copperfield* introduced an important structural change to the coming-of-age genre: it is the first of Dickens's novels "to be recounted entirely in the first person" (Gold 1972, 175), a feature that enables the ubiquitous voice of the protagonist to tell his own experience and the workings of his inner self. This innovation later becomes a staple of Diasporic Coming-of-age Novels, which seldom have a heterodiegetic narrator.

Even with these thematic and structure transformations, *David Copperfield* is quite a traditional *Bildungsroman*. As Buckley's plot diagrams, the novel begins in a suburban setting. There, a sensitive child, David, lives with his widowed mother Clara. They live well, as the Copperfield fortune belongs to his mother, until David is eight years old and his mother marries Murdstone, who manipulates her into accepting him as the owner of the household. This marriage—one of the many models David witnesses and contemplates—is certainly not *right* or well thought out, in the Austenian sense demonstrated earlier in this chapter. As Ross Dabney explains, "David's mother plunges fatuously into marriage with Murdstone" (1967, 68). The circumstances of Clara's death are never clear, but it is entirely possible that Murdstone murdered her in order to secure her possessions. Gail Houston is convinced of this murder, explaining that "in order to enter adulthood, the adolescent David must murder the 'murderer' stepfather," at least in the symbolic sense, which David does by exposing his villainy in the autobiographical form (1994, 107). In the literal sense, David bites Murdstone during a beating, which results in Murdstone sending David away, thus precipitating David's experiences of poverty and the new thematic expansion of the genre. After a brief period in a boarding house where Mr. Creakle, a friend of Murdstone, harshly mistreats David, the young protagonist goes to work in London in Murdstone's wine bottling factory. Because David cannot endure the conditions in London, he flees and almost succumbs to starvation before he reaches his aunt Betsy Trotwood's house in Dover, where he receives the first part of his education.

David then moves back to London, the metropolis, where he experiences another *Bildungsroman* convention: he has two important romantic relationships. The "bad" one ends with the death of his first wife Dora Spenlow, an incorrect marriage in the Austenian sense, "innocent and impulsive," in which David experiments with the disastrous marriage model his mother embodied: "David himself marries a helpless child very like his mother" (Dabney 1967, 66, 68). Dora's death is a convenient plot development that enables David to find the "good" relationship with his first love, Agnes Wickfield, whom David has to save from Uriah Heep, the novel's villain. His marriage to Agnes is idyllic and "carefully weighted" (67).

In accordance with Buckley's plot, at the end, the hero finds, among the roles that society has to offer, one in which he can feel accomplished and which completely represents an ideal and final version of himself, or of his identity, in terms of the social symbols and signs that he wishes to perform. David becomes a gentleman and a famous and respected writer, or "eminent author" (Dickens 1981, 746), as he is referred to in the second to last chapter. The last lines of the novel catch up to the present of the old narrator, who characterizes his final accommodations as a state of economic and social bliss: "And now my story ends. I look back, once more–for the last time–before I close these leaves. I see myself, with Agnes at my side, journeying along the road of life. I see our children and our friends around us; and I hear the roar of many voices, not indifferent to me as I travel on" (748).

The happy resolutions of *Pride and Prejudice* and *David Copperfield* underscore the importance of the correct marriage to the archetype of the traditional *Bildungsroman*. For both Elizabeth and David, a happy and socially advantageous marriage is a clear marker of maturity. In this sense, the enormous contribution of *Great Expectations* to coming-of-age novels comes at its endings since neither culminate in marriage. The original ending aligns with the unhappy tone of the novel and affords the protagonist no chance for romantic fulfilment. Only the revised ending implies a possibility of a "good" romantic relationship. The novel thus breaks from the classic expectations of plot to the extent that the "traditional *Bildungsroman*" label is no longer feasible. The structural transformation is so extreme that *Great Expectations* is better termed a "coming-of-age novel," a capacious term that encompasses novels built on introspective self-forging that do not necessarily culminate in marriage or idyllic citizenship, and are thus only occasionally moralizing.

The beginning of the novel matches the archetypal plot but introduces an eerie symbolic twist as readers find the protagonist Pip playing in a cemetery. Opening with an image of death, the novel announces itself as a story quite different from its predecessor *David Copperfield*. Nevertheless, Pip is, coordinating with Buckley's archetypal plot, a young imaginative child whose environment frustrates his prospects. Since he is an orphan living with his older sister Mrs. Joe and blacksmith brother-in-law Joe in a small village in Kent, his humble expectation is to become a blacksmith as well. Unknown to protagonist and readers, this expectation changes because of the events in the opening scene, where Pip helps the convict Magwitch, still wearing his shackles, by bringing him food and a file. Magwitch secretly becomes Pip's benefactor, paying for his education and bettering Pip's social station. In the first part of the novel, when young Pip still thinks he will spend his whole life in Kent, Magwitch secretly instructs Mr. Jaggers to begin Pip's education:

> "I am instructed to communicate to him," said Mr. Jaggers, throwing his finger at me sideways, "that he will come into a handsome property. Further, that it is the desire of the present possessor of that property, that he be immediately removed from his present sphere of life and from this place, and be brought up as a gentleman – in a word, as a young fellow of great expectations."
>
> (Dickens 1973, 245)

The archetypal plot points dwindle in the next section, when Pip goes to live in Satis House under the tutelage of Miss Havisham, a rich and eccentric dowager who keeps the house in almost absolute darkness and stops all the clocks, figuratively arresting the progression of time to the moment of her thwarted marriage, a symbol that is diametrically opposed to the formative process, always in motion. Of Satis House, Pip comments, "I began to understand that everything in the room had stopped, like the watch and the clock, a long time ago" (104). In this timeless environment, Pip's story strays from the archetypal plot as he meets the only romantic partner he will have, decidedly the "bad" one, Estella, Miss Havisham's adoptive daughter. When Pip meets her, she treats him with utmost distain, insulting his physical appearance, intelligence, and importantly his class. In their brief outdoor introduction, Estella says:

"He calls the knaves, Jacks, this boy!" said Estella with disdain, before our first game was out. "And what coarse hands he has! And what thick boots!" I had never thought of being ashamed of my hands before; but I began to consider them a very indifferent pair. Her contempt for me was so strong, that it became infectious, and I caught it. She won the game, and I dealt. I misdealt, as was only natural, when I knew she was lying in wait for me to do wrong; and she denounced me for a stupid, clumsy labouring-boy.

(Dickens 1973, 105–106)

Pip is hurt but also becomes fascinated by her beauty. He feels shame for his upbringing, blaming Joe for not teaching him Jacks "ought to be knaves" and his sister for making him oversensitive (108). Pip's anger at his humble beginnings, combined with a desire to become suitable for Estella, motivate his desire to rise in social station, thus diminishing the inner longing to self-forge as driver of plot.

Pip's motivations stray from those of the traditional *Bildungsroman*, thus expanding on the genre, but his formative process still bears a significant resemblance to that of the archetypal plot. He goes on to live in the metropolis where he furthers his education. He has marriage in mind and strives for happiness. However, the parallel coming-of-age of Estella subverts the horizon of expectations of traditional *Bildungsromane* since she does not strive for any kind of marriage. Towards the end of the novel, Miss Havisham complains that Estella is proud and hard, to which Estella replies, in impressive self-awareness, that it was Miss Havisham herself who had taught her to treat others unkindly and to strive to hurt men, in the way Miss Havisham had been hurt by the criminal Compeyson when he left her at the altar so many years ago:

"If you had taught her [your daughter], from the dawn of her intelligence, with your utmost energy and might, that there was such a thing as daylight, but that it was made to be her enemy and destroyer, and she must always turn against it, for it had blighted you and would else blight her; - if you had done this, and then, for a purpose, had wanted her to take naturally to the daylight and she could not do it, you would have been disappointed and angry?" Miss Havisham sat listening (or it seemed so, for I could not see her face), but still made no answer. "So," said Estella, "I must be taken as I have been made. The success is not mine, the failure is not mine, but the two together make me."

(Dickens 1973, 545)

Far from wanting a happy and advantageous marriage in the Austenian sense, Estella is, as a product of her upbringing, successful in both causing pain and resisting to feel or express affection.

The original ending of the novel is often celebrated in scholarship as corresponding to the general sense of unhappiness throughout the novel: an "austere ending consistent with the theme of vanished expectations"

(Meisel 1965, 326). In it, Estella has two "bad" relationships. The first is with her husband Drummle, a rich man who Pip characterizes as "heavy in figure, movement, and comprehension ... idle, proud, niggardly, reserved, and suspicious" (359). After an unhappy marriage that ends with his death, she marries a poor doctor and Pip remains single. As he recounts,

> It was two years more, before I saw her. I had heard of her as leading a most unhappy life, and as being separated from her husband who had used her with great cruelty, and who had become quite renowned as a compound of pride, brutality, and meanness. I had heard of the death of her husband (from an accident consequent on ill-treating a horse), and of her being married again to a Shropshire doctor, who, against his interest, had once very manfully interposed, on an occasion when he was in professional attendance on Mr. Drummle, and had witnessed some outrageous treatment of her. I had heard that the Shropshire doctor was not rich, and that they lived on her own personal fortune.
>
> (quoted in John Forster 1875, n. 270)

This ending opens a new door for the coming-of-age genre, where heroes could be represented at their end as incomplete and unfulfilled. The logic of marriage as the primordial objective of character development is thwarted for good and, although numerous coming-of-age novels have kept marriage as a fitting end, Diasporic Coming-of-age Novels follow in the example of *Great Expectations*, opting for other forms of social organization, sometimes unhappily, and diverse markers of maturity.

Perhaps too early for its time, Dicken's contemporary audience and critics rejected this original ending as too bleak. John Forster, Dickens's biographer and friend, shares an account of Dicken's contemporary writer Edward Bulwer-Lytton's objection to the original ending. In a letter to John Forster, Dickens wrote:

> You will be surprised to hear that I have changed the end of *Great Expectations* from and after Pip's return to Joe's, and finding his little likeness there. Bulwer, who has been, as I think you know, extraordinarily taken by the book, so strongly urged it upon me, after reading the proofs, and supported his view with such good reasons, that I resolved to make the change. You shall have it when you come back to town. I have put in as pretty a little piece of writing as I could, and I have no doubt the story will be more acceptable through the alteration.
>
> (John Forster 1875, 369)

The revised ending does not have Estella marry the doctor and instead, in a final meeting, Pip and Estella hold hands as Pip explains of the future that he "saw no shadow of another parting from her" (Dickens 1973, 865). This second ending implies marriage. However, as many critics have argued, it feels contrived and inconsistent with the story. John Forster himself argues that "the first ending nevertheless seems to be more consistent with the drift" (1875, 369), and George Bernard Shaw, the influential Irish playwright, similarly wrote that "It is too serious a book to be a trivially happy one. Its beginning is unhappy; its middle is unhappy; and the conventional happy ending is an outrage on it" (2006, 68). Regardless of which is aesthetically better, the great contribution to coming-of-age novels was the mere suggestion that a work depicting a formative process could be something other than a progression towards a stage of completion. Instead, for the first time, the ending could be a representation of despair, of the breeding of cruelty, and great expectations a synonym of misery.

The Forsterian Queer Break from Traditional *Bildungsromane*

Published posthumously more than a century after *Great Expectations*, E. M. Forster's *Maurice* shattered most archetypal plot points and the marriage ideal of the *Bildungsroman* and was likewise too early for its contemporary social setting. Instead of revising the novel as Dickens did, Forster decided not to publish it during his lifetime. It is understandable that after Oscar Wilde's infamous trials of 1895, Forster would keep this novel private, although it was suitable for publication by 1914 (Medalie 2017, 47). Its social commentary was far more acute than those of the previous novels. Far from representing an ideal citizen or having a moralizing end, *Maurice* broke away from most of the conventions of traditional *Bildungsromane* as it championed the individual happiness of a social outcast over all social conventions, thus building on the gender matters of *Pride and Prejudice*. Instead of pathologizing the homosexual man, removing him from society, or suppressing his sexual identity, the novel recasts "the situation by presenting society, rather than homosexuality, as the site of wrongdoing and perversity" (Medalie 2017, 47). Rejecting oppressive societal expectations and instead resorting to exile was a completely new generic development. Among protagonists like David Copperfield who invariably ended in some sort of accommodation within their societies, *Maurice* spearheaded the possibility of non-belonging, a central theme in Diasporic Coming-of-age Novels.

Despite its disregard for most archetypal plot conventions, *Maurice* is a coming-of-age novel in that it bears key characteristics of the genre, such as the thematic centrality of protagonist's formative process as the force that moves the plot forward. At the beginning, the hero leaves Sunnington, the preparatory school where he has learned that marriage is the ultimate goal of life from his teacher Mr. Ducie. In a strange scene that implies the perversion of heterosexual society, Ducie draws male and female genitals on the sand and then explains to Maurice: "To love a noble woman, to protect and serve her—this, he told the little boy, is the crown of life. 'You can't understand now, you will some day, and when you do understand it, remember the poor old pedagogue who put you on the track. It all hangs together—all—and God's in heaven, All's right with the world. Male and female! Ah wonderful!'" (E. M. Forster 1987, 14). Maurice entertains the idea of marriage for a moment, but then realizes Ducie lied about the simple joy of sex when Ducie starts "sweating with fear" at the realization that he "never scratched out those infernal diagrams" (15). Maurice calms his teacher reminding him of the tide, but he characterizes Ducie as a liar and coward. The first lesson on marriage is ambivalent. Maurice understands there is a hypocritical social expectation both to secretly desire heterosexual sex but also to be fearful of it.

Shortly after, Maurice starts his formal education at Cambridge, a conservative and traditional setting for a *Bildungsroman* that emphasizes societal mores and sharply contrasts with the informal education that Diasporic Coming-of-age protagonists will have to glean in vastly different settings. There, Maurice has two equally unaccommodated relationships in the Austenian sense of social suitability. However, in the sense of the endurance of affection, he has a short-lived and platonic "bad" one with Clive Durham, a fellow student, and a "good" one with Alec Scudder, Clive Durham's family servant, a poor man, son of a butcher, with whom Maurice eventually plans to escape, perhaps to Argentina, although the exact location is never specified.

Maurice's first affection for Clive Durham sparks a frightful desire that leads him to self-deprecation, a new possibility in the coming-of-age genre. For the first time, the protagonist must choose between his true self or society's prejudice. Because Maurice knows he will never be able to fit with societal expectations, he must struggle to either succumb to social forces and opt for self-annihilation or come out triumphant as a genuine version of himself. This difficult choice is often central to Diasporic Coming-of-age Novels, where the heroes must choose between assimilation to the social whole or a complex understanding of their culturally-hybrid identities. Maurice's choice is particularly apparent in three moments of the novel: when he and Alec have sex for the first time and he feels terrible guilt, when he almost immediately thereafter gives up on trying to cure his homosexuality, and finally when he chooses to flee with Alec—his diaspora.

Because Maurice meets Alec at the house of Clive Durham's family, Maurice feels that, when his relationship with Alec becomes sexual (as opposed to the platonic admiration that he had shared with Clive in the upper-class educational institution of Cambridge), he has violated the societal norm of hospitality: "Cambridge had left him a hero, Penge [name of the Durham's estate] a traitor. He had abused his host's confidence and defiled his house in his absence, he had insulted Mrs. Durham and Anne [Clive Durham's sister]. And when he reached home there came a worse blow; he had also sinned against his family" (E. M. Forster 1987, 206). Here,

Maurice momentarily abandons his brave process of liberation through self-forging to internalize society's prejudice. This lapse continues and promptly ends when he meets the hypnotist Mr. Lasker Jones for the last time. In Maurice's last session, he expresses frustration with his inability to change: "I swear from the bottom of my heart I want to be healed. I want to be like other men, not this outcast whom nobody wants" (210). However, since his desire for self-annihilation is of less power than his true affection and longing for Alec's body and companionship, Lasker Jones suggests the idea of exile to France or Italy, countries that had accepted the Napoleonic Code, which decriminalized same-sex activities. Jones starts,

> "France or Italy for instance. There homosexuality is no longer criminal"
>
> "You mean that a Frenchman could share with a friend and yet not go to prison?"
>
> "Share? Do you mean unite? If both are of age and avoid public indecency, certainly." "Will the law ever be that in England?"
>
> "I doubt it. England has been disinclined to accept human nature." Maurice understood. He was an Englishman himself and only his troubles had kept him awake. He smiled sadly. "It comes to this then: there always have been people like me and always will be, and generally they have been persecuted."
>
> (E. M. Forster 1987, 211)

By the end of the conversation, Maurice sadly agrees that there is no place in England for a homosexual man like himself and accepts the possibility of exile.

The good relationship leads Maurice to ponder and finally reject his position as a gentleman in society. Unlike David Copperfield's society, Maurice's society does not offer a suitable place for him, exposing both the strict social and sexual aspects of the term gentleman. If the ultimate goal is marriage, then a homosexual man cannot achieve a degree of completeness. Maurice is a character whose *Bildung* is incompatible with the expectations of his social environment. In the penultimate chapter of the novel, Maurice and Alec finally meet without remorse in a boathouse. Alec receives him in his arms and, mirroring the exact last phrase of the revised ending of *Great Expectations*, says: "And now we shan't be parted no more, and that's finished" (E. M. Forster 1987, 239). This coming-of-age novel thus ends subverting the archetypal plot with a happy and committed romantic relationship, but one that is not and indeed cannot be inscribed in the institution of marriage in this specific historic place. Modern mobility now provides alternatives; in the case of *Maurice*, moving to another country.

Coming-of-age novels underwent crucial thematic and structural transformations in England, which sowed the seeds for numerous variations. The Diasporic Coming-of-age Novel, one of the most exciting, varied, and relevant worldwide, finds its seeds in these works. They have bloomed into complex portrayals of culturally-hybrid characters and the nuanced representation of the topics of poverty, queerness, manifold romantic relationships, and the struggle to feel belonging in places where citizenship might not be readily available. Like the novels in the present chapter, the following ten novels use the thematic centrality of protagonist's formative process as the force that moves the plot forward. In their manifold settings, they subvert the conventions of the genre to represent experiences of poverty and hunger that, unlike those of Dicken's characters, are intersected by forms of oppression rooted in gender, sexuality, and ethnicity. They further expand on—and even reject—the Austenian concept of marriage as the access key to the social whole. If their settings do not allow them to exist, they follow in Maurice's footsteps and continue their formative processes elsewhere, thus expanding the possibilities of coming-of-age novels.

PART II

3 Diasporic Coming-of-age Novels of the Commonwealth Diaspora in Contemporary London

Hanif Kureishi and Zadie Smith

When the coming-of-age genre develops sufficiently away from some formal and most thematic conventions of its classic iteration, the traditional *Bildungsroman*, it becomes exceptionally flexible. In contrast to the traditional *Bildungsroman*, studied in depth in Part I, the vernacular and larger genre of the coming-of-age novel often disregards any edifying or moralistic intent, any effort to show a fully-formed upstanding citizen, spouse, parent, or role model. Instead, it focuses on the process—or plot—itself, bringing ontologically dominant questions to the forefront, but not necessarily providing definitive answers. The umbrella coming-of-age genre is a useful tool to dissect individual verbally-represented subjectivities and to understand marginal identities as they portray the construction of the self episodically. The coming-of-age genre's malleable capacity to encompass a vast range of formative processes, and its usefulness as an identity laboratory, makes it—historically and now—a global phenomenon.[1]

A crucial variation of the coming-of-age genre in increasingly globalized and cosmopolitan settings is the Diasporic Coming-of-age Novel. This is a broad, historically-sensitive category that encompasses the experience of first- and subsequent-generation diasporic characters in late twentieth and twenty-first centuries' globalized settings. It enables young people in diasporic communities, however scattered, to ponder how they fit into national and global narratives, to show the options and occupations that are available to them, and to ponder on how they might become adults in their particular environments. These novels focus on the internal development of culturally hybrid subjects as they puzzle over their processes of identification, negotiating with the varied and often contradictory expectations that other characters and contexts impose and inflict.

The Diasporic Coming-of-age Novel is only possible as a consequence of the changes that the social fabric of contemporary nations and regions have undergone due to postcolonial and post-World War II migratory movements, most often motivated by guest-worker programs (such as the *Bracero* program in the U.S. and the *Gastarbeiterprogramm* in Germany), economic hardship in their countries of origin, and war. Diasporic Coming-of-age Novels are a direct consequence of the culturally-hybrid subjectivities that emerge in globalized, postcolonial, and multicultural social settings where regional and national identities have become even more unstable and fluid.

While the formative processes of their characters may remain unfinished, Diasporic Coming-of-age Novels are sites for complex and intersectional exploration of the cultural practices, signs, and symbols that conform fluid identities. In *Reconstructing Childhood*, Julia Kushigian asks, "how can one consider the *Bildungsroman*, the novel of growth and youthful development, an important tool to renovate and challenge cultural scripts despite its eighteenth-century roots?" (2003, 13). Diasporic Coming-of- age Novels answer this question as they take the identity-laboratory element characteristic of traditional *Bildungsromane* and set it on the global stage, while disregarding the white male entrepreneur objectives. This chapter studies two bestsellers—read widely in England and abroad—that exemplify the zeitgeist of diaspora: Hanif Kureishi's *The Buddha of Suburbia* (1991) and Zadie Smith's *White Teeth* (1999). The two primary focal points are, on the one hand, the elements of character and ideas of the self, and, on the other, the plot as a depiction of the—partial—emancipation from restrictive stereotypes and xenophobic prejudice. These two novels are key examples of the subgenre because they so explicitly illustrate the arduous process of identification for subjects in the geographic and hegemonic center of the bygone empire and yet still at the margins of society.

In Diasporic Coming-of-age Novels, the representation of the protagonists' social environments is a key reason why they cannot fit into bourgeois accommodations. The heroes have experienced the often-traumatic movement of diaspora, either personally or in their families' recent histories. The literary settings of Diasporic Coming-of-age Novels, London in this particular chapter, are hybrid spaces, *borderlands*, as defined by Gloria Anzaldúa: "wherever two or more cultures edge each other, where people of different races occupy the same territory, where under, lower, middle and upper classes touch, where the space between two individuals shrinks with intimacy" (2007, 19), and famously "una herida abierta" [an open wound] (25). Useful for alerting readers to their participation in these variable literary spaces is Mary Louise Pratt's geographically mobile yet appropriate sensitive term *contact zone*, "social spaces where cultures meet, clash, and grapple with each other, often in contexts of highly asymmetrical relations of power, such as colonialism, slavery, or their aftermaths as they are lived out in many parts of the world today" (1991, 34). Pratt's term is of particular relevance to the geographies represented in Diasporic Coming-of-age Novels because they are fruitful sites of self-representations where marginalized characters can address "both metropolitan audiences and the speakers' own community" (35).

In *Buddha of Suburbia*, the protagonist Karim Amir is the son of an Indian immigrant and an English woman. He is therefore a "funny kind of Englishman, a new breed as it were, having emerged from two old histories ... the odd mixture of continents and blood, of here and there, of belonging and not" (Kureishi 1991, 3). Karim chooses to be an actor, a profession where aptitude is measured by the performance of a temporarily adopted subjectivity. It is a profession that at once glances backwards subtly to Wilhelm Meister, who ultimately discards this stepping stone, and powerfully marks its vast difference. While acting is a means for self-development for Wilhelm, Karim is invariably type-cast into stereotypical migrant roles, restraining the number of subjectivities that he is able to perform to a few undesirable characters: on the London stage, Karim plays Mowgli in Rudyard Kipling's *The Jungle Book* and in a soap opera, a rebellious teenager whose parents own a corner store. His formative process culminates in an ambivalent realization that the joy that can stem from his belonging in the London setting is mixed with misery.

In *White Teeth*, readers encounter three characters who undergo formative processes: Irie Jones, the daughter of Englishman Archie Jones and Jamaican immigrant Clara Bowden, and the twins Millat and Magid Iqbal, sons of Bangladeshi immigrants Samad and Alsana Iqbal. Irie goes through a long journey of self-hatred that leads her ultimately to a sense of joyful indifference towards her "substantial Jamaican frame, loaded with pineapples, mangos and guavas; the girl had weight; big tits, bug butt, big hips, big thighs, big teeth," features she inherited from her maternal grandmother Hortense (Smith 2001, 221). At the beginning of her story, Irie wears "elaborate corsetry" to lose weight because she sees England as "a gigantic mirror" where she has no reflection, "a stranger in a stranger land" (222). She initially conflates the rejection of her figure with that of her diasporic heritage, but eventually comes to tolerate—though never celebrate—both.

Concurrently, the twins Millat and Magid, puzzle over their identities. Millat is driven by "an ever present anger and hurt, the feeling of belonging nowhere that comes to people who belong everywhere" that splits him between his conflicting desires to be at once a gangster and an extreme ascetic Muslim. Eventually, he joins the "Keepers of the Eternal and Victorious Islamic Nation," a fundamentalist Muslim group that pushes him to an act of terrorism (225). Magid, having grown up in Bangladesh, is "more English than the English" and atheist (303), a commentary on the inauthenticity apparently inherent in the effort to assimilate and the failure of their father Samad Iqbal to raise what he perceives to be good Muslim men.

Postcolonial Melancholia and Convivial Multiculturalism

Both novels put in relief the intermingling of the melancholic and convivial visions of English society. In analyzing English immigration and multicultural policies, Paul Gilroy offers melancholia and conviviality as two opposing ways to understand English national identity. Gilroy argues that in order to understand contemporary English identity, a post-imperial melancholic vision emerged after World War II. This vision imagines England as the victim and survivor of Nazi aggression. In this "ethnic myth," Germans are characterized as "foes who [were] simply, tidily, and uncomplicatedly evil" (Gilroy 2005, 89). But the victory in the war also meant the loss of a homogenous British Empire that was, until then, fundamental for the understanding of London as the metropolis. This melancholic vision intends to make the victimhood of World War II "a privileged point of entry into national identity and self-understanding" for British citizens (89). Since then "the nation has been dominated by an inability even to face, never mind actually mourn, the profound change in circumstances and moods that followed the end of the empire and consequent loss of imperial prestige" (90). The inability to cope with change has been worsened by "successive political and economic crises, with the gradual breakup of the United Kingdom, with the arrival of substantial numbers of postcolonial citizen-migrants, and with the shock and anxiety that followed from a loss of any sense that the national collective was bound by a coherent and distinctive culture" (90). According to this melancholic vision of English identity, citizen-migrants, who used to be subjects of the British Empire, threaten the political body of England: they are imagined as an ethnic menace that destabilizes the identity of the former metropolis.

In this melancholic vision, "the history of the empire became a source of discomfort, shame and perplexity" (90). It aims to erase the brutality and guilt of the empire in order to enshrine a conception of imperialism as a noble effort to bring civilization: "that unsettling history was diminished, denied, and then, if possible, actively forgotten" (90). In turn, this erasure feeds racism and xenophobia because it imagines postcolonial people as "unwanted alien intruders without any substantive historical, political, or cultural connections to the collective life of their fellow subjects" (90). Further, the "national character" was built on colonialism as a force of good in the world, a burdensome responsibility. After the Second World War, this narrative of the use of force to expand civilization is effectively swept under the rug and post-imperial melancholia replaces, for many, the notion of English identity. This vision ignores the "hidden, shameful store of imperial horrors" and ultimately "seeks firstly to minimize the extent of the empire, then to deny or justify its brutal character, and finally, to present the British themselves as the ultimate tragic victims of their extraordinary imperial success" (94). In this melancholic vision multiculturalism constitutes a threat to national identity. The possible outcomes for this Diasporic Coming-of-age Novel are limited by the discrimination and stereotyping that Karim experiences along his formative process, especially in his work as an actor.

Conviviality, conversely, upholds the vision that, amid the contemporary cultural diversity of England, English identity should be regarded as multicultural; in other words, in order to be English it is not necessary to be white, Anglican, middle class, or a mouthpiece of the Queen's English. This vision presumes that the multiplicity of cultures and races that interact in both public and private spaces characterizes the routine and day-to-day life in England. It proposes that the normalization of the experience of multiculturalism can engender empathy across lines of difference and respect for contrasting worldviews, as

> processes of cohabitation and interaction that have made multicultural
> an ordinary feature of social life in Britain's urban areas and in

postcolonial cities elsewhere... . It does not describe the absence of racism or the triumph of tolerance. Instead, it suggests a different setting for their empty, interpersonal rituals, which, I suggest, have started to mean different things in the absence of any strong belief in absolute or integral races... . The radical openness that brings conviviality alive makes a nonsense of, closed, fixed, and reified identity and turns attention toward the always unpredictable mechanisms of identification.

(Gilroy 2005, XV)

Gilroy argues that conviviality does not eradicate a history of white supremacy and social hierarchies, but rather allows for a process of acknowledging the horrors of the empire that postcolonial melancholia so desperately tries to erase. Conviviality also finds fixed identities nonsensical. Thus, in a convivial representation of society in the novel, Englishness would have been more inclusive. In this vision of English identity, the components of everyday life are much more important than race or ethnicity to form notions of Englishness. However, most characters in *The Buddha*, on the contrary, support exclusionary national identities that leave Karim at the margins.

One of the blunter examples of postcolonial melancholia in *The Buddha* happens when Karim visits Helen, a young white girl he meets in Chislehurst, the London suburb of his childhood. Helen's father, whom Karim nicknames Hairy Back because he associates his hairy arms with Peter Sellers and Sean Connery, opens the door and tells Karim:

"You can't see my daughter again," said Hairy Back. "She doesn't go out with boys. Or with wogs."

"Oh well."

"Got it?"

"Yeah," I said sullenly.

"We don't want you blackies coming to the house."

"Have there been many?"

"Many what, you little coon?"

"Blackies."

"Where?"

"Coming to the house."

"We don't like it," Hairy Back said. "However many niggers there are, we don't like it. We're with Enoch. If you put one of your black 'ands near my daughter I'll smash it with a 'ammer! With a 'ammer!"

(Kureishi 1991, 40)

Hairy Back uses the disparaging terms "blackie," "wog," and "nigger" interchangeably. In doing so he eliminates any possibility for nuance in Karim's identities: Karim is flattened since his only relevant characteristic is the color of his skin, his otherness. Hairy Back simplifies people of color because doing so allows him to think they are all loathsome, foreign to English society, and a threat to the nation insofar as his house is a metaphor for his imagined country and Karim's presence an imagined invasion of that intimate space. In this sense, Karim "seeing" his daughter is also dangerous to Hairy Back's vision of Englishness since it makes the possibility for miscegenation intelligible. The Diasporic Coming-of-age Novel not only displays the too-pervasive xenophobic sentiments of this historical context, but also enables the hero to retort, in this instance with humor, to Hairy Back's violent rejection. Karim's ironic retort certainly diminishes the personal effect of Hairy Back's bigotry and serves to ridicule it. The interaction highlights Hairy Back's incapacity to understand Karim's wit. However ludicrous Hairy Back's comments are made by Karim's clever retorts, they are nonetheless representative of an exclusionary and pervasive view of national identity.

In order to eliminate the possibility of miscegenation, Hairy Back references Enoch Powell, whose famous speech "Rivers of Blood" epitomizes anti-immigrant sentiment. On April 20, 1968, Powell, a conservative English politician who served as member of Parliament from 1950 to 1978, spoke against the open immigration and antidiscrimination policies proposed by the English Parliament. His speech opened with the following: "The supreme function of statesmanship is to provide against preventable evils" (Rivers of Blood). Powell proposed that migration and multiculturalism were preventable if understood as social evils. And, while in some parts of the speech he explained why immigration was the seed of the destruction of Great Britain, his main objective was to set forth a plan to stop current immigration and start a process of re-emigration, by which immigrants would be returned to their home countries. Powell compared the previous twenty years of immigration policy to "watching a nation busily engaged in heaping up its own funeral pyre." He equated the growth of "immigrant-descended population" with the destruction of the British way of life and values, as well as an attack on white working-class families that were forced to compete with "commonwealth immigrants and their descendants" for jobs and access to healthcare and other governmental services.

In his pernicious xenophobia, Powell articulated normativity as masculine and white. He imagined a white "ordinary working man" who became "a stranger in his own country." In imagining this stereotypical symbol, Powell intended to instill fear among the everyman and went as far as saying that "in this country in fifteen or twenty years' time the black man will have the whip hand over the white man." Powell stated that the power dynamic would flip and what he viewed as the master would become the slave. The whip was particularly dramatic in evoking plurality as hierarchy in his recollection of the legal slavery of Great Britain's past. The melancholic vision of his plan involved a pure and ideal past distorted by cultural mix.

Kureishi's Hairy Back has internalized the fear of being unable to access public services and jobs. He accepts the notion that before Karim, his house and daughter, as symbols of the private and intimate, were safe and familiar. The relationship between Karim and his daughter Helen signifies the possibility of a new body politic. In the bodies of the younger generation, Hairy Back fears possible miscegenation, a threat to the power structures that Powell references. When Hairy Back states he is with Powell, he means the only possible outcome he imagines for Karim is re-emigration. The novel does not have a symmetrical episode that so clearly represents a convivial vision. This void is unsurprising because a convivial representation of Englishness would have allowed Karim to understand Englishness as a national identity that is not necessarily white.

A parallel example of postcolonial melancholia in *White Teeth* happens in Irie Jones's English class, when Mrs. Olive Roody has the class read William Shakespeare's Sonnet 127, the first of the "Dark Lady Sonnets." Irie already feels insecure about her body, as she is obsessed with her weight-loss regimen, an experimental program where some undisclosed institution pays for every pound she loses, and constantly repeats the mantra "Before. After." (Smith 2001, 222). Her rejection of her body is linked to the rejection of her mother's Jamaican heritage, as she describes the program as "a little Caribbean flesh for a little English change" (22). Irie wholly believes in her "ugliness, her *wrongness*," reinforced by her father's disappointment that the blue eyes with which she was born turned brown within two weeks and her "mountainous curves, buckteeth and thick metal retainer, impossible Afro hair" (223). As the sonnet is read aloud, it intermingles with Irie's distracted musings of her wrongness. But when the sonnet reaches the line "Thy black is fairest in my judgement's place," Irie's attention is sparked. In an effort to find a semblance of hope that her body could be considered beautiful by one of the fundamental voices of English literature, Irie naively asks Mrs. Roody whether the dark lady could in fact be Black:

"Is she black?"

"Is who black?"

"The dark lady."

"No, dear, she's dark. She's not black in the modern sense. There weren't any … well, Afro-Carri-bee-yans in England at the time, dear. That's more a modern phenomenon, as I'm sure you know. But this was the 1600s. I mean I can't be sure, but it does seem terribly unlikely, unless she was a slave of some kind, and he's unlikely to have written a series of sonnets to a lord and then a slave, is he?"

[…]

And the reflection that Irie had glimpsed slunk back into the familiar darkness. On the way out of class, Irie was passed a note by Annalese Hersch, who shrugged to signify that she was not the author but merely one of the many handlers. It said: "By William Shakespeare: ODE TO LETITIA AND ALL MY KINKY-HAIRED BIG-ASS BITCHEZ."

(Smith 2001, 227)

Her hope is met with utter rejection by Mrs. Roody. Her existence is practically nullified in historical terms, except "as a slave" to whom no poems could ever be written. As a figure of authority and gatekeeper of Englishness, Mrs. Roody shuts Irie out of the body politic, a marginalization that is reinforced by the derision of Irie's peers. Here, "body politic" should be understood in terms of Thomas Hobbes as the counterpart to the "natural" and individual body, "a *Commonwealth* [...] made by the wills and agreement of men" (quoted in Zarka 1996, 76). By excluding Irie's natural body from the cultural hegemony of England, Mrs. Roody also excludes symbolically from participation in the political and civil body of the nation. For Mrs. Roody, the existence of a person like Irie in the space of her classroom, and indeed potentially in English literature, is but a modern quirk, a "phenomenon" outside of the English canon and thus outside of conventional nationhood. Her existence unsubstantiated, Irie sinks back into the darkness.

In tension with the disdain in the note, the students' wit can be read as mocking not Irie, but rather Mrs. Roody. In this reading, the note celebrates a reading of Shakespeare's sonnet that Mrs. Roody's nostalgic view of the national literary canon cannot even consider, one that highlights desire for non-white bodies and features. As such, Mrs. Roody mirrors Hairy Back's lack of understanding of the world around him. Wit becomes a site of epistemological resistance to bigotry, turning Hairy Back and Mrs. Roody into laughable characters. And yet, regardless of how powerful wit can be, the novels do not let readers lose sight of the pervasiveness and real violence of postcolonial melancholia, which seeks to eradicate the existence of diasporic populations in the national social body.

Miserable Joy in *The Buddha of Suburbia*

But the existence of migrants like Irie and Karim Amir is undeniable even in the durable literary form of the coming-of-age novel. In *The Buddha of Suburbia*, the title itself brings into focus the presence of diaspora in the day-to-day life of London. Buddhism's importation from Asia and the referent—the father rather than the protagonist—point to a multicultural past, as well as the perplex juxtaposition of the religious and secular social of "suburbia."

In the first part of *The Buddha*, readers encounter the expectations Karim's father Haroon has for him. Haroon's expectations illustrate his ideal image of an immigrant: a professional worker who accesses the middle class by means of education. As Karim muses,

> Dad was still convinced I was trying to be something—a lawyer, I'd told him recently, because even he knew that that doctor stuff was a wind-up. But I knew there'd have to come a time when I broke the news to him that the education system and I had split up. It would break his immigrant heart, too.
>
> (Kureishi 1991, 94)

Haroon has lived in England for twenty years and works for the English government as a "badly paid and insignificant" Civil Service clerk (Kureishi 1991, 7). He thinks that higher education and the social status it entails is an essential part of the ideal goal of an immigrant. An essential facet of the formative processes of the gentlemen David Copperfield, Pip, and Maurice in the works of Charles Dickens and E. M. Forster, discussed in Chapter 2, higher education in *The Buddha* is merely one of many paths set for Karim. He rejects it because he associates educational institutions with racial abuse: "I was sick too of being affectionately called Shitface and Curryface, and of coming home covered in spit and snot and chalk and wood-shavings" (63). We may conclude from Haroon's expectations that he sees his son as an immigrant like himself. For Haroon there is no possibility of hybridity, a definition of an Englishman that can include his son.

But Haroon's expectations are not the only way this character influences Karim's path: Haroon serves as the first model of imitation—and dis-identification. Early in the narrative, Haroon abandons Karim's mother Margaret and his job to live with Eva Kay, a white suburban middle-class woman. By means of Eva's help and encouragement, Haroon starts doing "gigs" where he leads yoga sessions and lectures the white inhabitants of the suburbs on Eastern philosophy. Eva sees Haroon as the embodiment of everything exotic and of an ancient and Eastern kind of wisdom. When she introduces him to her friends in the context of his first "gig," Eva says, "My good and deep friend Haroon here, he will show us the Way. The Path" (13). Haroon readily performs these expectations and leads shirtless yoga where he displays his lean and muscular body in Eva's house: in doing so Haroon becomes the *Buddha of Suburbia* of the title.

Karim's mother Margaret conversely dislikes it when Haroon practices yoga and exposes his body: "Oh God, Haroon, all the front of you is stick-ing out like that and everyone can see!" (4). Her dissension condemns Haroon's inauthentic performance as an incorrect model of imitation. A key feature of Diasporic Coming-of-age Novels, role models are often both praised and criticized, thus disorienting rather than narrowing the protago-nist's formative process. While Eva wants to exhibit Haroon's exoticism, Margaret would prefer to keep it hidden from the neighbors. Karim dresses similarly to his father and is eager to go with him, but Haroon is an imitation model only in the first few pages. Karim swiftly recognizes that Haroon is performing an oriental caricature to seem wise to Eva and her uniformly white middle-class friends. Karim tries to resist this model because he thinks it is fake and ridiculous: "I wanted to see if Dad was a charlatan ... whether ... Dad really did have anything to offer other people, or if he would turn out to be merely another suburban eccentric" (Kureishi 1991, 22). But despite this initial rejection, at the end of the novel, Karim does something very similar to his father: in his work as an actor he also adopts and performs a stereotype, a form of inner betrayal that contradicts his resistance throughout the novel.

Within his family, Karim also finds the expectations and an imitation model in his cousin Jamila. She is about the same age as Karim, but she is very different in that she is the daughter of two immigrants (52). This parallel coming of age story depicts, if secondarily, the recognition of the intersectionality of gender in any nuanced depiction of diasporic identities, as is more forefronted in other Diasporic Coming of Age novels to be explored. At the beginning of her coming-of-age, we encounter Jamila filling shelves in her father "Anwar's shop, Paradise Stores" (50), an unsuccessful business. Through the influence of activists such as Angela Davis, Jamila's formative process takes her out of the store and into the streets, where she enthusiastically demonstrates against neo-fascist groups and right-winged politics: "She was preparing for the guerilla war she knew would be necessary when the whites finally turned on the blacks and Asians and tried to force us into gas chambers" (56). Jamila rejects the beliefs and lifestyle of her father, as is made clear in the episode where she initially rejects the husband Anwar had chosen for her. In retaliation, Anwar goes on a hunger strike in order to force his daughter into marriage with another Indian immigrant, thus avoiding miscegenation and countering genetic and cultural hybridity.

Jamila is worried that her father's type of backlash furthers the Indian stereotypes she tries to fight and eventually agrees to marry Changez. However, she finds ways to emancipate herself from the oppressive institution of marriage by means of the political act of having many sexual partners and finally moving to a sexually-liberated commune. In her own coming-of-age, Jamila shows the bravery liberation requires: she does not sit quietly at home but rather looks for a family model that best fits her desires and takes to the street to demonstrate and march against racism and fascism.

Also within the realm of Karim's family, his mother Margaret enunciates entirely different expectations of Karim's performance of national identity. The first is early on, when his mother reacts to the traditional Indian attire that Karim wears to please his father: "When she saw me she too became tense. 'Don't show us up, Karim,' she said continuing to watch TV. 'You look like Danny La Rue'" (Kureishi 1991, 7). Danny La Rue was an English comedian known for his representation of feminine characters.

Even though Karim is dressed exactly like his father, his mother finds the outfit strange on Karim. Margaret implies that the attire corresponds to her husband Haroon's body, but looks queer on her son's body. Margaret wants Karim to dress as a non-effeminate Englishman. Much later in the novel, she again calls attention to Karim's choice of clothing, but does not focus on gender:

> "You weren't in a loin-cloth as usual," she said. "At least they let you wear your own clothes. But you're not an Indian. You've never been to India. You'd get diarrhoea the minute you stepped off that plane, I know you would."
>
> "Why don't you say it a bit louder," I said. "Aren't I part Indian?"
>
> "What about me?" Mum said. "Who gave birth to you? You're an Englishman, I'm glad to say."
>
> "I don't care," I said. "I'm an actor. It's a job."
>
> "Don't say that," she said. "Be what you are."
>
> (Kureishi 1991, 232)

Margaret sees Karim as an Englishman because of her blood in him and his upbringing. She ignores his paternal Indian heritage, his clothes, and the characters he represents, and instead emphasizes that he has never gone to India and that he would be physically incapable to adapt to it. Karim does not want to shed his "Englishness" but he does not want to reject his "Indianness" either: "Aren't I part Indian"? In a convivial environment he would not have to, because these identities would not be mutually exclusive.

From his family's expectations we can conclude that different characters have different, and often contradictory, ideas of him. The family, rather than being a guide for the protagonist's *Bildung* plot, confuses Karim and signifies the impossibility of cultural hybridity. Outside of his family, the melancholic vision of national identity is unmistakably present in his audition with Jeremy Shadwell, a white and racist theater director, who hires Karim to play Mowgli. Shadwell expects Karim to be exotic, as evidenced by an uncomfortable discussion of language:

> Instead of talking about the job he said some words to me in Punjabi or Urdu and looked as if he wanted to get into a big conversation about Ray or Tagore or something. To tell the truth, when he spoke it sounded like he was gargling. "Well?" he said. He rattled off some more words. "You don't understand?"
>
> "No, not really."
>
> What could I say? I couldn't win. I knew he'd hate me for it. "Your own language!" ... "What a breed of people two hundred years of

imperialism has given birth to. If the pioneers from the East India Company could see you. What puzzlement there'd be. Everyone looks at you, I'm sure, and thinks: an Indian boy, how exotic, how interesting, what stories of aunties and elephants we'll hear now from him. And you're from Orpington."

(Kureishi 1991, 141)

Shadwell expects Karim to talk about elephants, to perform what Indian means in his mind, but is violently disappointed by Karim's "breed." Shadwell is the only character to recognize that Karim is something new, a product of the contact zone: neither Indian nor English. However, Shadwell thinks this "newness" is a monstrous brood, which is why he gives Karim the disguise of dark makeup, "shit-brown cream" (146), and an exaggerated Indian accent. Shadwell imposes his idea of Indianness as a costume on Karim's body, which Karim flaccidly protests:

"What d'you mean authentic?" "Where was our Mowgli born?" "India." "Yes. Not Orpington. What accent do they have in India?"

"Indian accents."

"Ten out of ten."

"No, Jeremy. Please, no."

(Kureishi 1991, 147)

Shadwell erases what he deems a monstrous hybridity and compels Karim to become a completely Indian caricature, flattening his complexities. Karim feels miserable and at first explains his resistance is a political matter to him: that, like Jamila, he does not want to reinforce the old and offensive Indian stereotype. However, at the end of the novel he adopts the stereotype and plays a character that is a rebellious teenager, son of a traditional Indian couple who owns a small convenience store.

The final scene of the novel epitomizes the incomplete resolution to the identity crisis. Karim is in a restaurant with his brother Allie, Haroon, Eva, Margaret, and her new boyfriend, a white Englishman. Haroon has just announced that Eva and he are getting married and they are all seemingly happy: "And so I sat in the centre of this old city that I loved, which itself sat at the bottom of a tiny island. I was surrounded by people I loved, and I felt happy and miserable at the same time" (Kureishi 1991, 284). At the end of the plot process, Karim has seemingly finished his *Bildung* and found a suitable place within immediate social group and in society. Indeed, the diversity of the group appears to point to the emergence of a multicultural English society in which "Englishman" can include white Englishmen and women, Indian immigrants, and two people in-between, Allie and Karim.

This analysis, however, ignores the interlaced misery of the scene. Haroon has found an accommodation and a way to quit his government job, but to do so he has been forced to portray a caricature of Indian culture, to feed a fetish that corresponds to a melancholic vision of Englishness where the exoticism of the former empire persists. Karim is happy to feel love, but he is miserable because his job has taken him backwards, forced him to undo the part of his *Bildung* that taught him to resist inauthenticity and stereotype. In one of the final scenes of the novel, his father asks him whether he lives "an untrue life" (265), to which Karim assents. Like his father, Karim performs a melancholic stereotype that flattens his identity, fetishizes his body, and erases his cultural hybridity.

This historically embedded novel closes with hope for a better future, with Karim articulating, "I thought of what a mess everything had been, but that it wouldn't always be that way" (284). But this hope is expressed on March 29, 1979, the day after the vote of no confidence in the government of James Callaghan, then leader of the Labour Party, which would lead to the election of Margaret Thatcher, leader of the Conservative Party, two months later. This is what Jamila had rallied against and what Karim's friend Terry characterizes as England falling apart and "the rise of the Right" (Kureishi 1991, 258).[2]

The Diasporic Coming-of-age Novel does not offer an unequivocal solution to the problematic expectations and models the protagonists have encountered. At the end of *The Buddha*, the question of Englishness is open, like Karim's formative process. The novel's ending does not correspond to one of Gilroy's visions of society, but rather keeps both visions in tension, portraying a convivial micro-universe at the dinner table and a pessimistic foreshadowing of the decade to come.

Mixed Outcomes in *White Teeth*

The novel *White Teeth* also represents convivial and melancholic visions of Englishness in tension. However, Smith's novel shows how the heroine can liberate herself from the identity crisis altogether in the case of Iris Jones, and what can happen when there is no resolution to the crisis in the case of the Iqbal twins. The novel starts with the depiction of the family sagas of the Joneses and the Iqbals. The heads of both families, English Archibald Jones and Bangladeshi Samad Iqbal meet in World War II, where they fail to kill Dr. Marc-Pierre Perret, a French eugenicist who collaborated with the Nazis. This is a relevant fact since the cultural and religious implications of eugenics, as well as miscegenation, are two of the main themes in the novel. A significant portion of the novel follows the marriage of these two characters to much younger women, an unusual feature of Coming-of-age Novels, which almost always focus on the young protagonists and largely disregard the parents' stories. These marriages are unhappy and abusive, diametrically opposed to the "marriage of true affection" that Elizabeth

Bennet pursues in Jane Austen's *Pride and Prejudice* (Austen 2016, 70). In *White Teeth*, marriage is transformed from a beneficial accommodation into an abnegated prison. It is thus not a desirable model of imitation for the three young protagonists who consequently remain unmarried at the end of the novel.

At age forty-seven, Archibald Jones marries nineteen-year-old Clara Bowden, a Jamaican immigrant trying to escape her strict mother Hortense, a Jehovah's Witness obsessed with the end of days. Clara sees in Archie "a savior … a man to whisk her away, to choose her above others so that she might *walk in the white with Him*" (Smith 2001, 52). Clara does not find joy in her marriage but she is not miserable either. As she sarcastically words it, citing Corinthians I, "It is better to marry than to burn" (53). Samad Iqbal has an arranged marriage with fellow Bangladeshi immigrant Alsana Begum. Such a marriage would be impossible in traditional *Bildungsromane*, which depicted the bourgeois European ideal of *choosing* one's partner based indeed on socioeconomic suitability but also on affection and compatibility. Although the marriage starts off peacefully, it deteriorates to the point where the spouses cease to talk to each other directly and communicate almost exclusively with physical violence both privately and publicly. As Alsana explains,

> "I was married to Samad Iqbal the same evening of the very day I met him. Yes, I didn't know him from Adam. But I liked him well enough… I thought he had a good face, a sweet voice, and his backside was high and well formed for a man of his age. Very good. Now, every time I learn something more about him, *I like him less*."
>
> (Smith 2001, 90)

While marriage in traditional *Bildungsromane* ensures the reproduction of social structures, the inheritance of wealth, and the incorporation of the protagonist into his social whole, in *White Teeth* marriage is an undesirable accommodation.

It is in this dysfunctional family context that the three young protagonists, Irie Jones, and the identical twins Magid and Millat Iqbal are born. Irie's body is a disappointment to her parents from the very beginning. Her father wants her to have blue eyes as it would be "a piece of him slugging it out in the gene pool with a piece of Clara and *winning*" (Smith 2001, 78). Irie's brown eyes are thus a failure in her father's view and the very foundation of her deep self-hatred. Although low self-esteem is not completely new to the coming-of-age genre, as evidenced by the guilt the titular character of E. M. Forster's *Maurice* experiences over his sexual identity, the feeling of one's body being completely wrong is a unique development in Diasporic Coming-of-age Novels. Irie's body does not fit into the aesthetic and racial expectations of the host society, embodied in her father's rejection.

During the first centuries of the genre's existence, the success of heroes in coming-of-age novels depended directly on their bodies' acceptance in their social setting. There are scarce physical descriptions of characters in traditional *Bildungsromane* because their bodies are always assumed to be "right:" able, white, and attractive. Irie's formative process is instead focused on her incorrect body and her attempts to make it fit. Most strikingly, Irie tries to change her body in an episode involving her hair. She wants to straighten her afro as she believes it will make her more attractive to Millat Iqbal, whom she has always desired. Upon arrival to the hair salon, the conversation with the stylist Jackie makes Irie's unplaceable foreignness evident:

"Pale, sir! Freckles an' every ting. You Mexican?"

"No."

"Arab?"

"Half Jamaican. Half English."

"Half-caste," Jackie explained patiently.

(Smith 2001, 228)

The episode ends badly as Irie has her scalp burned, loses most of her natural hair, and needs to get a wig. Although she expects praise for her new hair, Millat continues to ignore her. Unexpectedly however, her new hair brings the hope for a twist of fate, which puts her on track towards a sense of indifference for societal expectations—a positive option for the children of diasporas. Millat's unapologetically lesbian and feminist cousin Neena, who like Jamila in *The Buddha* has found a sense of self-worth in the writings of Germaine Greer and Simone de Beauvoir, tells Irie, "You're a smart cookie, Irie. But you've been taught all kinds of shit. You've got to reeducate yourself. Realize your value, stop the lavish devotion, and get a life Irie... The Afro was cool, man. It was wicked. It was *yours*" (Smith 2001, 237). After this pivotal conversation, Irie's obsession with her incorrect body disappears entirely. The omniscient narrator stops mentioning it, and, instead, her formative process turns its attention to her relationship with the Iqbal twins.

Often in Diasporic Coming-of-age Novels, several characters in concurrent processes of development come in and out of focus in the diegesis. Their processes are intertwined, supporting and informing each other. In *White Teeth*, the focus on one single subjectivity of traditional *Bildungsromane* is substituted by collective utterances that contain distinct alternatives for Diasporic adulthoods. The progress of Irie's story is intimately linked to that of the twins who, in turn, have complex formative processes of their own. In terms of Irie's story, Millat is of key relevance since she loves him unrequitedly "as if he were an island" and she was "shipwrecked" (382).

This "bad" relationship culminates in passionate sex that ends "as suddenly and feverishly as it had begun" with both springing back "in horror for different reasons" (381). Millat regrets it due to his recent turn to religious fundamentalism while Irie becomes "embarrassed and ashamed because she could see how much he regretted it" (381). In an act of anger not at Millat but at his older-by-two-minutes twin Magid, whom she blames for Millat's incapacity to love her, Irie marches over to Magid's home "maliciously determined to make Magid the second son for once" (382). Irie makes "love to him angrily and furiously, without conversation or affection" (382). Irie becomes pregnant but since they are twins, no paternity test can tell her who the father is. Initially this makes Irie sad but, after "weeping and pacing and rolling it over and over in her mind, she thought: *whatever*, you know?" (427). Her *whatever* might seem inconsequential, but after years of trying to control her body, to protect and attract Millat, to hold on tight to the past and her resentment, Irie's *whatever* is a release and an important marker of maturity.

While traditional *Bildungsromane* would offer the unequivocal maturity markers of marriage and professional success, the Diasporic Coming-of-age Novel can offer a myriad of untraditional markers of maturation. In Irie's case, the release of control and the tolerance for the unknown demonstrate her development. Her story ends seven years later with Irie "sitting by the Caribbean sea" with her grandmother Hortense and her lover Joshua, an English classmate (perhaps a "good" relationship, although readers know nothing about it), while her "fatherless little girl writes affectionate postcards do *Bad Uncle Millat* and *Good Uncle Magid* and feels free as Pinocchio, a puppet clipped of paternal strings" (Smith 2001, 448). This return to the Caribbean is peaceful and signifies a reconciliation with the Jamaican ancestry she had previously rejected. This reconciliation does not imply a rejection of her Englishness either, as this blissful snapshot notably embraces Joshua. The Diasporic Coming-of-age Novel enables this strange and blissful family portrait, the unmarried couple, the fatherless daughter, and the grandmother at the sea. There are no final accommodations that would suit traditional *Bildungsromane*, but, in this particular case, the formative process is joyously complete, not by the achievement of model adulthood, but rather by the powerful liberation from the preoccupation with body, race, and ethnicity inscribed in the word *whatever*.

Unlike Irie, the Iqbal twins do not reach such a point of contentment. While Diasporic Coming-of-age Novels often have optimistic conclusions, characters can find themselves just as confused as at their beginning without models of adulthood. This is particularly visible in the case of the younger twin Millat. Millat's first description is that of a neglected child, invisible to his father, but respected in the streets, "the DON, the BUSINESS, the DOG'S GENITALIA, a street boy, a leader of tribes," enamored with trouble (Smith 2001, 181–82). In the streets, he finds belonging with the *Raggastanis,* a "new breed, just recently joining the ranks of the other street crews: Becks, B-boys, Indie kids, wide-boys, ravers, rudeboys, Acidheads, Sharons, Tracies, Kevs, Nation Brothers, Raggas, and Pakis; manifesting itself as a kind of cultural mongrel of the last three categories" (192). Added to the mix, Millat feels a profound religious guilt for his consumption of drugs and of women's bodies as disposable objects that is exceptionally clear when he starts dating Karina Cain. This is a relationship unlike any other since "he liked her and she liked him," and he only cheats on her "with three other women ... a personal record" (419). This could evolve into the "good" relationship, caring and affectionate, but it is around the same time that he joins KEVIN, the Keepers of the Eternal and Victorious Islamic Nation, a fundamentalist political group. KEVIN's brothers convince Millat that his relationship is sinful. Quickly Karina goes from being "a darling of a girl" to one who "had irritated him more than she had managed in the whole year they'd been shagging" (420). His love for Karina turns into disgust to the point where he tells her, during sex: "Don't do that...don't offer it to me like a whore. Haven't you heard of unnatural acts? Besides, I'll take it if I want it—and why can't you be a lady, don't make all that noise!" (422). Millat's relationship with women is profoundly founded on a misogyny first inherited from his father, imitated from his parents' relationship, and cultivated to the extreme in the religious radicalism of the streets. Millat's misogyny does not prevent him from seeking more sexual relationships with women, but rather enhances his search for vacuous relationships that do not help him grow. Misogyny contributes thus to his arrested development. Millat's cousin Neena unsurprisingly describes him as a person who does not know himself: "One day he's Allah this, Allah that. Next minute it's big busty blondes, Russian gymnasts, and a smoke of the sinsemilla. He doesn't know his arse from his elbow. Just like his father. He doesn't know who he is" (237).

By the end of the novel in 1999, Millat is just as confused and angry as at the beginning. Supported by his KEVIN brothers, he tries to shoot a eugenicist who happens to be the same French doctor his father failed to kill in World War II. Millat, repeating his father story, fails to kill the doctor and is finally sentenced to 400 hours of community service. Unlike Irie who is able to liberate herself from her internalized prejudice and the obsession with identity definition in terms of national heritage, Millat ends up repeating history and taking his parents' religion to a perverse extreme. His lack of final accommodation or peace illustrates the danger of a Diasporic Coming-of-age process with damaging guidance, where the models and mentors are likewise angry and confused.

Conversely, Magid grows up far from London's mean streets. The twin's Samad only has enough resources to send one of his children to study in Bangladesh, so he chooses his favorite. Samad kidnaps Magid without his wife's knowledge and sends him away in hopes that he will become what he has always wanted from his children, "two good Muslim boys" (444). Millat and Magid have only two things in common: their deoxyribonucleic acid and their endless capacity to disappoint their father. Instead of a pious man, Magid returns "more English than the English," an atheist scientist-apprentice working on a eugenics project that aims to improve the life expectancy of mice, under the tutelage of none other than Dr. Marc-Pierre Perret, the French eugenicist (303). All stories converge in the presentation of the research project. It is at the presentation of "FutureMouse" that Millat attempts to kill Dr. Perret. In the confusion, witnesses are unable to identify whether it is Millat or Magid who attempts the shot, so the judge sentences both twins to community service. Magid's formative process seems to be the exact opposite of his brother's, but they both end in the same place, the non-accommodation of court-mandated community service. Neither is content with his place in society and while one takes his parents' heritage to the extreme, the other rejects it categorically. At his end, Magid is just as ashamed of his Bangladeshi origin as when he was a small child and used to change his name to Mark in order to fit in with his exclusively white friends.

The endings of *The Buddha* and *White Teeth* illustrate how varied the formative processes of Diasporic Coming-of-age protagonists can be. Karim Amir's story concludes with him still trying to fit his body and person into the nation. His partial success as a member of his family and a somewhat prosperous actor sparks the contradictory emotions of bliss and misery. Quite distinctly, Irie Jones lets go altogether of the identity conflict that had mired her *Bildung* to the point where "roots won't matter anymore" and she can just exist happily and untethered (Smith 2001, 437). And alternatively, the Iqbal twins hold on steadfast to their identity struggle and find no sort of accommodation or hint of peace. Diasporic Coming-of-age Novels thus offer a myriad of paths for their heroes, as varied as there are possibilities for model and reprehensible adulthoods for the children of diasporas.

Notes

1 Examples can be found, to name a few, in the meatpacking factories of Chicago in Upton Sinclair's *The Jungle* (1906), the Umuofia clan of Chinua Achebe's *Things Fall Apart* (1958), the streets of Mexico City in José Emilio Pacheco's *Las Batallas en el Desierto* [*Battles in the Desert*] (1981), or Iran's Islamic Revolution in Marjane Satrapi's graphic novel *Persepolis* (2000).

2 Karim's hope for a better future takes place in the context of the beginning of a conservative government led by Prime Minister Margaret Thatcher, who repeatedly expressed sentiments against immigrants, especially people of color. "She thought it quite wrong that immigrants should be given council housing whereas white citizens were not ... She made clear, however, that she had 'less objection to refugees such as Rhodesians, Poles and Hungarians, since they could more easily be assimilated into British society'" (Swaine 2009).

4   Diasporic Coming-of-age Novels of the Mexican Diaspora in the United States

Sandra Cisneros and Yuri Herrera

Diaspora is a defining brushstroke in the portrait of the United States body politic. President John F. Kennedy famously imagined the countrywide community as a nation of immigrants, a vision that has persisted in discourses of the Union's character to this day enshrined in Emma Lazarus's 1883 poem New Colossus, which famously states "Give me your tired, your poor / Your huddled masses yearning to breathe free." Yet multicultural visions of the U.S. exist in tension with an "anti-immigrant sentiment in the general population," which has become in recent years "more virulent, more sustained, and more clearly targeted at Hispanics" (Gonzalez 2011, xiii). José David Saldívar underscores the presence of such "colonialist discourses whereby U.S. Latinos, Chicanos, Mexicanos, Central Americans, and Asian Americans are cast as an illegal outside force, an alien nation 'polluting' U.S. Culture" [*sic*] (x). State-sanctioned xenophobia is exemplary expressed in Donald Trump's speech announcing his presidential candidacy in 2015:

> "When Mexico sends its people, they're not sending their best. They're not sending you. They're not sending you. They're sending people that have lots of problems, and they're bringing those problems with us. They're bringing drugs. They're bringing crime. They're rapists. And some, I assume, are good people."
>
> (Trump 2015)

This tension, evidenced by the conflicting messages of Lazarus and Trump, is key to understanding why coming-of-age processes of culturally hybrid protagonists in novels of Latin-American diasporas are complex, difficult, and often painful. The protagonists in the two novels showcased in this chapter and the two novels in the next do not have clear paths to adulthood and belonging laid before them. The expectations of the characters in their social context are often contradictory and informed by racist, xenophobic, and misogynistic imaginings of social hierarchies.

In the context of the Mexican diaspora, comprised both of "early settlers on U.S. soil *and* the largest group of new arrivals," the coming-of-age processes take on new political dimensions where the characters not only attempt to define themselves but must ponder how their heritage communities fit into—and distort—national narratives of race, ethnicity, and culture (Gonzalez 2011, 96). In order to provide a range of experiences in the context of the Mexican diaspora, I analyze first the coming-of-age of a young working-class Latina in the northern U.S., Humboldt Park, Chicago, in Sandra Cisneros's *The House on Mango Street* (1984) and then Yuri Herrera's U.S.-Mexico border depiction of the perilous journey of Makina, the undocumented migrant young woman who is the protagonist in *Señales que precederán al fin del mundo* [*Signs Preceding the End of the World*] (2011).

The particular case of Mexican diaspora in the U.S. is intimately linked to the ways the U.S. has shaped its foreign policy through the centuries. Juan Gonzalez argues that the present state of immigration is a consequence of U.S. colonialist practices in Latin-America: "the United States expanded into an empire during the nineteenth century through seizing and exploiting Latin American territories" (xix). This expansion secured the "U.S. economic and political domination over Latin America," which inadvertently "has been—and continues to be—the underlying reason for the massive Latino presence here ... the unintended harvest of the U.S. empire" (xvii). In particular, Gonzalez ascribes Latin-American diasporas to two interrelated colonial processes that respond to colonial, political, or economic needs:

> The Latino migrant flows were directly connected to the growth of the U.S. empire as responded closely to its needs, whether it was the political need to stabilize a neighboring country or to accept its refugees as a means of accomplishing a broader foreign policy objective (Cubans, Dominicans, Salvadorans, Nicaraguans), or an economic need, such as satisfying the labor demands of particular U.S. industries (Mexicans, Puerto Ricans, Panamanians).
>
> (Gonzalex 2011, xviii)

Gonzalez further argues that rather than moving from an immigrant to a mainstream position, individuals of Latin-American diasporas are often marginalized into "a linguistic/race caste status, mostly as a result of how language and race conflicts have been dealt with throughout the United states and Latin American history" (Gonzalex 2011, xviii). Indeed, Esperanza Cordero sees her subsistence-class Humboldt Park community of Mango Street as an almost hermetic-pocket-universe within the larger Anglo and bourgeois Chicago context. Mango Street and Chicago acknowledge each other's existence only in accidental interactions riddled with fear. Similarly, Makina acknowledges this caste status, yet she resists it when she ironically calls Mexican immigrants barbarians, drawing attention to the linguistic difference of many of the migrants she encounters in her journey.

In contrast to the hegemonic identities of the protagonists of traditional *Bildungsromane*, the relegated status of Latin-American migrants is furthered by the colonial notion that the U.S. is a modern civilization while Latin-America is pre-modern and uncivilized. The notion is rooted in colonialist discourses that place Western Civilization, as Walter Mignolo explains, "not just as another civilization in the planetary concert, but as the civilization destined to lead and save the rest of the word from the Devil, from barbarism and primitivism, from underdevelopment, from despotism, and to turn unhappiness into happiness for all and forever" (Mignolo 2011, 28). As such, the U.S. is considered to be in the upper tiers of an epistemological hierarchy that imbues discourses like Donald Trump's quote in his candidacy speech with enunciative privilege. In a colonial vision of the world order, this sort of discourse, insofar as it is produced in the U.S., is at the "epistemic zero point," and "every way of knowing and sensing (feeling) that do not conform to the epistemology and aesthetics of zero point are cast behind in time and/or in the order of myth, legend folklore, local knowledge, and the like" (80).

The notion that Latin America is premodern and should strive to become more like the U.S. insidiously ignores the complex histories and cultures of the twenty-six sovereign states and territories south of the U.S.-Mexico border. The notion persists as an heir to the racist ideology that validated European colonialism as the "white man's burden."[1] This colonial imagining appears in literary representation, as Vicente Luis Mora explains of *Señales que precederán al fin del mundo*, where he views the U.S.-Mexico border not only as a geographical one, but "una línea que separa dos momentos o, si se prefiere, dos estados de la globalización económica" [a line that divides two moments or, if one prefers, two stages of economic globalization] (Mora 2011, 50).[2] In contrast, a decolonial vision of the world would be polycentric and "no one civilization is imposed over all the rest" (Mignolo 2011, 28). Esperanza Cordero in *The House on Mango Street* assumes the "epistemic zero point" to make herself and her Latino community to fill a literary void and is thus decolonial. Makina in *Señales* sarcastically reclaims the "barbarian" label for herself in order to assert her humanity in a powerful marker of maturity that I analyze later in this chapter.

Intersected by the marginalized identities of her class, race, and gender, Esperanza Cordero grows up in a working-class Latino community in Chicago. As expected, her formative process does not yield a completed and ideal adult, but rather enables fluid and intersecting identities up to the very end. Esperanza's autodiegetic voice weaves her own experiences with depictions of her community and the voices of the people around her. In doing so, the novel presents a shift from the individual focus from the central capitalist aspect of Western coloniality, as defined by Mignolo, to a collective utterance.

In *A House of My Own* (2015), Sandra Cisneros states she started to write *The House on Mango Street* at the Iowa University Writer's Workshop during "the spring of 1977, Iowa City" (Cisneros 2015, 125). Sonia Saldívar-Hull observes that in this "elitist writing program in the Midwest"

Cisneros "was alien because of her race and ethnicity, alien as a working-class woman—alien, that is, as a product of her specific history" (Saldívar-Hull 2000, 83). Cisneros confirms that this triple alienation prevented her from understanding many of the texts assigned because "none of the books in this class ... had ever discussed a house like mine" (Cisneros 2015, 125). She cites the unfamiliar houses of Vladimir Nabokov's *Speak, Memory*, (Karen Blixen's pen name) Isak Diensen's *Out of Africa*, and Gaston Bachelard's *The Poetics of Space* (Cisneros 2015, 126). The latter was especially challenging since it described a "house of memory" using the metaphor of an attic, a room that none of Cisnero's apartments ever had. The "class" in this passage refers to the university space, but can also be understood as socioeconomic class because all the other students came from backgrounds and had experiences that allowed them to understand and relate to canonical literary texts even if none had been to Nabokov's country estate Vyra, Diensen's house in Kenya, or the architectural masterpieces Bachelard describes.

In this process of realizing and subsequently coming to terms with her "otherness," Cisneros explains in an interview with Jim Sagel that she found a voice distinct from that of her classmates:

> It was not until this moment when I separated myself, when I considered myself truly distinct, that my writing acquired a voice. I knew I was a Mexican woman, but I didn't think it had anything to do with why I felt so much imbalance in my life, whereas it had everything to do with it! My race, my gender, my class! That's when I decided I would write about something my classmates couldn't write about.
>
> (Cisneros 2015, 74)

Cisneros decided to tell the story of her class, race, and gender. She would fill the "literary void" she had found as a teenage reader. Cisneros was "trying to write the stories that haven't been written," and felt "like a cartographer" who would draw the map of her community of attic-less houses and, instead of streets and avenues, she would use experiences and stories (quoted in Sagel 1991, 74). Therefore, the novel is not only a coming-of-age of the character but also a coming-into-existence of the Latino community of Humboldt Park. At the end of the novel the three sisters, old wise ladies who Esperanza meets at a wake, will tell Esperanza she "will always be Mango Street" (Cisneros 2015, 105). The process of becoming Mango Street turns Esperanza into a point of convergence for stories. Her narrative is a collective utterance where she threads together different experiences of Latin-American Diasporas in Humboldt Park. In becoming both place and storyteller, Esperanza assumes the responsibility of voicing those underrepresented, untold tales, specifically linked to the place where she grew up. Paradoxically, it is her departure from this specific place that enables her to become its storyteller.

Saldivar-Hull keys in on the fact that Esperanza assumes the responsibility to tell the stories as the main factor that disables assimilationist interpretation of the text. Saldivar-Hull explains that when the book was first published Juan Rodríguez, "editor of the notoriously sexist Chicano newsletter *Carta Abierta*," misread the novel when he affirmed "that Esperanza chooses to leave Mango Street, chooses to move away from her social/cultural base to become more 'Anglicized,' more individualistic" (quoted in Saldívar-Hull 2000, 85). Saldívar-Hull disputes Rodríguez's interpretation explaining that Esperanza's escape from Mango Street "does not have to be a bourgeois escape to an academic ivory tower." Rather, higher education constitutes an option that allows "the Chicana working-class intellectual the possibility of a return" (102). Saldívar-Hull then clarifies that "the return, of course, is the book itself. The house Esperanza seeks is … a site that offers countless Chicanas and other women a mirror of their own lives under Chicano (male) rule and signals how it is possible to resist and to build new structures as women" (102). Saldívar-Hull underscores the significance of the return-in-letters, but Rodríguez argument is not so easily shaken, as it becomes clear in the last vignette that the protagonist does not return-in-person. Even if it is not necessarily a "bourgeois escape," the access to higher education and to English letters enables a self-determination not afforded to the other women in her community, oppressed both by the larger Anglo context and the men in Mango Street.

The stories of the girls and women in Esperanza's community represent the possible outcomes for the coming-of-age process. The depiction of the multiplicity of stories and voices that converge in Mango Street enable Esperanza not to assimilate, but rather to revise the genre so that the collective can escape oppressive gender roles. The power of storytelling enables nuanced self-representation for marginalized and often stereotyped identities.

The Diasporic Community of Mango Street

The novel begins with a bilingual dedication: "A las Mujeres / To the Women." In intermingling Spanish and English, Cisneros announces a hybrid identity and, therefore, cultural hybridity that manifests itself throughout the novel. The bilingualism of the dedication indicates the novel is intended not exclusively but rather especially for readers who grew up speaking as bilinguals, Spanish-English bilingual in particular, experiencing their distant home culture simultaneously with the one of their host country. Hybridity is also at the center of the novelistic style, as its forty-four vignettes, built with incomplete sentences, phrases, and fragments of thought, mix short story and poetry. Saldívar-Hull argues hybridity inserts the novel in a U.S. feminist working-class tradition: "Cisnero's mestiza text is both lyrical and realist; it has the rhythms of poetry and the narrative power of fiction. It participates (borders on) a variety of genres—historia, testimonio, and poetry, as well as working-class, U.S. feminist fiction closely allied to (working-class feminist writer) Tillie Olsen's novel of the 1930's

Yonnondio" (Saldívar-Hull 2000, 87).[3] *The House on Mango Street* is relentlessly liminal; the Diasporic Coming-of-age genre parallels this liminality in its subversion of traditional genre expectations and inclusion of elements of other genres.

Inscribing herself into and yet subverting the larger coming-of-age genre, Cisneros begins Esperanza's formative process with a discussion of her strange name—strange to the Anglo context. This clashes with traditional *Bildungsromane* that often start with a name containing lineage and implying inheritance. Esperanza's name exemplifies her difference and marginalization, "In English my name means hope. In Spanish it means too many letters. It means sadness, it means waiting" (Cisneros 1984, 10). Her name represents the initial impossibility of reconciliation with her hybrid identity. While "the English definition is motivating and positive," the Spanish definition is associated with sadness (Betz 2012, 19). Coloniality operates in the intimate facet of name, as it places the Spanish meaning in a subordinate position in relation to the dominant English meaning of "hope." Further, the name implies the possibility of unintentionally repeating the story of the woman who had it before her, her great-grandmother:

> It was my great-grandmother's name and now it is mine. She was a horse woman … I would've liked to have known her, a wild horse of a woman, so wild she wouldn't marry. Until my great-grandfather threw a sack over her head and carried her off. And the story goes she never forgave him. She looked out of the window her whole life, the way so many women sit their sadness on an elbow … Esperanza. I have inherited her name but I don't want to inherit her place by the window.
>
> (Cisneros 1984, 11)

Male violence traps the woman's wildness, taming the "wild horse." In Esperanza's process of identification, her great-grandmother functions as a model of imitation and rejection. Esperanza wants her strength, but she does not want to repeat her story. Her name carries both admiration and refusal as she tries to reject what being from Mango Street could mean for her: becoming a submissive wife.

The linguistic ambiguities that participate in the confusing process and goals of Diasporic Coming-of-age Novels persist in the vignette. Esperanza's name collides with the English-speaking world and the school, the repeated site of social mores in *Bildungsromane*:

> "At school they say my name funny as if the syllables were made out of tin and hurt the roof of your mouth. But in Spanish my name is made out of a softer something, like silver, not quite as thick as sister's name—Magdalena—which is uglier than mine. Magdalena who at least can come home and become Nenny. But I am always Esperanza."
>
> (Cisneros 1984, 11)

Esperanza envies the linguistic and cultural possibility her sister has of becoming a Nenny sometimes, to hide her identity under her nickname. Nenny's name mutates to assimilate into the cultural space she inhabits. But Esperanza has to carry her great-grandmother's story at all times.

For Luz Aurora Pimentel, the name of a character starts out as a word devoid of meaning, a blank slate, and acquires significations throughout a narration. By the end, readers associate the name of a character with the constellation of characteristics that the text has built (Pimentel 2001, 56). Much like a magnet, the name of a character is a noun that attracts adjectives. Esperanza's desire to shed her name, her semantic magnet, disappears in the end, when she achieves what her great-grandmother never could. Esperanza goes to the world outside the window and promises to come back to bring the change to Mango Street that outside forces cannot bring: "I have gone away to come back. For the ones I left behind" (Cisneros 1984, 110).

Esperanza's choice to access the bourgeois context and leave Mango Street behind is hastened by the male violence that she and generations of women before her experience in her community. This motivation is a new development of the Diasporic Coming-of-age Novel, where self-forging is not only a natural impulse of a young male hero, but a necessity to avoid material danger and survive. Starting with the story of Esperanza's great-grandmother, readers encounter the violent nature of most of the men in Esperanza's life. Except for her father, who displays vulnerability when he hears news of the death of Esperanza's grandfather (56), men are depicted as violent and abusive of women. Further, several men sexually assault Esperanza, mirroring her great-grandmother's story of abuse, as in the vignettes "The First Job" and "Red Clowns."

In "The First Job" Esperanza is isolated from the rest of the workers because her age and inexperience make her afraid to build work relationships. She "was scared to eat alone in the company lunchroom with all those men and ladies looking" (54). A man takes advantage of her isolation and asks her for a kiss on account of it being his birthday. Esperanza explains, "I thought I would because he was so old and just as I was about to put my lips on his cheek, he grabs my face with both hands and kisses me hard on the mouth and doesn't let go" (55). Even men who seem benign are violent. Esperanza ends the vignette with the kiss and does not explain what happened to the man or whether she stayed at the job. The lack of a follow-up signifies a lack of consequences for the man. Her family's financial struggles intersect with her gender to create this particularly vulnerable situation in an unlawful job that offers her no protections from harassment or abuse.

In one of the most ambiguous vignettes, "Red Clowns" Esperanza tells, or rather is unable to tell, her story of assumed rape. Esperanza is again isolated, this time at a fair, since her friend Sally has left her alone. In this scene, Esperanza's intersectional identity comes into play, as the stranger who grabs her emphasizes his assumption of her ethnicity, "I love you,

Spanish girl, I love you, and pressed his sour mouth to hers" (Cisneros 1984, 100).[4] Violent masculinity is inescapable in the stories of Esperanza's great-grandmother and, as represented later in the novel, Sally. Male violence functions like the idea of destiny that predominates in Proto-*Bildungsromane*, but the protagonists of Diasporic Coming-of-age Novels swerve, avoiding this outcome and creating a new way of learning. Sally is abused first by a father who hits her when he finds out she has been talking to boys, "he just went crazy, he just forgot he was her father between the buckle and the belt" (93); then by her husband—"sometimes her husband gets angry and once he broke the door where his foot went through" (101). As evidenced by Sally's father and husband, and Esperanza's great-grandfather, male violence is normalized in society at large and institutionalized in marriage, thus subverting the accommodation of the "marriage of true affection" that Elizabeth Bennet pursues in Jane Austen's *Pride and Prejudice* (Austen 2016, 70). In this sense, Esperanza's escape from her community and her quest for a house free of men is a quest not only for higher education or the means to become a storyteller, but also for security and physical wellbeing.

In her process of identification, Esperanza selects two other characters that fulfill the function of mentors: her aunt Lupe and her Puerto Rican neighbor Alicia, who studies at a university. Esperanza's aunt, who lives by herself in a "dark apartment, second-floor rear building where sunlight never came," is extremely sick, and is the only adult who listens to Esperanza's poems and encourages her to work on her art (Cisneros 1984, 60):

> She listened to every book, every poem I read her. One day I read her one of my own. I came very close. I whispered it into the pillows:
>
> I want to be
> like the waves on the sea,
> like clouds in the wind,
> but I'm me.
> One day I'll jump
> out of my skin.
> I'll shake the sky
> like a hundred violins
>
> That's nice. That's very good, she said in her tired voice. You just remember to keep writing, Esperanza. You must keep writing. It will keep you free, and I said yes, but at the time I didn't know what she meant … And then she died, my aunt who listened to my poems. And then we began to dream the dreams.
>
> (Cisneros 1984, 60–61)

Even though Esperanza does not understand at that point that writing will set her free from the oppressive roles in the stories of her great-grandmother or Sally, she does start to "dream the dreams." The rich vagueness of these dreams coordinates with the alternative formative process that enables Esperanza to define the artistic adulthood she eventually builds. For the first time, she accepts the notion that the possibility of dreaming to go away does not necessarily mean the same thing as jumping out of her skin or shedding her name. However, she can only fully accept this at the very end, when she is able to acknowledge that she is Mango Street but that she can go away nonetheless. In her last vignette she says,

> I like to tell stories. I am going to tell you the story about a girl who didn't want to belong. I didn't always want to live on Mango Street ... Mango Street, sad red house, the house I belong but do not belong to ... One day I will go away. Friends and neighbors will say, What happened to that Esperanza? Where did she go with all those books and paper? Why did she march so far away? They will not know I have gone away to come back.
>
> (Cisneros 1984, 109–110)

Esperanza recognizes that she can refrain from repeating her great-grandmother's story without having to reject her name, but rather becomes the new story of the re-signified name of her own sewing.[5] The meaning of the name becomes more flexible since she recognizes the possibility to have her own home and live by herself: to not marry. Where a traditional *Bildungsroman* would enshrine marriage as a fundamental part of the respectable accommodations of the middle-class protagonist, *The House on Mango Street* enables readers to understand singleness as a possible and desirable accommodation.

Alicia is the first to present to Esperanza the possibility of escaping by means of education through her own practices. Alicia lives with her father who thinks "a woman's place is sleeping so she can wake up early with the tortilla star" (Cisneros 1984, 31). Since Alicia's mother is dead, she has the responsibility of cooking. Alicia "inherited her mama's rolling pin" (31). However, Alicia "is smart and studies for the first time at a university" (31). Alicia's decision to go to college shows that educated women become ostracized in the diasporic community, as evidenced by Esperanza's earlier perception in the fifth vignette: "Alicia is stuck-up ever since she went to college" (12). Her education is by no means an easy feat because of not only her gender, but also her class position, geographically in the city, which forces her to take "two trains and a bus" to arrive. But Alicia is willing to do it "because she doesn't want to spend her whole life in a factory or behind a rolling pin" (31–32). Her aunt and Alicia represent the possibility of empowerment that Esperanza will later possess.

In addition to her great-grandmother, aunt, and Alicia, Esperanza's social environment disperses modeling among several other women. Unlike traditional *Bildungsroman*, where the figure of the mentor is one successful and wise citizen-worker, young diasporic protagonists must evaluate multiple role models to build their own definition of adulthood. Esperanza's mother and Minerva, an older married girl, are ambivalent models while her neighbor Marin is a negative model. Both her mother and Minerva are storytellers. In the first vignette, where Esperanza yearns for a middle-class suburban house, she says "this was the house Mama dreamed up in the stories she told us before we went to bed" (4). In the vignette "A Smart Cookie," Esperanza's mother is shown to have an artistic sensibility that she was never able to develop. Her mother recalls, "I could've been some-body ... [I] can sing an opera" (90). Esperanza's mother often sings, mean-ingfully Puccini's *Madame Butterfly,* an opera about a Japanese woman who also waits by the window, in this case for her husband to return, and who eventually kills herself. "That Madame Butterfly was a fool," exclaims Mama (90). The reference to *Madame Butterfly* inserts the novel into a centuries-old and global history of lack of positive models for young girls. It is a model distinct from but related to her mother's shame of her social class, which prevented her from finishing her education. Esperanza's mother embodies the potential of talent and the paralysis that stems from class shame.

Minerva is also a writer but, even though she "is only a little older than" Esperanza, she already has two children and depends on an irresponsible man who leaves her time and again (84). These women depict two ways in which class and gender can halt the development of talent, imprisoning them. Esperanza's neighbor Marin recalls the image of Esperanza's great-grandmother because, like her, she is also looks out and waits. But, unlike her great-grandmother, Marin hopes to find a man who will marry her "and take [her] to live in a big house far away" (Cisneros 1984, 26). Marin "is waiting for a car to stop, a star to fall, someone to change her life" but she cannot imagine the possibility of changing it herself (26).

Diasporic Coming-of-age Novels often show concurrent formative processes that the protagonists can imitate or reject. The stories of Sally and Mamacita, which serve Esperanza as models of disidentification, depict the most despairing outcomes for women in Mango Street. Sally's story depicts marriage as a false escape from male violence. Her story appears in three non-consecutive vignettes. In the first one, "Sally," Esperanza depicts her friend as a beautiful girl who only wants "to love and to love and to love" (83). For this reason, she is called a nasty name and the boys tell lewd stories of her in the coatroom. In "What Sally Said," Esperanza reports a particularly bad beating her father gave Sally when he "catches her talking to a boy" (93). This beating is described in unclear terms but suggests the possibility of sexual abuse when Esperanza explains, "he just forgot he was her father between the buckle and the belt" (93). In "Linoleum Roses," Sally gets married to a "marshmallow salesman" she met "at a school bazaar" (101). They have to go to another state, "where it's legal to get married before the eighth grade" and Esperanza explains she thinks "she did it to escape" (101). The outcome is despairing, as her husband is just as violent as her father and isolates her: "He doesn't let her look out the window. And he doesn't like her friends, so nobody gets to visit her unless he is working" (102). Sally's isolation is more brutal than that of Esperanza's great-grandmother because Sally is forced to look inside her house; she is not even allowed to imagine the possibilities out the window. Sally's thwarted escape presents a grim alternative for the women in Esperanza's community, jumping from one abusive household to the next, dependent on men and their desires. It also portrays an imprisonment made possible by socioeconomic conditions: the only escape from her father's house that Sally can imagine is another man's house. Sally becomes a linoleum rose, as the title of the vignette suggests, in a household that cannot afford real flowers, as beautiful and unmovable as the rose.

Mamacita is also imprisoned in her apartment. It is not however her husband who restrains her, but her Spanish monolingualism, which alienates her from the larger Anglo Chicago context and from the bilingual community of Mango Street. The immediacy of her diaspora marginalizes her linguistically. As opposed to Esperanza, Mamacita cannot escape any of the oppressing forces of her life because in the larger context of Chicago she is unable to communicate. Mamacita's husband had come to Chicago before her. He worked and "saved and saved because she was alone with the baby boy in that country [Mexico]" (76). When *Mamacita* arrives she instantly becomes secluded. Esperanza mentions that when her own father first came to *this* country he ate "hamandeggs" for three months because it was the only word he knew. Mamacita's desire is to go home but her husband is annoyed with what he assumes to be her nostalgia. He tells her, "*!Ay, caray!* We *are* home. This *is* home. Here I am and here I stay. Speak English. Speak English. Christ!" (Cisneros 1984, 78).

Afterwards, Mamacita's greatest fear is realized when her little son "starts to sing the Pepsi commercial he heard on T.V." (78). The protection from linguistic marginalization she has built within her house crumbles when English invades her intimate space in the form of the capitalist structure that educates her son as a consumer: "No speak English, she says to the child who is singing in the language that sounds like tin. No speak English, no speak English, and bubbles into tears" (78). The broken English signifies a broken relationship with her son, who is learning how to interact with the outside world and possibly forgetting his Mexican heritage.

Mamacita is an extreme example of the marginalization that the English-speaking Chicago exerts on the immigrant community of Mango Street, but Esperanza also draws one vignette where the rest of the city interacts with Mango Street and vice versa. Esperanza explains: "those who don't know any better come into our neighborhood scared. They think we're dangerous. They think we will attack them with shiny knives. They are stupid people who are lost and got here by mistake" (28). Mamacita cannot interact with the city because she cannot speak English; but, conversely, the "stupid" outsiders who speak only English cannot interact with this street either. Mango Street seems dangerous to outsiders, but the people of Mango Street are also scared: "All brown around, we are safe. But watch us drive into a neighborhood of another color and our knees go shakity-shake and our car windows get rolled up tight and our eyes look straight. Yeah. That is how it goes and goes" (28). Chicago is fearful of the Mango community. The community becomes a marginal "them" to the ones who get there by mistake. Esperanza defies this typification by saying,

> "But we aren't afraid. We know the guy with the crooked eye is Davey the Baby's brother, and the tall one next to him in the straw brim, that's Rosa's Eddie V., and the big one that looks like a dumb grown man, he's Fat Boy, though he's not fat anymore nor a boy."
>
> (Cisneros 1984, 28)

Esperanza gives names to the people in Mango. By acquiring a name or nickname, they also acquire collections of adjectives that turn them into individuals.

The inexorable segregation that characterizes Chicago's neighborhoods to this day plays a key role in this short vignette. Chicago is depicted as a city reigned by fear of difference and delimited by both racism and social class. This is how it goes and goes: everyone is guilty of the ubiquitous lack of sympathy and solidarity between races. The vignette thus signifies a necessity for fair and nuanced storytelling. Resisting the violent stereotype associated with people of color can foster solidarity and understanding.

Esperanza suffers from different kinds of oppression, a key motivator in Diasporic Coming-of-age Novels that accelerates the need for self-awareness and confidence: as a woman she is abused; as the daughter of immigrants living in a segregated U.S. city, she is feared and ridiculed. Experiences of class shaming, which bookend the novel, further expedite her process of growing up. In the first vignette, a nun in her school asks Esperanza to show her where she lives. Esperanza points to the "third floor, the paint peeling, wooden bars Papa had nailed on the windows so we wouldn't fall out," and the nun says "You live *there?*" (Cisneros 1984, 5). This experience parallels the reason her mother left school: "Shame is a bad thing, you know. It keeps you down. You want to know why I quit school? Because I didn't have nice clothes. No clothes, but I had brains. Yup, she says disgusted, stirring again. I was a smart cookie then" (91). Esperanza's mother was paralyzed by the shame of her class, written in her clothes for everyone to read. Like her mother, at the beginning of the novel Esperanza learns to be ashamed of where she lives and what her name represents: roughness and marginalization in school, marriage and imprisonment in the house. However, at the end of the novel Esperanza has found a way to accept her name. This acceptance empowers Esperanza to continue her education, the path that will ultimately enable her not to repeat her mother's story of frustration and shame.

In a conversation that she has towards the end of the novel, in the vignette "The Three Sisters," one of the old ladies tells her "You will always be Esperanza. You will always be Mango Street. You can't erase what you know. You can't forget who you are" (105). Esperanza does not know how to respond: "It was as if she could read my mind, as if she knew what I had wished for, and I felt ashamed for having made such a selfish wish" (105). Esperanza feels ashamed that she had wanted to get rid of her name, like her sister Nenny, in order to become someone else. In the final vignettes, the identity Esperanza has constructed enables her to imitate the characteristics that she had admired in her great-grandmother, her strength and wildness, but to reject the roles of wife and mother. In her rejection of the secluded nature of Mango Street and the static longing of her great-grandmother gazing through the window, Esperanza imitates brave women like her aunt Lupe and neighbor Alicia. From her aunt, Esperanza learns to recognize the value of her poetry and the possibility to have a house of one's own, even if it is small and dark. Alicia embodies the possibility of social mobility through education. Esperanza's process of identification enables her to escape the brutality of men and to get a house that is "Not a man's house. Not a daddy's. A house all of my own" (Cisneros 1984, 108).

Esperanza's story follows some aspects of Jerome Buckley's plot, except for the love affairs and the final accommodation characteristic of the most traditional *Bildungsroman*. Esperanza's repudiation of marriage subverts one of the main objectives of Elizabeth Bennet in Jane Austen's *Pride and Prejudice* and the eponymous protagonist in Charles Dickens' *David Copperfield*. In these novels, marriage is a key marker of maturity and represents the protagonists' exemplary standing in their communities and social wholes. Instead of the imprisonment that marriage would entail, Esperanza's need to tell stories and survive is what frees her from her marital destiny. However, she still feels a responsibility, at the end, to "come back. For the ones I felt behind. For the ones who cannot out" (110). As she explains in one of the last conversations of the novel, there are no outside powers that can change the conditions that Mango Street represents:

Like it or not you are Mango Street, and one day you'll come back too.

Not me. Not until somebody makes it better.

Who's going to do it? The Mayor?

And the thought of the mayor coming to Mango Street makes me laugh out loud.

Who's going to do it? Not the mayor.

(Cisneros 1984, 107)

Since the mayor, as a representative of the power structure that marginalizes Mango Street, is not going to do anything to change Mango's conditions, she believes it is her responsibility to speak for those who don't have a voice.

Betz argues that the acquisition of English "is perceived as a chance to escape poverty and restraint in such a misogynist culture, so author and heroine establish English as mother-tongue" (Cisneros 1984, 32). I disagree with Betz on this point. Neither Cisneros nor Esperanza are sellouts, as was suggested by many critics when *The House on Mango Street* was first published. Saldívar-Hull disapprovingly explains of such critics,

> When Chicana feminist writers begin to examine Chicano "tradition" and criticize wife battering, child abuse, "drunk husbands," the misogyny that is embedded in the culture, they are branded "vendidas," sellouts, who betray their people and contribute to the damaging stereotypes of Mexicans and Mexican Americans that Anglo America already believes.
>
> (Saldívar-Hull 2000, 83–84)

Esperanza's narration does not adopt English in order to further the stereotypes associated with Latino communities in segregated U.S. cities, but rather to show the constellation of characters and experiences that constitute the community. Her voice is predominantly in English, but it is woven with Spanish terms of endearment. Her name signifies the English word hope, but it also carries the story of her ancestry and her fight against repressive models. The power Esperanza acquires during her process is not the adoption of the privileged language, but rather the capacity to be the one who tells her story. Esperanza decides which adjectives she wants and which adjectives she does not for herself and for her community. In the context of a collision between us (Mango Street) and them (the Chicago majority), the possibility to represent implies the power to build an identity as rich as the storyteller desires, and that has spoken to and about diasporic communities.

Through that collision, Esperanza's coming-of-age challenges the conventions of the *Bildungsroman*. Rather than a standard role model, she adopts piecemeal aspects of partial models in her community. Afterwards, when she leaves her community, she subverts the original expectation of the *Bildungsroman* to teach how to be a respectable role model in one's own social context. Her self-inflicted exile is not entirely grim, however, because she has found a way to resist the oppressive family structures that her great-grandmother could not, and she does return, in the book itself.

Unlike the imagined white middle-class male readers of *Bildungsromane* of the eighteenth century, Cisneros' imagined readers are people like her, whose class, race, and gender identities are confusing and marginal, who exist in liminal places where they are often less certain of who they are or should be. The Diasporic Coming-of-age conventions enable explorations with identities and open-ended conclusions that allow fluid notions of adulthood. Cisneros does not tell readers what they ought to become, but rather enables her marginalized readers to understand their identities as complex and nuanced. Cisneros fills the "literary void" in telling the story of "My race, my gender, my class!" (Sagel 1991, 74).

The Lived Experience of Diaspora across the U.S.-Mexico Border

Unlike Esperanza Cordero, born north of the U.S.-Mexico border, the story of Makina, born south of it, in *Señales que precederán al fin del mundo* [*Signs Preceding the End of the World*], illustrates the formative process of a poor female migrant who experiences several forms of direct and constantly life-threatening intersecting oppressions as she crosses the border. The Diasporic Coming-of-age Novel can encompass this experience because of its extraordinary malleability. Like Esperanza, Makina experiences intersecting forms of oppression due to her minority identities of class, race, and gender. Both novels show the reality of male violence against women in diasporic communities, regardless of whether they are well-established communities in urban geographical demarcations or inscribed in the process of border-crossing. As such, the protagonists actively reject or overlook marriage as an ideal path to belonging or citizenship, subverting early expectations of women in *Bildungsromane*.

Throughout the borderland, Makina witnesses the dire and often opprobrious spaces other migrants inhabit. Unlike traditional *Bildungsromane* where names are of great importance, *Señales* depicts a coming-of-age where the hero chooses to forego her name, the identity she has created throughout the process.[6] Further, instead of starting with the birth of the character, the novel begins with Makina's voice explaining "estoy muerta" [I am dead] (Herrera 2010, 11), a reversal of the traditional temporal unraveling of any formative process.

The Diasporic Coming-of-age framework enables a sensitive reading of this novel, which focuses on the possible alternatives that Makina encounters throughout her journey. Such a reading diverges significantly from other approaches to Herrera's work. Ivonne Sánchez Becerril, for example, interprets the story as a metaphor for crossing into the Mictlán, the underworld of Aztec mythology. The nine sections of the novel mirror the nine levels of the journey whereby the souls of the dead become detached from their bodies, material possessions, and cultural identities. This allegorical interpretation, supported by the nebulous atemporal setting, underscores that the location of the U.S. is, similar to the Mictlán, "debajo de la tierra y hacia el norte" [underground and northward] (Sánchez Becerril 2014, 109). Sánchez Becerril indicates that this is not a mere coincidence, but rather proposes that Makina's arrival at the "región norte, al inframundo, a Mictlán" [North region, to the underwold, to the Mictlán] is also her arrival at the "vida clandestina, subterránea—*underground*—de los migrantes mexicanos en Estados Unidos" [clandestine life, subterraneous—underground—of Mexican migrants in the U.S.] (Herrera 2010, 112). Extending this allegorical reading, Sánchez Becerril proposes that the ambiguous names of the "lords" in Makina's town can be read as Aztec divinities that help her soul across. Makina enlists Dobleú, Tlaloc, God of water and rain, to help her cross the river; Hache, Huitzilopochtli, the foundational patron of Mexico

City and God of War, to help her find her brother (whom she finds in a military base); and Q, Quetzalcoatl, the feathered serpent, God of life, wisdom, and duality, to help her return.

This allegorical reading underscores the symbolic dimension of the characters in the story and is helpful in illuminating the connection between Makina's initial death and her journey into a "subworld" of material and social inequality. Such a reading valuably shows the pertinence of an allegorical interpretation of the characters' names and plot. It pays tribute to the mythical quality of Herrera's novel and to the foundational tension in the *Bildungsroman*, in which the protagonist is at once a realistic, historically-situated character and an everyperson.

Makina grows up in *la provincia*, the derogatory way Mexico City inhabitants refer to the rest of the country, outside of the metropolis. We know little about her education, but the novel portrays a "sensitive child," multilingual and prudent in the way she speaks to dangerous characters and what information she should share or conceal. Makina is well respected by the lords and inhabitants of her village for her capacity to keep secrets and deliver messages without questioning the content or recipients: "Una no hurga en bajo las enaguas de los demás" [One does not poke around in other people's underskirts] (Herrera 2010, 19). Makina is therefore ideal for her job: "estaba a cargo de la centralita con el único teléfono en kilómetros y kilómetros a la redonda" [she was in charge of the only telephone switchboard for kilometers and kilometers around] (19). Makina receives all messages and phone calls, even the ones from the migrants in the U.S. who "ya se habían olivdado de las hablas de acá" [had already forgotten the local language here] (19). Makina speaks three languages: "la lengua," an indigenous language; "la lengua latina," Spanish; and "la lengua gabacha," English. And most importantly for the role she plays in her community, she knows when to remain silent in all of them: "Makina hablaba las tres, y en las tres sabía callarse" [Makina spoke all three and in all three she knew how to keep quiet] (19). Makina thinks of herself as a messenger, a door between distant worlds, but she does not want to be the one who crosses into either side: "Una es la puerta, no la que cruza la puerta" [One is the door, not the one who crosses it] (19). Her multilingualism enables her coming-of-age because she is able to cross borders and communicate in every liminal space she traverses.

Unlike the hero in Jeffers's plot, Makina is content with her life. It is a request from her mother Cora that upturns her world. She must go to "el gran Chilango" [Mexico City] and then to "el gabacho" [the U.S.] to find her brother and give him a letter asking him to come back.[7] Makina fears losing herself in foreign lands:

No quería ni quedarse por allá ni que le sucediera como a un amigo suyo que se mantuvo lejos demasiado tiempo, tal vez un día de más o una hora de más, en todo caso bastante de más como para que le pasara que cuando volvió todo seguía igual pero ya todo era otra cosa, o todo era semejante pero no era igual: su madre ya no era su madre... . Hasta el aire, dijo, le entibiaba el pecho de otro modo.

[She did not want to stay over there nor to repeat the experience of a friend of hers who was there for too long, maybe only a day or an hour too long, but in any case long enough that when he came back everything remained the same but was already something else, or everything was similar but was no longer the same: his mother was no longer his mother ... . Even the air, he said, warmed his chest differently.]

(Herrera 2010, 21)

Despite her fear of estrangement, powerful elements compel her to leave her village: her poverty, the same pressure that compelled her brother to migrate, and gender, as her mother tells her she cannot entrust the message to a man. Herrera brilliantly articulates the reluctance of the protagonist's journey in a metaphor of treading lightly: "plantaba el pie suavecito porque no era ése el sitio donde quería dejar huella" [she treaded lightly because this was not the place where she wanted to leave footprints] (Herrera 2010, 27). This metaphor finds its counterpart at the end, when she walks in a park in the U.S. and "al andar sus pies—pat, pat, pat— dejaban huella sobre la tierra" [when she walked, her feet—pat, pat, pat— left footprints on the ground] (115). The sound, "pat," is a nod to Makina's transformation since it is not a term used in Spanish and is thus a multilingual point.

Makina's process further subverts Jeffers's plot in the matters of love and sex, as she does not have "at least two love affairs, one good and one bad, which help him revalue his values" (52). In the bus to the border, Makina encounters her first "love affair," the "bad one." To consider this encounter a love affair one must do so with irony, as the male character does not express love, but a form of sexual violence that Makina learns to reject. At the line to buy the bus tickets a man comes up to Makina and tells her: "Me apellido ¡Merezco!" [My last name is I deserve you!] (Herrera 2010, 32). In the bus he sits next to her and starts brushing his hand against her thigh "como por descuido, pero ella conocía esa clase de descuidos" [as if by accident, but she knew about this kind of accidents] (33). When "el idiota" puts his whole hand on her leg,

Makina se volvió hacia él, lo miró directamente a los ojos para que supiera que lo que venía no era accidental, se puso un dedo en los labios, calladito, eh, y con la otra mano prensó el dedo medio de la mano con que la había tocado y lo dobló hasta acercarlo a un par de centímetros de su reverso ... No me gusta que me manoseen pinches desconocidos ¿puedes creerlo?

[Makina turned towards him, she looked him directly in the eye so he would understand that what was about to happen was not accidental, she placed her finger over her lips, be quiet, ok?, and with her other hand she grabbed the middle finger of the hand that had touched her and she bent it back until it almost touched the back of his hand ... I don't like getting touched by fucking strangers, can you believe it?]

(Herrera 2010, 33–34)

Makina learns that the society on the border imposes sexual violence on her body: the man thinks it is permissible to assault her and foresees no consequences: "I deserve you." The violation of her body emerges as a possible outcome of her journey, but Makina violently rejects this possibility and asserts her agency.

Her light reference to the possibility of a second love affair, the "good one" in Buckley's archetypal terms, starts when she meets Chucho, the man who helps her across the U.S.-Mexico border. (In an allegorical reading, Chucho, short for Jesus, becomes a Christian symbol of the passing of souls.) Unlike the man in the bus, Chucho does not make a pass at her, which makes her feel safe at first and soon makes him desirable. After they have crossed the river, Chucho and Makina go to a shack where she changes out of her wet clothes in the same room as Chucho:

> Makina comenzó a desvestirse de espaldas a Chucho, que fumaba y miraba por la ventana al cabrón en vigilia, y pensó que era cosa rara no sentir ni miedo ni rabia por tener que encuerarse sin pared de por medio ... Makina supo que él seguía mirando por la ventana pero su voz caía sobre ella. Sintió que ese segundo de tensión duraba y duraba, y ahora se sorprendió de que ya hubiera pasado tanto tiempo y ella no comenzara a sentirse culpable de querer lo que quería.

> [Makina started to undress with her back to Chucho, who smoked and looked out the window for the bastard who was watching them. She thought it was weird not to feel fear or anger for having to take her clothes off with no wall separating them ... Makina knew he was still watching out the window but his voice fell on her. She felt that second of tension kept going on and on, and now she was surprised that so much time had passed and she had not felt guilty of desiring what she desired.]

(Herrera 2010, 51)

Makina is surprised to find no guilt associated with her desire. This is the last instance where we encounter Makina in a situation sexually charged. Thus her experiences with the man on the bus and with Chucho succinctly portray a sexual coming-of-age, not expressed through the social and institutional act of marriage but rather through an internal realization of self-identity. She violently rejects a relationship where she is the object of power imbalance but desires the man who respects her privacy. The relationship has a positive outcome for Makina, one that is in a different mode from the expectations readers might have. Afterwards, Chucho protects her from a racist farmer and police officers that open fire against them. Makina is wounded in the brawl, but she survives because Chucho enables her to escape.

Importantly to the subversion of the classic plot, the good relationship with Chucho does not end in institutionalized marriage. In Diasporic Coming-of-age Novels, love is often not a means for the protagonist to learn how to adhere to the capitalist and heterosexual social order. Marriage is no longer a criterion to measure the "goodness" or suitability of romantic relationships. These, nonetheless, can be tools for protagonists to explore and eventually understand their desires and test what they want in a partner—even if they want one or many, as is the case of Jamila in *The Buddha of Suburbia*, or no partner if asexuality or aromance is consistent with their sense of self. Romantic and sexual relationships can still be means of exploration and enable maturation, but in a myriad of ways and to a broader range of ends that the traditional *Bildungsromane* never explored.

During her crossing, Makina finds two possible outcomes for diasporic individuals and, therefore, alternatives that she could unwillingly embody. She lights upon the first one when she encounters what she thinks at first to be a pregnant woman lying peacefully under a tree. Makina thinks she sees the woman's "vientre antes que las piernas o su rostro" [womb before the legs or face], which can easily be read as an image of serenity, "un buen augurio" [a good omen] (Herrera 2010, 47). Soon thereafter and suddenly, Makina realizes it is not a woman but rather a "pobre infeliz hinchado de putrefacción al que los zopilotes ya le habían comido los ojos y la lengua" [unfortunate wretch, swollen and rotting, whose eyes and tongue had been eaten by buzzards] (48). The dead body is an omen of the bodies of many migrants, men or women, pregnant with putrefaction rather than life.

Another possible outcome occurs to Makina when she drives by a baseball stadium with an old Mexican migrant. She asks him what the "gabachos" are doing, and the man explains they gather every week in the stadium to celebrate who they are. He explains that baseball is a metaphor for imperialism, where a player has to visit bases around the world and come back home victorious. In a question that enunciates the possibility of assimilation, Makina asks whether the man enjoys the game. He explains that "yo aquí nomás estoy de paso" [I am only passing through] (66). Makina asks him how many years he has lived there and he answers "voy para cincuenta años" [almost fifty years] (66). This dis-placement, a feeling of being a passer-by despite decades of residence, enunciates an alternative for Makina that she rejects in the next chapter. Assimilation is impossible for this man who does not adopt the culture or the love of baseball. And while Latin-American men have played baseball professionally, the "American pastime" is implicitly less available as a pastime to Makina as a woman and certainly unavailable to her and other Latina women professionally.

The more she experiences the U.S., the more Makina becomes comfortable with hybridity. "Son paisanos y son gabachos" [they are countrymen and they are gabachos], she explains about the Mexicans living in the U.S. Southwest (73). These identities are not mutually exclusive but rather coexist in the same bodies: "Hablan una lengua intermedia con la que Makina simpatiza de inmediato porque es como ella: maleable, deleble, permeable, un gozne entre dos semejantes distantes" [They speak an in-between language with which Makina immediately sympathizes because it is like her: malleable, erasable, permeable, a hinge between two distant neighbors] (73). The prevalence of this in-between language is a contrast to her singularity in speaking three distinct languages in her native town. Her hometown distinguishes between the languages and considers both Spanish and English foreign, as evidenced by their epithets "lengua latina" and "lengua gabacha." In this border space, the distinction between languages fades. In her discovery of this linguistic dimension of cultural hybridity she begins to consider the possibility of belonging in the U.S.

In the subsequent chapter, Makina comes across a Gay and Lesbian rally, which further shows her the possibility of a marginal identity. It demonstrates the ways in which identities such as sexual or political are not easily parsed and carry different meanings in the U.S. Southwest from the ones in her hometown.

> había mucha gente con banderas multicolores ... se matrimoniaban. Tan deslumbrada estaba Makina con la belleza del rito que tardó en reparar en que las parejas eran de hombres o eran de mujeres pero no de hombre y mujer; y al advertirlo le conmovió cuánto largaban lágrimas, como flores de ojos, por cuán difícil debía de haber sido llegar ahí, y pensó que ojalá la gente que había conocido en esa situación hubiera podido estar así de contenta.
>
> [there were many people with multicolor flags ... they were getting married. Makina was so dazzled by the beauty of the rite that she took a while to notice that the couples were either men or women but not man and woman; in noticing she was moved by the shedding of tears, like flowers blooming from their eyes, for how difficult it had been to get there, and she wished that the people she knew in this situation could be as jubilant.]
>
> (Herrera 2010, 90)

The joy of this sight moves Makina to tears because she sympathizes with the same-sex couples. Makina is aware of the marginal place they occupy in her own society and this rally allows them openness and participation in what Makina has experienced as a quintessentially heterosexual rite, marriage. Sexual fluidity becomes a possibility for Makina, adding to the hybrid identity she has only recently discovered, even though these marginal sexual identities are not ones she adheres to specifically.

After these transformative experiences, which shift her focus to puzzle over her own place in the U.S., Makina resumes the objective of her journey. She eventually finds her (unnamed) brother, whose process of identification is again surprising. Now a U.S. army soldier, her brother is vastly different from Makina's memory and expectation. He embodies an option for diasporic populations in the host country, a citizenship path not available to Makina. The brother tells her he found their plot of land but it was worthless. Ashamed of his failure to re-conquer the land, he enlisted when a white suburban family paid him to go to the war in place of their son. Makina realizes he has no intention of coming back to Mexico. When they say their final goodbyes, he hugs her "como si no fuera su hermana" [as if she were not his sister], fulfilling the fear of estrangement that Makina experienced at the beginning of the novel (Herrera 2010, 98).

These plot elements find their resolution in the penultimate chapter, when Makina has an epiphany where she understands her place in the U.S. Southwest. A policeman has gathered Makina and several migrants and tells them he will teach them a lesson. While she is on the floor, the policeman takes a little notebook from one of the subjugated men. The policeman realizes it is a book of poems and in an attempt to humiliate the poet he tears a piece of paper, gives it to the man, and orders him to write. Makina takes the paper from the man's shivering hands and quickly scribbles the following lines:

> Nosotros somos los culpables de esta destrucción, los que no hablamos su lengua ni sabemos estar en silencio. Los que no llegamos en barco, los que ensuciamos de polvo sus portales, los que rompemos sus alambradas. Los que venimos a quitarles el trabajo, los que aspiramos a limpiar su mierda, los que anhelamos trabajar a deshoras. Los que llenamos de olor a comida sus calles tan limpias, los que les trajimos violencia que no conocían … nosotros, a los que no nos importa morir por ustedes… . Nosotros los oscuros, los obesos, los anémicos. Nosotros, los bárbaros.

> [We are guilty for this destruction, we are the ones who don't speak your language nor know when to be silent. We do not arrive in boats, we sully your gates with dust, we cut through your wires. We come to take your jobs, we aspire to clean your shit, to work at late hours. We fill your clean streets with the smell of food, we bring violence you didn't know … we, who don't mind dying for you… . We the dark ones, the obese, the anemic. We, the barbarians.]

> (Herrera 2010, 109–110)

Instead of conforming to the barbarian stereotype imposed on migrants, her sarcasm signifies the utmost alterity and the wide spectrum of possibilities

for self-construction. In this climactic moment for her process of identification, Makina uses her written words to get rid of the policeman, who reads
the lines out loud, losing volume as he reads, at the end whispering, until he
finally tosses the paper, calls someone on his radio, and leaves. She finds an
effective voice to resist the oppressive force of this state apparatus and ironically calls herself the barbarian—the savage who cannot speak—when she
is the eloquent one. In her written speech she describes the place of migrants
at the lower tier of working conditions, but she denounces the portrayal of
Mexicans as dirty, of their bodies as imperfect and sick. Makina has found a
way to stay in a place that offers her social and sexual possibilities that she
had not encountered before by ironically proclaiming: We, the barbarians.
In ironically accepting this imposed characterization, she has found a way to
resist it. Indeed, the mere act of fighting back constitutes her resistance to
the stereotype she is enunciating and a recognition of the model identities
unavailable to her. Her formative process, characteristic of the Diasporic
Coming-of-age Novel, yields a deep understanding of migrant experiences in
the U.S. At the end, Makina decides to stay in the U.S. for the time being,
the price for which is to change her name and acquire new documents.

Up to this point, "Makina" has been a semantic magnet that signifies her
network of experiences and characteristics. At the beginning of the novel her
name told readers little about her past and upbringing. Her name translates
as *machine* but is misspelled—*máquina* would be the correct spelling. The
spelling points to a phonetic rather than orthographic emphasis, which
could be interpreted as a result of the illiteracy of Makina's mother Cora.
However, many of the characters have nicknames—Lord Q, Lord H,
Chucho—and "Makina" could be an acquired epithet, the name the village
gave her because of her function: receiving calls from abroad and relaying
messages. The lack of a written accent shifts the stressed syllable to the
penultimate, which suggest "Makina" is a verb rather than a noun.
Maquinar translates as *to plot maliciously*, an ironic name for someone
whose intention was for everything to stay as it was. Nevertheless, when the
wheels of the plot start to turn, Makina begins to plot her departure, visit-
ing the lords' houses. And by the end of the novel, *Makina* has acquired the
meaning of the woman who learned to use the power of physical violence to
resist the possibility of sexual assault and the power of self-definition in
order to resist police abuse. In the loss of her name, Makina loses her outer
layer, her semantic magnet: "me han desollado" [they have flayed me], she
responds at the very end, after she has received her new identity (Herrera
2010, 119). But this metaphorical shedding of identity represents for Makina
a new beginning: a birth. Unlike the classic *Bildungsroman*, the first sentence
of Makina's coming of age is "I am dead," and, through an arduous journey
of self-discovery that ends with a character that is ready to accept hybridity,
Makina is finally born under a different name.

Migration contains the signs that preceded the end of Makina's world.
The process of coming-of-age while crossing into a different world

underscores the protagonists' cultural hybridity; her experiences of inter-secting forms of oppressions due to marginal identities of class, race, and gender, among other cultural constructs; the conflicting expectations of her role models inside and outside her family; the clash between the inherited culture from ancestors and the culture of the host society; the possibility of self-representation, nuance; and the resistance to stereotypes. Makina and Esperanza constitute two examples of an exciting development of the coming-of-age genre not concerned with the creation of moral entrepreneurs and family men, but rather the constant becoming of culturally-hybrid pro-tagonists as they experiment and puzzle over their multiple identities. As evidenced by these examples, the study of the coming-of-age genre as it develops in global diasporas enables abundant decolonial understandings of diasporic identities as well as nuanced readings of an even larger set of novels that have emerged worldwide from the end of the twentieth century.

Notes

1 "The White Man's Burden: The United States and The Philippine Islands" by British novelist and poet Rudyard Kipling encouraged the U.S. to continue the "burden" of empire in the footsteps of Britain in order to "serve your captives' need" and civilize "sullen peoples, / Half devil and half child" (Kipling 2019).
2 All translations from Spanish are mine.
3 The connection with other working-class women writers is particularly relevant in light of the literary voids Cisneros tries to fill. Tillie Olsen's *Yonnondio* could be approached fruitfully from a *Bildungsroman* framework as it depicts the lives of a working-class family, the Holbrooks, (and is therefore a collective utterance) although it, unlike *The House in Mango Street*, focuses particularly on the coming-of-age of the younger daughter Mazie. *Yonnondio* remains unfinished, much like Penelope's tapestry in Homer's *Odyssey*, as if Olsen had not been able to find a suitable final accommodation for this family.
4 This man elides Esperanza's ethnicity calling her not Mexican or Chicana, but *Spanish*. Like the character Hairy Back in *The Buddha of Suburbia*, discussed in Chapter 3, who uses the racist slurs "wog" and "nigger" interchangeably to deni-grate Karim Amir, all "others" are the same for this man. He does not care for nuance. His attack is motivated both by misogyny and racism.
5 The book cover of the Vintage edition shows three women of color holding what could be either a veil or white threads that partially cover their faces. The threads evoke the image of Penelope in Homer's *Odyssey*, unwilling to complete the tapestry therefore taking control of her own destiny.
6 For Luz Aurora Pimentel the name of a character starts out as a word devoid of meaning and acquires a network of significations throughout a narration. The narrative discourse takes a blank name and fills it with meanings. By the end of the narration, readers associate the name of a character with the constellation of characteristics that the text has built (Pimentel 2001, 56).
7 According to the dictionary from the Real Academia Española, "Gabacho" is derived from the Occitan word *gavach* meaning "que habla mal" [one who speaks incorrectly]. It is generally used in Spain and Hispano-America to refer to for-eigners, calling attention to their linguistic difference. In this sense, it is equivalent to the English "barbarian," which is derived from the Greek word for foreigners and is also marked by linguistic difference.

5 Diasporic Coming-of-age Novels of the Greater Antilles Diasporas in the United States

Piri Thomas and Reinaldo Arenas

The two Diasporic Coming-of-age Novels in this chapter demonstrate the political power of the genre when it aims to affect the setting it represents. They also push the boundaries of the Diasporic Coming-of-age Novel to the limit by intermingling with the narrative genres of the *testimonio* and memoir, especially in the case of Reinaldo Arenas' *Antes que anochezca* [*Before Night Falls*] (1992). Departing from the fundamental convention of the traditional *Bildungsroman*, and many Diasporic Coming-of-age Novels, of depicting the protagonist's formative process up to a degree of completion, the novels in this chapter show two incomplete formative processes where the protagonists give up on the introspection necessary to understand themselves profoundly. The novels of the Mexican diaspora studied in the previous chapter represent the marginalization of a Latino community in a major northern U.S. urban setting in Sandra Cisneros's *The House on Mango Street* (1984) and the opprobrious spaces of undocumented migrants at the southern border in Yuri Herrera's *Señales que precederán al fin del mundo* [*Signs Preceding the End of the World*] (2009). The Diasporic Coming-of-age Novels in this chapter likewise represent segregated urban spaces and the perils of migration, but they demonstrate, importantly, the thematic complexities of the genre as they additionally foreground the intricacies of race relations in the case of Piri Thomas's *Down These Mean Streets* (1967) and explicitly aim to bring about the downfall of a political regime, that of Fidel Castro, which Reinaldo Arenas characterizes as cruel and oppressive in particular towards gay men like himself. Unlike the protagonists in previous chapters, young Piri and Reinaldo rarely look far into the future. Instead of pondering on the adults they ought to become and how to marry, key issues in traditional *Bildungsromane*, the violent settings they inhabit force them to be present-oriented, as death is a very real possibility. Piri witnesses his friends' early deaths mainly due to addiction and gang violence, while Reinaldo sees his gay and artist friends incarcerated, tortured, and executed.

The novels further subvert the expectations on the genre in their transformation of the key features of role models and romantic relationships. Piri does not find suitable models of imitation because there is not one single professionally successful or happily married dark-skin Puerto Rican in his social setting. In addition, Piri fails to build any long-term affectionate relationships because of his deep-ingrained misogyny. Reinaldo's role models are swiftly imprisoned and killed. Reinaldo has numerous sexual relationships but they never develop into a "good" relationship in the Austenian sense: one both socially suitable and "of true affection" (Austen 2016, 70).

In the context of the Puerto Rican diaspora, whose individuals Juan Gonzales characterizes as de jure "citizens yet foreigners," Piri Thomas depicts the poignant struggle of young Piri, born in the barrio of East Harlem, New York in 1928, to reconcile his dark skin, read by other characters as incompatible with latinidad (Thomas 1968, 81). Much like Cisneros, Thomas employs a hybrid of Spanish words and English grammar representative of his protagonist's cultural hybridity. In the context of the Cuban diaspora, Reinaldo Arenas depicts the politically-nuanced exile of a homosexual artist, whose coming-of-age is marked by a voracious sexual appetite that is part and parcel of his opposition to Castro's Cuba. This text has not been traditionally read as a novel, in part due to Arenas's statement in the introduction, written three years after the main body, that it is intended as an autobiography: "Cuando salí del hospital terminé mi autobiografía (con excepción, desde luego, de esta introducción)" [When I came out of the hospital I finished my autobiography (with the exception, of course, of this introduction)] (12). Moreover, as an explanation for the title, Arenas states that he named it *Antes que Anochezca* [*Before Night Falls*] because "la tenía que escribir antes de que llegara la noche ya que vivía prófugo en un bosque. Ahora la noche avanzaba de nuevo en forma más inminente. Era la noche de la muerte. Ahora sí que tenía que terminar mi autobiografía antes de que anocheciera" [I had to write it before night fell because I lived as a fugitive in the woods. Now the night was approaching again more imminently. It was the night of death. Now I really had to finish my autobiography before night fell] (11). The text is indeed autobiographical and a testimony of the horrors of his marginal life in Cuba and his sickness in the U.S. However, the text has a formative process at its core, and its overt fictional quality and myriad rhetorical devices—perhaps hyperbole being the most salient of all—justify a reading in the context of Diasporic Coming-of-age Novels, as I will explain further in the section that addresses Arenas's critical reception. Like Yuri Herrera's novel *Señales que precederán al fin del mundo* [*Signs Preceding the End of the World*] (2009), *Antes que anochezca* [*Before Night Falls*] is in Spanish, a language more indicative of a process of first-hand diaspora than of a second-generation coming-of-age. To avoid confusion and to drive the point home that these texts, although autobiographical, are indeed novels, I will refer to Piri Thomas, the author, by his last name Thomas and to Piri, the character, by his first. Similarly, I will refer to Arenas, the author, by his last name and to his fictionalized young self as Reinaldo.

Unlike the novels in the previous chapter, the novels here follow male protagonists and therefore ponder the formation of masculinity. On the one hand, Thomas's novel shows the lack of suitable accommodations for a dark-skin Puerto Rican in New York, but an appropriate-for-the-environment—though extreme—performance of masculinity in its violence and heterosexual desire. On the other, Arenas's depicts the instances of queer marginalization and possibilities for the fulfilment of homosexual desire both in Cuba, due to the repressive regime, and in the U.S., due to the HIV/AIDS pandemic.

The novels both in the previous and the present chapters portray degrees of queerness, a key trend in Diasporic Coming-of-age Novels, defined in general terms by Eve Sedgwick as "the open mesh of possibilities, gaps, overlaps, dissonances and resonances, lapses and excesses of meaning when the constituent elements of anyone's gender, of anyone's sexuality aren't made (or can't be made) to signify monolithically" (Sedgwick 1990, 10). As illustrated in depth in Chapter 4, the experience of heterosexual relations in *The House on Mango Street* is imminently intersected by violence and rape, which gives way to a focus on homosocial relationships and female mentors; and Makina in *Señales* celebrates a pride parade she stumbles upon and identifies with its participants due to their shared marginalization. In this chapter, Piri participates in an orgy with queer men whom he and his friends later violently attack, as if to reassert their heterosexuality, an episode that I will discuss in depth. And Reinaldo identifies and portrays homosexual desire and its consummation as one of the main drivers of plot. In particular, Reinaldo praises the desire that structures homosexual relations in heteronormative terms. He takes on a feminine-perceived role of *pájaro* or *loca*, a complex identity marker that performs gender-bending and necessarily implies madness, and his partners a masculine-perceived one of *bugarrón* or *macho*, as described in this passage, which merits full quotation:

> En Cuba, cuando uno iba a un club o a una playa, no había una zona específica para homosexuales; todo el mundo compartía junto, sin que existiera una división que situara al homosexual militante. Esto se ha perdido en las sociedades más civilizadas, donde el homosexual ha tenido que convertirse en una especie de monje de la actividad sexual y ha tenido que separarse de esa parte de la sociedad, supuestamente no homosexual que, indiscutiblemente, también lo excluye. Al no existir estas divisiones, lo interesante del homosexualismo en Cuba consistía en que no había que ser un homosexual para tener relaciones con un hombre ... al que le gustaran los hombres de verdad, también podía alcanzar a ese macho que quería vivir con él o tener con él una relación amistosa, que no interrumpía para nada la actividad heterosexual de aquel hombre. Lo normal no era que una loca se acostara con otra loca, sino que la loca buscara a un hombre que la poseyera y que sintiera, al hacerlo, tanto placer como ella al ser poseída.

[In Cuba, when one went to a club or a beach, there was no specific area for homosexuals; everyone shared together, without a division that situated the militant homosexual. This has been lost in more civilized societies where homosexuals have had to become a sort of sexual activity monks and have had to split from that part of society, supposedly non-homosexual that, indisputably, excludes them as well. Without these divisions, the interesting thing about homosexuality in Cuba was that there was no need to be a homosexual to have inter-course with a man ... those who liked real men, could also attain a *macho* that would want to live with him or have a friendly relationship, without this interrupting that man's heterosexual activities. It is not normal for a *loca* to sleep with another *loca,* but rather for a *loca* to search for a man to possess her and for him to feel as much pleasure in possessing her, as she would by being possessed.]

(Arenas 2003, 133)

Reinaldo describes homosexuality in Cuba with a sense of loss and nos-talgia. He preferred to desire in heteronormative terms with men he would define as real, that is, who would carry on their heterosexual lives. Unable and unwilling to enact the socially-acceptable double life of *bugarrones,* Reinaldo lives his coming-of-age as an outcast, mostly unconcerned with becoming a role model of adulthood.

Winding Identities Down These Mean Streets

Before Reinaldo is even born in 1943, young Piri is already roaming the streets of New York in the late thirties. The son of a Cuban father and a Puerto Rican mother, Piri's diasporic heritage differs greatly from others discussed in previous chapters because Puerto Ricans "are both American citizens and colonial subjects by birth according to international law" since the U.S. intervention in 1898 (Sánchez González 2001, 1). The Puerto Rican nation is unique in that "well over a third of this population today lives in the continental United States, forming one of the nation's most significant 'minority' communities" grouped often under the self-defining term "Bor-iqua" in general, which refers to the indigenous name of the main island Boriquén, or "Nuyorican" specifically for the New York community (1). Given that there are almost as many Puerto Ricans living in Puerto Rico and Mainland United States, Carmen Whalen characterizes Puerto Rico as a "divided nation ... a result of a long history of colonialism and the massive migration that accompanied it" (1). Piri is legally part of the New York social body but is simultaneously marked by the decidedly racist hegemony of the mid-twentieth century as outsider and other by his bilingualism, national heritage, and—at first glance—his skin tone. New York appears to have no place for him, except for the streets, a world of drugs and gangs that Cisneros also represents in *Mango Street.* The titular "mean streets" appear as a metaphorical place that exists all throughout the urban landscape but that is also a non-accommodation where marginalized people, especially people of color, are relegated to and simultaneously try to escape.

Down These Mean Streets illustrates the complexities of the Puerto Rican diaspora, with which Thomas identifies explicitly, practically disregarding his father's Cuban heritage, in the incomplete formative process of young Piri. The old narrator, a Piri that reconstructs the instances by which he came to become an adult, depicts the young Piri as a confused child craving belonging yet powerless before the marginalization that his intersecting racial and ethnic identities trigger. Old narrator Piri presents himself as a victim of circumstances, but does not ever acknowledge his own role in the violence he perpetrates towards women and queer people. In depicting the real forces that oppress him, old Piri in turn excuses the oppression that he exerts on others, rendering the moments of realization about racial solidarity and complexity somewhat contrived. The old narrator uses the Diasporic Coming-of-age Novel as an apology for the shortcomings of his character, who nevertheless undergoes a formative process in which young Piri's growth as citizen and worker is stunted by racism and xenophobia.

Like his Cuban father, Piri has dark skin, what Piri's brother José will eventually describe as "Indian" (Thomas 1968, 145), while his siblings and Puerto Rican mother are light-skinned and indeed *white*, as Piri's brother José explicitly identifies. José tells Piri, "'Yeah, you're my brother, and James an' Sis, and we all come out of Momma an' Poppa—but we ain't Negroes. We're Puerto Ricans, an' we're white'" (144–145). To this, Piri replies, "'Boy, you, Poppa and James sure are sold on that white kick. Poppa thinks that marrying a white woman made him white. He's wrong. It's just another nigger marrying a white woman and making her as black as him'" (145). Characters in the larger Anglo New York context identify him solely as Black American. He internalizes this taxonomy as it is often imposed in interactions that involve extreme physical and verbal violence and sometimes employment discrimination and disregard his latinidad. Piri's mother conversely rejects Piri's Blackness as an offensive category and insists rather that he is "not black ... you're brown, a nice color, a pretty color" (135). This creates in Piri a disconnect from his own skin, racially categorized one way in the streets and another at home. His family rejects the label of Black because his Puerto Rican heritage, as Garland Mahler explains, "affords him a higher status in the U.S. racial hierarchy" (138). Piri's coming-of-age process of acceptance is to eventually be able to identify "as a black Puerto Rican" and to view his "experience of racial discrimination as an impetus for political solidarity with African Americans" (Garland Mahler 2018, 138).[1] Throughout his process however, colonial discourse often reduces the complexities of non-hegemonic identities to stereotypes, obliterating the nuance necessary to understand that latinidad and Blackness can coexist in one single body and subjectivity.

The disparity between his racial categorizations is evidence of the lack of a clear path into adulthood. The heroes of traditional *Bildungsromane* never need to question their racial or even national identity. While the white male bourgeois heroes of *Bildungsromane* chose their professions and relationships based on their interests and passions, Piri's range of choices are limited to what is available to marginalized individuals, as he realizes when he unsuccessfully applies for a job and is rejected on account of his perceived race. In Diasporic Coming-of-age Novels, protagonists have to puzzle over how they fit into segregated social spaces in order to find accommodations. Piri's story thus subverts the archetypal plot where the hero can wander freely, as in the case of Wilhelm Meister in *Wilhelm Meisters Lehrjahre*, who is able to experiment with both commerce and theater without fear of poverty or discrimination. Piri further subverts this archetypal plot with unhealthy love affairs, which remind him of racial hierarchies that he cannot dismantle or fit into. As will be analyzed in depth, these love affairs arrest his development rather than bring him closer to the institution of marriage—as would be the expectation in traditional *Bildungsromane*. Unlike the horizon of expectations from the archetypal plot, Piri shows no inclination towards marriage, and instead his need for belonging most often occurs in homosocial spaces and groups.

Down These Mean Streets is a novel that portrays the impossibility of an ideal bourgeois adulthood in a world in which there are no represented models for dark-skinned Puerto Ricans and that yields no clear example for young readers. Unlike the Young Lords and artists such as Miguel Piñero, a leading member of the Nuyorcan literary movement, which did provide complex models for young Puerto Ricans, Thomas neither problematizes violent and rigid masculinity nor strives for decolonization of the mind.[2] The novel ends in a flicker of enthusiasm, with Piri reflecting on the person he has become through his travels and experiences. In particular, Piri is able to finally reject drugs and avoid prison, two stereotypical stories for young Latinos that he has experienced but successfully emerged from. However, readers are left with uncertainty for the future.

With a category of race in his house, another outside, Piri attempts in the earlier chapters of the novel to unravel the confusion of his split identity:

> I hate the paddy who's trying to keep the black man down ... But I'm beginning to hate the black man, too, cause I can feel his pain and I don't know that it oughtta be mine ... I'm trying to be a Negro, a colored man, a black man, cause that's what I am. But I gotta accept it myself, from inside. Man, do you know what it is to sit across from a dinner table looking at your brothers who look exactly like paddy people?

(Thomas 1968, 124)

He hints at a possible solution when he imagines acceptance of his Blackness from within, rather than as a classification that is imposed by his social environment. This acceptance would be possible if his society did not consider Puerto Rican and Black American mutually exclusive. Piri cannot think of himself a "new mestizo," a possibility Gloria Anzaldúa usefully defines in *Borderlands* as "a malleable species with a rich gene pool ... characterized by movement away from set patterns and goals and toward a more whole perspective, one that includes rather than excludes" and that has "a tolerance for contradictions, a tolerance for ambiguity" (Thomas 1968, 99–101).

When Piri is thirteen years old, he desires the bourgeois accommodation that would characterize a traditional *bildung* process. Buying into the white identity that his family claims, Piri hopes his "ancestors were noble princes born in Spain" (Thomas 1968, 10). Piri recognizes the colonizer-colonized dichotomy in his environment and wants to belong with the colonizers, as his family does. But through his formative process, he realizes that people group his body with the colonized. The realization that he cannot participate in the fantasy of noble white ancestry comes soon, both from within and outside the house. Piri's mother calls him a "funny morenito" [funny little brown one] as a term of endearment, and jokingly tells him that only she could love him, "un negrito and ugly" [a little black one and ugly], contradicting her own categorization (19). Later, as he is walking in the predominantly Italian neighborhood on 114th Street, a group of kids ask him about his ethnicity: "'Ah, Rocky, he's black enuff to be a nigger. Aint that what you is, kid?' 'I'm Puerto Rican. I was born here'" (26). He tries to explain that he was born in Harlem Hospital, since "there's all kind of people born there. Colored people, Puerto Ricans like me, an' even Spaghetti-benders like you" (26). To this, the kids respond that Harlem Hospital is where "all them black bastards get born at" (26). The hostility escalates to the point where the kids throw a fistful of ground asphalt in Piri's eyes. As he is taken to the hospital, somebody exclaims: "He got much heart for a nigger" and Piri corrects them, thinking "A spic" (32). His eyes heal but Piri is left with the realization that he was not even ascribed with the *correct* racial slur, the slur that his siblings might be called. Perhaps Piri insists on the *correct* slur because he wants to claim the societal privilege that a monolithic Puerto Rican identity holds.

In an attempt to protect Piri and his siblings from the violence of the city, epitomized by the incident just described, the family moves to the suburban setting of Long Island. This is a disastrous move for Piri who is again faced with discrimination, but this time in the context of romance, and in an all-white setting. The comment by Piri's mother's about him not being loved by anyone but her becomes a reality. Piri meets Marcia, an Irish girl, at a school dance. She asks him "Are you Spanish? I didn't know. I mean, you don't look like what I thought a Spanish looks like." Piri responds that he is not Spanish from Spain, but rather a Puerto Rican from Harlem. She is surprised that his English is so good, thus demonstrating her lack of understanding of both the social setting she represents and what it means to be a Puerto Rican from Harlem: "I told you I was born in Harlem," Piri clarifies. "No, your accent is more like Jerry's." "What' she trying to put down?" Piri wonders. "Jerry was this colored kid who recently had moved to Bayshore" (83–84). Marcia rejects Piri's invitation to dance and Piri heads outside where he overhears Marcia's conversation:

> I hear Marcia say "Imagine the nerve of that black thing" "Who?" someone asked. "That new colored boy" … "Just as if I was a black girl" … "Christ, first that Jerry bastard and now him. We're getting invaded by niggers" said a thin voice. "Ha—he's probably passing for Puerto Rican because he can't make it as white" … "no really!" a girl was saying "I heard he's a Puerto Rican, and they're not like Neg—"
>
> "There's no difference," said the thin voice "He's still black."
>
> (Thomas 1968, 85)

This is a crucial moment of self-determination, fueled not by the archetypal impetuous to self-forge in *Bildungsromane* but by his hurt pride and romantic rejection. Piri scraps his family's plan and moves back to Harlem. This "bad relationship," a characteristic of the archetypal *Bildungsroman* plot per Jerome Buckley, devoid of suitability or affection, makes Piri want to be in Harlem where he feels able to find a sense of belonging in meaningless sexual relationships with women of color and among his Latino friends. This path leads to drug addiction and dangerous run-ins with racist police. This path, too often forced on young men of color, violently subverts the archetypal plot as it leads to stunted development, or premature death, before *any* adulthood can be reached, accommodated or not.

Diasporic Coming-of-age Novels do often employ the conventions of traditional *Bildungsromane* such as travel as a catalyst of self-discovery. It is through this convention that Piri achieves a more sophisticated conceptualization of race in the U.S. South, particularly during a contrived conversation with two characters who seem to exist only for this occasion and who later disappear. The first man is Brew, an African American *Deus ex machina*, who fulfills a trope that Christopher John Farley defines as the "Magical African American Friend," the caricature of a wise man with no identity or purpose of his own, but who rather exists in the plot to help the main character tap into a fountain of wisdom (Farley 2000, 14). Brew explains that even though Piri is a Puerto Rican, he is "a member of the black man's race an' hit don't make no difference he can talk that Porty Rican talk. His skin is dark an' that makes him jus' anudder rock right along wif the res' of us" (Thomas 1968, 159). Indeed, for Brew, culture does not bear significance to the "the color of your skin" (159). Piri begins to unravel the problem of race and national heritage coexisting in the same body when he is later asked by a Pennsilvanian white-*passing* man, called

Gerald Andrew West, whether "Oh—er—do Puerto Ricans—er—consider themselves—uh—negro"? To which Piri replies, "word for word, *amigo* ... I'm a Puerto Rican Negro" (173).

Piri understands race here—and only in this contrived and artificial moment—more complexly as a network of signifiers. Race is not only skin color, but rather a number of identities that can converge. Although this realization would be a logical end to his struggle, later in prison Piri regresses to outright acts of racism against his Black cellmate. This later regression would be impossible in the sequence of traditional *Bildungsromane*. Whether a mistake on the part of the author or a deliberate choice to make the protagonist move backwards on his learning process, it shows a character who cannot commit to his formative process and who seems to utterly lie to his readers in order to present himself wiser than he actually is.

In her essay on the solidarity that Piri claims to experience between the disporic Puerto Rican and African American communities who "lived in close quarters in the Harlem," Garland Mahler states that Thomas's text "ultimately aims to break completely with racial or geographic determinism and instead to propose a transnational, transracial, and transethnic subaltern, resistant subjectivity" (Garland Mahler 2018, 139, 140). Her argument is substantiated in the "marked representations of AAVE" (African-American Vernacular English) with which Piri performs Blackness, first in a stereotypical way that "maintains a difference between himself and African Americans" but later indicating an "ideological transformation" in which "Thomas argues for the existence of a transnational system of oppression and proposes a resistant political solidarity" (147, 149). In her reading, Piri's experiences of racial solidarity result in his realization while in prison that hierarchies are constructed, grounded on the religious idea that "God looks like all of us ... Around the world, hear this, North and South, East and West: We are all the same in our souls and spirits and there's nobody better than anybody else, only just maybe better off" (Thomas 1968, 299). Garland Mahler sees this statement as an indication that he has accepted the religion of his parents. But it should not be interpreted as an epiphany as it occurs 100 pages after the conversation with Brew. The formative process has by the end of the novel enabled a repressed peaceful relationship with the chaos that racial identity precipitated. However, it does not answer questions of hybrid identity and ideal citizenship because there is no successful adult. Instead, it shows a character who has not finished puzzling over who he ought to be, what he ought to do, or his sexuality. On the contrary, he does not give any indication that he wants to reach maturity, as evidenced by the following episodes regarding sexuality.

In an episode seemingly out of place that does not further Piri's understanding of his sexuality and is never addressed again—but is later mirrored when he is in prison—teenage Piri has a sexual encounter that he describes as an example of "some improbable stories of exploits with faggots" (Thomas 1968, 54–55). In it, one "stud, Alfredo" suggests going to "the faggots' pad and cop some bread," a plan in which Piri does not want to partake (55). Piri so wants to belong and follow in the steps of his peer-mentors, however, that he agrees. The narrator seems to be scared that readers might think he goes willingly as he constantly, and in unusually vulgar terms for him, reminds us of his heterosexuality: "Oh shit, I ain't gonna screw no motherfuckin' fag. Agh—I'm not gonna get shit all over my peter, not for all the fuckin coins in the world" (55). In the midst of a drug haze and the proximity of Concha, one of "two faggots," both "boys in their twenties," Piri tries "to stop his pee-pee's growth, but it grew independently" (55, 61). The episode concludes with the sounds of the *stud* "Alfredo's anger beating down against La Vieja—blap, blap, blap—and the faggot's wail, 'Ayeeeee, no heet me, no heet'" (61). As though it were a dream, Piri is suddenly walking down Fifth Avenue, and never discusses the scene again. Piri only processes this event as though a dream in order to minimize its effect on his concerns of identity.

The matter of homosexual desire appears again when, in prison, Piri explains that "there always was the temptation of wanting to cop some ass" (262). But, when the possibility of making another inmate his "steady," Piri tells this man,

> if I gotta break your fuckin' jaw, I will. They've put a wall around me for fifteen years, but I've got something real outside, and it makes no difference when I get out, married or not, she's mine and there'll be no past for the two of us, just a stone present and a cool future. Meanwhile, I'll jack off if I gotta, but I ain't gonna marry you, faggot, no matter what.
>
> (Thomas 1968, 263)

Both episodes demonstrate Piri's homophobia as a guideline for his construction of masculine identity intimately tied to his unstable racial identity. His inner desire is not exclusively heterosexual, but his sharp repression and disgust, his use of slurs, and his indifference to Alfredo's violence all signal a process of decided disidentification with queer and thus more fluid identities, which cancels all possibility for kindness or solidarity towards queerness. Although there is a real chance that Piri could explore his latent desire, when it comes to sexual orientation Piri strictly upholds social hierarchies, a contrast with the process of nuancing of race and culture.

Piri's repudiation of queerness exemplifies what could have happened with his blackness, especially in consideration of his brother's self-identification as white. Piri could have listened to his brother and adopted a rejection of blackness, but instead he pondered over it and was able to eventually have a more sophisticated—if inconsistent—understanding. But any sort of discussion of queerness could signify non-belonging in his all-male-of-color groups, in which any type of deviating masculinity is forbidden. Misogyny and homophobia, often ugly brothers, guide the adult that Piri becomes.

And although race is a fundamental question of his coming-of-age, sexuality is not, because he is never introspective enough to explore it.

Down These Mean Streets depicts the incomplete coming-of-age of a character unable to look deeply into who he is. The lack of introspection necessary to become an adult is a real possibility for the protagonists of Diasporic Coming-of-age Novels who, instead of resisting the violence in their environment, replicate it, never build a "good relationship" or a profession. A parallel example takes place in Zadie Smith's *White Teeth*, studied in depth in Chapter 3, where the young Bangladeshi immigrant to England, Millat Iqbal, chooses misogyny and religious fundamentalism over introspection and thus ends his formative process in the non-accommodation of court-mandated community service. Piri's process similarly ends in non-accommodation: he has nowhere to live, no relationships, no job. Thomas's novel contrasts with the didactic purpose of traditional *Bildungsromane* to teach intended readers how to be successful and fulfilled adults, citizens, and workers. Marginalized young male readers of Thomas's work, likely the intended audience, learn little from Piri about what jobs and careers are available to them, what healthy masculinity looks like, or how to live a happy life. Although there is hope in Piri's rejection of drugs, the end of the novel is open, unable to answer how this Puerto Rican from Harlem fits into New York's pocket of the globalized work.

Coming-of-age as Queer Political Testimony

In contrast to Piri, Reinaldo has the introspection necessary to self-forge but the cruelty of his social context thwarts his path to adulthood. Thirty years after Piri, Reinaldo finds himself in the same city, in the middle of the non-accommodation of the HIV global pandemic, after a life of marginalization in Cuba and a perilous exile. No other Diasporic Coming-of-age story and ensuing identification processes in this book is as explicitly political as Arena's *Antes que anochezca* [*Before Night Falls*]. Arenas's voice has the explicit objective of a collective utterance and testimony aiming neither to represent the bourgeois values of the social setting in an exemplary individual, as was the case of traditional *Bildungsromane*, not to direct the readers' education, but to materially affect the setting. Arenas's portrayal of his peculiar coming-of-age is intentionally propagandistic. His life, mentorships, models of imitation, desires, and final accommodations are intimately linked to the history of Cuba and the effect of the Revolution years 1953–1959 on his development as public figure and counterrevolutionary. Arenas's autobiography is a denouncement of the abuses of the Revolution of Fidel Castro, whom Arenas categorically blames in his suicide letter printed at the end of text. This letter subverts the horizon of explications of the *Bildungsroman* and destabilizes the easy categorization of the work as a novel. As expected, almost every dimension of the archetypal plot is included only to be turned on its head, corrupted by hunger, persecution, and disease.

The young man, here the collapsed author and protagonist, finds models of imitation who are all eventually crushed—in both body and mind—many of whom betray Reinaldo. The paths set out before him lead to silence or death, a complete annihilation of the material personhood and his voice, enabling no possibility of an ideal adult that the young artist ought to become.

In Reinaldo's story, the institution of marriage, a key objective in early and traditional *Bildungsromane* such as Dickens' *David Copperfield* and Austen's *Pride and Prejudice*, is turned into a sham to enable the rent of an apartment that is only available to married couples: "Lo pedí [un cuarto] a través de la UNEAC, pero sólo podían dárselo a una persona que estuviese casada ... La Revolución no le iba a dar un cuarto a un homosexual" [I requested it [an apartment] through the UNEAC but they could only give it to a married person ... the Revolution was not going to give a room to a homosexual] (Arenas 2003, 177).[3] And, perhaps most heartbreaking of all, even the possibility of migration leads to Arenas contracting HIV in the mid 1980s when the epidemic was rapidly spreading in New York City. Reinaldo describes the virus as a "mal perfecto porque está fuera de la naturaleza humana y su función es acabar con el ser humano de la manera más cruel y sistemática posible ... esta perfección diabólica es la que hace pensar a veces en la posibilidad de la mano del hombre" [perfect evil because it is outside of human nature and its function is to annihilate human beings in the most cruel and systematic way possible ... this diabolic perfection makes one think at times of the possibility of human design] (15). His migration is better described as self-enacted exile, a form of diaspora that emphasizes its political urgency and absence of clear volition.

Given its sharp political character, Arenas's autobiography has been read from the framework of *testimonio* and in the context of writers of the Cuban exile. What then does the framework of Diasporic Coming-of-age Novels enable in the reading of this text? It is not to deny or undermine the possibilities that *testimonio* facilitates, but rather to explore how Diasporic Coming-of-age Novels can interact with a proximal narrative genre while keeping the formative process as the thematic core and main driver of plot. The taxonomy of *testimonio* underscores the urgency of the narrative, the reality that must be unveiled so that it may affect readers' lives and catalyze liberation or justice. Arenas played with genre, an essential act in the development and endurance of the family of Proto-*Bildungsromane*, traditional *Bildunsromane*, the larger category of coming-of-age novels, and Diasporic Coming-of-age Novels. He wrote not one but many expressly fictional and non-fictional accounts of the repression in Cuba such as *Otra vez el mar* [*Farewell to the Sea*] (1982), *El color del verano* [*The Color of Summer*] (1982), and *El Asalto* [*The Assault*] (1990). The last line of the last document of his life, his suicide note, embodies the intensive and collective urgency that characterized this work: "Cuba será libre. Yo ya lo soy" [Cuba will be free. I already am] (Arenas 2003, 343). Arenas's work thus corresponds to John Beverley's definition of *testimonio*, which emphasizes political urgency:

La situación del narrador en el testimonio siempre involucra cierta urgencia o necesidad de comunicación que surge de una experiencia vivencial de represión, pobreza, explotación, marginalización, crimen, lucha. En la frase de René Jara, el testimonio es una 'narración de urgencia' que nace de esos espacios donde las estructuras de normalidad social comienzan a desmoronarse por una razón u otra... . A veces su producción obedece a fines políticos muy precisos. Pero aun cuando no tiene una intención política explícita, su naturaleza como género siempre implica un reto al *statu quo* de una sociedad dada.

[The narrator's situation in the *testimonio* always entails a certain urgency or necessity to communicate which arises from an experience of repression, poverty, exploitation, marginalization, crime, struggle. In the words of René Jara, the *testimonio* is a "narrative of urgency" that is born from those spaces where the structures of social normality start to crumble for any reason ... sometimes their production obeys very precise political ends. But even when it does not have an explicit political intention, its nature as genre always entails a challenge to the *statu quo* of a given society.]

(Beverley 1987, 9)

Antes que anochezca [*Before Night Falls*] is both a Diasporic Coming-of-age Novel *and* a *testimonio* in which the narrator undergoes a formative process in an opprobrious environment and ends not in an idyllic accommodation but in a suicide that he expressly blames on Fidel Castro: "Sólo hay un responsable: Fidel Castro. Los sufrimientos del exilio, las penas del destierro, la soledad y las enfermedades que haya podido contraer en el destierro seguramente no las hubiera sufrido de haber vivido libre en mi país" [There is only one responsible: Fidel Castro. The sufferings of exile, the pains of banishment, the loneliness and sicknesses that I have contracted in banishment, surely I would not have suffered if I had lived freely in my country] (Arenas 2003, 343).

The Diasporic Coming-of-age Novel's malleability enables *Antes que anochezca* to be both a story of a young boy who tries to become an adult and a *testimonio*, defined in George Yúdice's terms, that unearths a repressed story, abandons the bourgeois I, and collaborates in the articulation of collective memory (Yúdice 1992, 211). The protagonist as the writer of collective memory is the innovative fulfilment of the ideal citizen of traditional *Bildungsromane* in an oppressive setting. The contemporary blending of genres reminds of the perennial malleability of the coming-of-age genre.

Reading Arenas's text as a Diasporic Coming-of-age Novel does not diminish its validity or character of truth, just as there is no implication of falsehood in calling Cisneros's *The House on Mango Street* or Herrera's *Señales que precederán al fin del mundo* [*Signs Preceding the End of the World*] novels. All three stories represent the strife-ridden process of vibrant characters based on real people. But Arenas is the only author with the explicit intention of showing the complexities of his formative process as a homosexual man who grows up in a repressive environment in order to change that environment. From the start, coming-of-age novels have held, as it were, a mirror up to society. As Thomas Jeffers argues in a frequently-quoted statement, "In the event-racked revolutionary years of the late eighteenth century, the emergence of the hero's character increasingly mirrored the emergence—socially, economically, politically, ideationally—of the world around him" (Jeffers 2005, 2). *Antes que anochezca* [*Before Night Falls*] critically depicts the world of the narrator and is no less true because (at times) it fictionalizes experiences; for example, when his mother—transubstantiated into the Moon—protects the narrator from stepping on landmines as he fails to escape Cuba, trying to walk across the border from Guantanamo village into the U.S. Guantanamo Bay naval base (Arenas 2003, 339).

Reading Arenas's text as a Diasporic Coming-of-age Novel also enables a complex analysis of identity development: the tension between the burgeoning adult and an environment that violently suppresses his intellectual development and the voracity of his desire. The young homosexual artist attempts to self-forge in a social setting that would prefer him quiet or, better yet, dead. The drive of the social setting to suppress and kill the protagonist's will to live and grow is a new possibility in Diasporic Coming-of-age Novels in severe contrast to the settings in traditional *Bildungsromane* that support or (in the worst of cases) are merely indifferent towards the protagonist's goal. In his study of the autobiography, Emilio Bejel argues that the text is, rather than a mere example of a discourse produced by a soldier of the Cold War, a furious clash between homosexual desire and political power:

> En este texto se entrelazan con furia el deseo homosexual y el poder político dentro de una textualidad cuya creatividad se nutre precisamente de sus paradojas y del vació de autoridad en el que se desliza dicha obra. En ésta se enfrentan fuerzas que van mucho más allá (o más acá) de la rebeldía de un homosexual que dedica su producción literaria a vengarse, con indignación, de un sistema político que lo discriminó y asedió. Verlo exclusivamente de esta manera sería reducir la obra de Arenas a un mero ejemplo de discurso producido por un soldado de la guerra fría.

> [In this text homosexual desire and political power furiously intertwine in a textuality whose creativity is nurtured precisely by its paradoxes and the power vacuum on which the work glides. In it, forces clash, which go beyond (or are closer to) the rebellion of a homosexual who dedicates his literary production to take indignant revenge on a political system that discriminated and besieged him. To see it exclusively in these terms would be to reduce Arenas's work to a mere example of discourse produced by a soldier of the cold war.]

(Bejel 1996, 29)

Reinaldo's is indeed an intricate formative process and a moving account of resistance and brave self-determination.

Arenas's text begins with an introduction that he wrote years after finishing the body of his autobiography, four months before he died of an intentional overdose on December 7, 1990. Much like the story of Makina in Chapter 4 of this book, whose first sentence is "Estoy muerta" [I am dead], Arenas's opening statement subverts the expected order of the coming-of-age novel, foreshadowing a desolate outcome (Arenas 2003, 11): "Yo pensaba morirme en el invierno de 1987" [I thought I would die in the winter of 1987, alternatively, I was thinking of dying in the winter of 1987] (9). The tone of the introduction is of despair, a vengeful voice which has achieved success in its recognition but is devoid of a personal peaceful resolution and citizenship, both essential in classic didactic and bourgeois *Bildungsromane*.

After the introduction, the novel starts as a traditional *Bildungsromane* would: a young precocious child, whose imagination far exceeds those around him, begins his formative process in the countryside, in this case the barrio of Perronales, between the towns of Holguín and Gibara. Abandoned by his father, Reinaldo's young mother and first mentor soon becomes distant, physically violent, and suicidal. Bored and lonely, Reinaldo begins to develop stories from a very young age: "Para llenar aquella soledad tan profunda que sentía en medio del ruido, poblé todo aquel campo, bastante raquítico por cierto, de personajes y apariciones casi míticos y sobrenatrales" [To fill the profound loneliness that I felt in the midst of the noise, I populated all that field, rather rickety by the way, with almost mythical and supernatural characters and apparitions] (Arenas 2003, 23). Reinaldo's grandfather partially fills the absence of parental figures whom the narrator describes with youthful admiration as an "antirreligioso, liberal y anticomunista" [anti-religious liberal and anti-communist], an avid reader, and a farmer (51). Reinaldo's later longing for nature and political conviction are shaped on this early model.

Veering from the archetypal plot, his parallel early experiences of desire foretell his later voracity as young Reinaldo recognizes pangs when he sees teenagers bathing naked and experiments sexually with his older cousin Orlando. His is a world charged with sensuality; and his suspicion of his own homosexuality is confirmed when a classmate tells him that he is indeed a *pájaro*, someone who prefers a submissive role in sex and is thus perceived as feminine by heteronormative standards. Preceded by *Maurice* (written in 1913–914 and published posthumously in 1971) by E. M. Forster, Arenas's depiction of desire is much more extreme because, unlike Maurice's, Arenas's homosexuality becomes central to his counterrevolutionary identity. He eventually understands sexual acts as acts of resistance. An affectionate long-term relationship, like that of Maurice with Alec Scudder, is unimaginable for Reinaldo because his promiscuity is intertwined with his political project to write and live, in such a way that he challenges the hegemony of the Cuban Revolution. In Diasporic Coming-of-age Novels, the project of self-forging may be in direct opposition to the earlier objective of marrying into the social whole or a single sustained relationship.

His formative process continues to drive the plot forward when, as a teenager, Reinaldo develops his fascination with storytelling at the movie theater and begins to write novels on a second-hand typewriter. Like protagonists of traditional *Bildungsromane* who need to move to cities to continue their education, Reinaldo's family moves to the small city of Holguín.[4] However, unlike traditional heroes driven by a desire for education and betterment, his family is driven by hunger and poverty. After the defeat of the Batista regime, the social setting guides Reinaldo's formative process as he displays an initial enthusiasm for the Revolution.

Driven by this enthusiasm, Reinaldo enrolls in an agricultural accounting program for young men which serves like standard institutions upholding hegemonic systems in *Bildungsromane*. In it, he finds a model of dis-identification in the humiliating treatment that his classmates undergo when they are discovered to be homosexuals: "Los muchachos que eran sorprendidos en esos actos tenían que desfilar con sus camas y todas sus pertenencias rumbo al almacén, donde, por orden de la dirección, tenían que devolverlo todo; los demás compañeros debían salir de sus albergues, tirarle piedras y caerle a golpes" [The young men who were caught in the act would have to march with their beds and all their belongings to the warehouse, where, ordered by the administration, they had to give everything back; the other students had to go out of their shelters, throw rocks at him and beat him up] (Arenas 2003, 71). In these circumstances, he initially internalizes the prejudice of society and even considers seeking a cure. His first impulse is to seek belonging into the social whole by means of self-repression, but unlike Piri in *Down These Mean Streets* who violently represses his sexuality in order to belong, Reinaldo is introspective and true to his desires. Reinaldo's secrecy and self-denial do not last long.

This time motivated by his imagination, Reinaldo moves to the larger urban center of La Habana where he begins an apprenticeship under Virgilio Piñera, an older gay writer who has been in El Morro, a dreadful prison that Reinaldo will eventually occupy. Mentors are an essential figure in traditional *Bildungsromane*, often successful adults whom the heroes can imitate, but Virgilio represents rather an undesirable outcome: a defeated artist, harassed by the regime and therefore silent, and unable to escape this setting. Under the guidance of this mentor, however inadequate, Reinaldo is able to develop his artistic trade to the point of winning several international literary prizes. It is in these years that Reinaldo overcomes his earlier prejudice and unleashes his sexual voracity, explaining that by the year 1968, at the age of twenty-five, "Yo llegué, haciendo unos complicados cálculos matemáticos, a la convicción de que, por lo menos, había hecho el amor con unos cinco mil hombres" [I arrived, through complicated mathematical calculations, to the conviction that, at least, I had made love with about five thousand men] (119). Reinaldo purposefully portrays the context in which he grows up as oppressive and successfully renders a world of violence against difference. In going from a young revolutionary, blind to the oppression of the new regime, to a decided voice of dissidence, sexual liberation is key. It cannot be read as an accident of innocence to have had 5,000 partners by the age of twenty-five because all acts of illegal homosexual sex acquire political and subversive qualities.

In a traditional *Bildungsroman,* readers would expect the formative process to progress through the novel towards the goal of adulthood. However, the marginalization of the protagonist and the cruelty of his setting have the opposite effect: as the plot presses on, Reinaldo's situation worsens. Like many young men, he is forced to work in ruthless conditions in sugar cane fields. Back in La Habana, the increasing international success of his novels, translated and published in France, lands him under surveillance, putting him on track to replicate his mentor Virgilio's story. His success in the globalized literary market exacerbates the local risk of imprisonment and death.

The increasing difficulty of finding a place to live leads him to marry Ingrávida González, a woman who can barely support her two children. Reinaldo explains the affiliation of women and homosexuals as inferior beings within the Castro system: "las mujeres y los homosexuales se unieran, aunque sólo fuera una manera de protegerse" [women and homosexuals would unite, even if it was only a way to protect each other] (Arenas 2003, 178). The civil union of marriage is here stripped of its idyllic heterosexual and capitalist privileges and instead is a form of solidarity and protection for disenfranchised groups, marginalized by the sexism that sees all femininity as inferior, regardless of the body. Marriage as protection from the state is one of numerous functions that the institution acquires in Diasporic Coming-of-age Novels where it is no longer the fundamental path to bourgeois accommodations. In other Diasporic Coming-of-age Novels, marriage is also restructured. In *The House on Mango Street*, marriage signifies women's captivity and is thus a path that protagonist Esperanza avoids. The protagonists of *The Buddha of Suburbia, White Teeth,* and *Down These Mean Streets* overlook marriage, in their own different ways, as a path into adulthood.

Instead of marriage, Reinaldo's final years in Cuba, between 1973 and his exile in 1980, lead him to prison, which (along with assassination) is the only represented outcome for a homosexual counterrevolutionary intellectual who does not self-repress, hide, or commit suicide. Arenas and his friend Coco Salas, robbed by two teenagers with whom they had sex, foolishly contact the police to help them recover their stolen possessions. When found, the teenagers accuse Arenas and Coco of sexual assault, which gives the aptly-named *Seguridad del Estado* [State Security] a perfect excuse to imprison them. Fearing El Morro, the prison where his mentor Virgilio's spirit was broken, Reinaldo manages to escape from jail and tries to swim to the sea to perhaps find a boat, an attempt that ends with his first suicide attempt, an outcome that parallels his mother's depression and the multiple suicides cited as an option for Cuban artists and intellectuals. His subsequent failed attempt to self-exile through Guantanamo lands him in the streets, a common space that marginalized people inhabit in Diasporic Coming-of-age Novels in contrast to the capitalist institutions (such as universities, corporations, and heterosexual nuclear families) that traditional *Bildungsromane* heroes occupy. Reinaldo lives in Lenin Park for months before he is eventually found and taken to El Morro.

El Morro means a myriad of indignities from hunger to torture that bring Reinaldo's formative process to a halt. Reinaldo's body and spirit are crushed to the point that his voracious sexual desire, synonymous with resistance and joy, comes to a halt:

> Las relaciones sexuales se convierten en la cárcel, en algo sórdido que se realiza bajo el signo de la sumisión y el sometimiento, el chantaje y la violencia; incluso, en muchas ocasiones, del crimen ... el propio sistema carcelario hace que el preso se sienta como un animal y cualquier forma de sexo es algo humillante.

> [Sexual relations become in prison something sordid, done under the sign of submission and compulsion, blackmail and violence; even, in many cases, of crime ... the very prison system makes the prisoner feel like an animal and any form of sex is humiliating.]

> (Arenas 2003, 205)

The *Seguridad del Estado*, unable to convict him for long due to the activism of his international community of readers releases Reinaldo after two years—a reminder of the importance of the globalized setting of Diasporic Coming-of-age Novels. In the years that follow, Reinaldo is constantly under surveillance, his manuscripts burned or lost. His mentor Virgilio dies as a direct consequence of state harassment.

Self-enacted exile is a longstanding device in coming-of-age novels when protagonists need to continue their formative processes and their social settings are unendurable and restrictive. Stephen Dedalus in James Joyce's *A Portrait of the Artist as a Young Man* (1916) and the eponymous protagonist in *Maurice* are two examples where the protagonists resort to exile in the hope of more fulfilling lives. Reinaldo's own opportunity for exile happens in a collective exodus at Port of Mariel with 105,000 people who, like him, "lo que querían era vivir en un mundo libre y trabajar y recuperar su humanidad perdida" [wanted to live in a free world and work and regain their lost humanity] (Arenas 2003, 304). In this formative process, diaspora does not mean the destabilization of identity, but the search for lost humanity. In this sense, the genre of the Diasporic Coming-of-age enables the hope of building the dignity necessary for subjectivity beyond the confines of the place of birth.

Yet, as is sometimes the case in Diasporic Coming-of-age Novels, diaspora results in further dehumanization, a possibility throughout the globe. The last few chapters take place in Miami and then New York, where Reinaldo grows increasingly depressed. Diasporic Coming-of-age Novels often lead to the nuanced understanding of hybrid identities in complex social settings, but they can also lead to the defeated realization that the protagonists' marginalization prevents them from fully and joyfully belonging anywhere. Reinaldo's diaspora corrodes his sense of self into phantasmal subsistence and eventually nothingness:

> Para un desterrado no hay ningún sitio donde se pueda vivir; que no existe sitio, porque aquél donde soñamos, donde descubrimos un paisaje, leímos el primer libro, tuvimos la primera aventura amorosa, sigue siendo el ligar soñado; en el exilio uno no es más que un fantasma, una sombra de alguien que nunca llega a alcanzar su completa realidad; yo no existo desde que llegué al exilio; desde entonces comencé a huir de mí mismo.

> [For an exiled person there is no place where he can live; there is no place because the one we dream of, where we discovered a landscape, read the first book, had the first love adventure, is still a dreamscape; in exile one is no more than a ghost, a shadow of someone who never achieves complete reality; I do not exist since I was exiled; since then I started to run from myself.]
>
> (Arenas 2003, 314)

The introspection that characterizes most of the coming-of-age genre and Reinaldo's process is thwarted when the protagonist starts running from himself. Diasporic Coming-of-age Novels enable the task of introspection to become too painful. Or, as is the case of Piri in *Down These Mean Streets*, introspection requires the bravery to reject belonging in a misogynistic or homophobic group, which Piri lacks.

These novels do not yield model adults for young readers to imitate. They neither embody the values of their societies nor teach them how to marry properly in terms of social suitability or affection. However unsuccessful as traditional *Bildungsromane*, they are groundbreaking as Diasporic Coming-of-age Novels: Thomas shows how a racist and misogynistic setting conspires with the character's flaws, his lack of introspection, and his internalization of hegemonic systems, to prevent him from reaching a developed sense of self. As such, it shows the formative process in the context of diaspora can denounce the injustice of the social order even despite the protagonist's lack of maturity. Arenas uses a failed formative process, where the character gives up on introspection because he is exhausted by the cruel forces that have crushed him, in turn, to elevate its political effectiveness by showing beyond reasonable doubt how harsh and perverse his setting is. In chilling contrast to the blissful older narrator of Dicken's *David Copperfield* who reflects on a joyful (albeit sometimes sinuous) life, Arenas' suicide note is the culmination of a painful formative process. In depicting a failed formative process and convincingly placing the blame of such failure on the setting, Arenas uses a fundamental characteristic of the Diasporic Coming-of-age Novel, its reliance on a diasporic formative process as driver of plot, to substantiate his *testimonio*.

Notes

1 Similarly to racial solidarity, in *Señales que precederán al fin del mundo* [*Signs Preceding the End of the World*] Makina develops a sense of solidarity with queer people who, like herself, have shared experiences of marginalization.
2 The Young Lords, also addressed in Chapter 7 of this book, are defined by Johanna Fernández as a 1970s "group of poor and working-class Puerto Rican radicals brought an alternative vision of society to life in their own neighborhood. Their aim was to reclaim the dignity of the racially oppressed and elevate basic human needs—food, clothing, housing, health, work, and community over the pursuit of profit. In the course of a fight with East Harlem's First Spanish United Methodist Church (FSUMC), they found an unlikely but irresistible setting for the public presentation of their revolutionary project" (Fernández 2020, 1).
3 The UNEAC is the Unión de Escritores y Artistas de Cuba [National Union of Writers and Artists of Cuba] founded by poet Nicolás Guillén in 1961.
4 Pip epitomizes the need for metropolitan relocation in Charles Dicken's *Great Expectations* (1861), studied in depth in Chapter 2.

PART III

6 Diasporic Coming-of-age Novels of Eastern European Diasporas in Contemporary Berlin

Yadé Kara and Wolfgang Herrndorf

Emerging from medieval narratives that depict the formative processes of children whose destiny was to become knights and kings, Johann Wolfgang von Goethe's *Wilhelm Meisters Lehrjahre* [*Wilhelm Meister's Apprenticeship*] (1795) was the first to forego destiny as the main driver of plot and instead focus on the internal, rather than external, coming-of-age of the hero. Discussed in depth in Chapter 1, *Wilhelm Meisters Lehrjahre* contains the seeds of the great variability of the contemporary coming-of-age genre and compellingly challenges conventions of the marriage institution and the family of the eighteenth- and early-nineteenth-centuries. *Wilhelm Meister* thus heralded the capacity of the coming-of-age genre, enabling play and experimentation with individual and national identity, which vibrantly continues in Germany to this day. In the region that gave birth to the genre, writers continue to create energetic representations of the formations of individuals at a time when Germany has become a de facto multicultural country and a home for various contemporary diasporas. The great number of people and cultures that now convivially belong to the German national body stimulates the task to rethink and redefine Germanness without universally-agreed ethnic, cultural, socioeconomic, religious, or even linguistic standards.

The ever-malleable genre of the Diasporic Coming-of-age Novel is an ideal site for the representation of the convivial multiculturalism and intricacy of the contemporary German social body. Contemporary Diasporic German Coming-of-age Novels reflect the current state of Germanness—which is one of flux and fluidity. *Selam Berlin* (2003) by Yade Kara ponders how the son of a Turkish marriage can fit into the social context of Berlin shortly after the reunification of Germany and concludes not with marriage as a marker of maturity but the realization that the protagonist Hasan Kazan is not "zwischen den Kulturen hin- und hergerissen war, jemanden der nicht dazugehörte" [split here and there, between cultures, someone who did not belong], but rather has "alles von beidem. Von Ost und West, von deutsch und türkisch, von hier und da" [everything from both. From East and West, from German and Turkey, from here and there] (Kara 2003, 223).[1] Hasan develops a cheerful tolerance for the tension between cultures that characterizes his culturally hybrid upbringing. Published in the same decade, *tschick* (2010) by Wolfgang Herrndorf also disregards marriage and instead foregrounds the parallel formative processes of two friends whose joyful resolutions strengthen their individual sense of self and their fraternal bond.[2] Their quest for belonging is not to the nation as citizens, but with each other.

Instead of representing full inclusion to the national body politic, completeness, or accommodation, *Selam Berlin* and *tschick* enable their protagonists to develop a complex and personal understanding of their identities and how they fit into their social setting. They keep at their center the formative process as driver of plot and complex portrayals of hybrid and fluid identities, with little concern for ideal depictions of citizens and workers. The images of Germanness are flexible and thus representative of diasporic identities, which Stuart Hall describes as "constantly producing and reproducing themselves anew, through transformation and difference" (Hall 1989, 80). In these Diasporic Coming-of-age Novels of contemporary Berlin, the Germanness of the young protagonists is not an "already accomplished fact" or an inner truth already formed and that is slowly discovered; rather, it is a "production, which is never complete, always in process" (68).

Selam Berlin and *tschick* embody the most salient structural and thematic transformations of the coming-of-age genre in contemporary Berlin. In *Selam Berlin*, Hasan Kazan, starts his formative process in Kreuzberg, West Berlin, in 1971. His coming-of-age is an exploration of both the significance of the reunification of Germany of 1991 and the culturally hybrid identities of Germans with *Migrationshintergrund* [migration backgrounds], the term the German Federal Statistical Office uses to classify individuals whose immediate ancestors came from abroad. *tschick* follows the shorter, but far more complex, coming-of-age story of two fourteen-year-olds, Maik Klingenberg and Andrej Tschichatschow, "Tschick," a Russian repatriate, who steal a car and drive aimlessly around the German countryside. In the process, they figure out how they fit in their families, heterosexual social structures, and the variegated German social body. This is a challenging task as they must account for their intersecting marginalized identities of queerness, poverty, and *Migrationshintergrund*.

The literature of diasporic groups often centers on the unraveling of complicated and split identities, violence, hybridity. Literature of diasporas puzzles over national identity and people's places in their body politic. Such literature asks the questions of who can access and belong in particular nations as citizens and, in the case of Germany, whether a contemporary literary canon can secure the transcendence of novels written by and about Germans with *Migrationshintergrund*. Although the word *hintergrund*— "grounded in the past" being the most literal translation applied to immigrants—might imply a going-back or a stubborn attachment to the culture of their immigrant parents, these young protagonists take national subjectivity to new horizons, expanding how Germanness can be defined. Their subjectivity is only partially regional and only marginally based on the canonical German literary tradition. *Selam Berlin*, a novel about the Turkish diaspora in Germany, showcases the conflicts of the definition of Germanness and the problem of cultural erasure often implied in full assimilation. Similar in topic but focused on different circumstances, *tschick* puzzles over these problems but in the context of the less-studied Russian diaspora in Germany and intersecting marginalized identities. As expected, German society is depicted in contrasting strokes, at times with scenes of convivial intermingling of cultures, at times with bigoted characters who long for a pure and homogeneous nation that never in reality existed, a longing pointedly not shared by the protagonists.

Germany as a *De Facto* "Country of Immigrants"

The history of diaspora in Germany in the second half of the twentieth century enables the assertion that two Diasporic Coming-of-age Novels, one written by Yadé Kara, born in Çayırlı, Turkey in 1965, and another by Wolfgang Herrndorf, born in Hamburg also in 1965, can be read within the contemporary German literary tradition. A great influx of foreign workers during the 1950s and 1960s transformed Germany: "temporary guest workers recruited to work in West Germany between 1955 and 1973 became de facto immigrants, thus transforming the Federal Republic of Germany into an immigration country" (Triadafilopoulos and Schönwälder 2006, 1). Douglas Klusmeyer and Demetrios Papadimitriou likewise assert that "between 1950 and 1994, approximately 80 percent of the increase in the West German population resulted from migration" (Klusmeyer and Papademetriou 2009, xii). In 2006, the Federal Statistical Office reported of the reunified contemporary Germany "that nearly one-fifth (19 percent) of the population in Germany had a migration background (Migrationshintergrund)," a number that excluded the "approximately 12 million ethnic German refugees and expellees, who came to Germany as a result of World War II and its aftermath" (Klusmeyer and Papademetriou 2009, xii). In the early 1990s, "the introduction of jus soli [right of the soil] granted former guest workers and their children greater access to German citizenship and, in so doing, transformed the boundaries of German nationhood" (Triadafilopoulos 2013, 3). As a consequence of the guest worker policy, "the continuing crisis of German identity since unification and the de facto settlement of Turkish and many other 'other' Germans make it imperative to rethink Germanness" (Cheesman 2007, 32). The picture painted by these statistics is of a de facto immigration land, despite reactionary efforts by a xenophobic minority to define it otherwise.

The length and social impact of the guest worker program meant the emergence of what has been termed Gastarbeiterliteratur or guest worker literature. This taxonomy "was coined in 1980, simultaneous to the founding to two publishing houses PoLiKunst (Politische Literatur und Kunst) and Südwind Gastarbeiterdeutsch," which made the accounts of guest workers' experiences available to a larger public (Mani 2002, 113).[3] *Gastarbeiterliteratur* was marked by "documenting experiences of culture-shock and problems of integration, exploitation at work and social discrimination, domestic clashes due to conflicting social values, and financial and emotional hopes and aspirations of guest workers in Germany" (113). While *Gastarbeiterliteratur* might no longer be a fitting term because guest workers and subsequent generations have become full citizens, many of the themes in Kara's and Herrndorf's novels fall into the aforementioned list. However, Kara and Herrndorf also expand it, pondering the German political situation at large and "the larger community of immigrants in Europe" (114). *Gastarbeiterliteratur* paved the way for a now-complex literary corpus that challenges its subcategorization and has broken into mainstream contemporary German art and literature. The works of Kara and Herrndorf, in addition to such authors as the prolific novelist Feridun Zaimoğlu and the award-winning poet Zafer Şenocak, are now included in syllabi across Germany and abroad, and they populate bookshelves of bookstores and libraries alike. In cinema, the films of acclaimed directors Fatih Akin and Yasemin Şamdereli depicting stories of multiculturalism in Germany are among the most successful blockbusters of the last ten years.

Despite—and in reaction to—the success of these authors in showcasing the cultural reality of Germany, there are sectors of the population that have unjustly adopted reactionary and bigoted rhetoric. It is relevant to acknowledge the existence of such rhetoric in contemporary Germany not because it is representative of the sentiments of the country as a whole, but rather because it is significant to understanding why the protagonists of *Selam Berlin* and *tschick* struggle at times to feel a sense of unquestioned and unequivocal belonging to the nation. The exclusionary rhetoric of the right-wing political party Alternative for Germany [*Alternative für Deutschland*, AfD] has only been adopted by a minority of the population in Germany. Indeed, Germany has enthusiastically and uninterruptedly welcomed more asylum applicants than any other nation in the European Union since 2008, a testament to the citizenry's heartfelt adoption of convivial multiculturalism (Eurostat). In spite of this convivial effort, two examples from 1977 and 2016 illustrate the xenophobic minority's assertion of a monocultural and homogeneous German national body politic represented in Diasporic Coming-of-age Novels. The first is the West German stance officially adopted in a "1977 policy report of a joint commission of the federal government and the states on migrant workers" (Klusmeyer and Papdemetriou 2009, xxi). This report proclaimed that West Germany was "not a country of immigration" but instead a "country in which foreigners reside for varying lengths of time before they decide on their own accord to return to their home country" (Katzenstein 1987, 239–240). The report proclaims a national vision at odds with the reality of the guest worker program, which facilitated the permanent settlement of workers primarily from Turkey and changed the traits of the German body politic. Triadafilopoulos challenges this report by correctly informing that by the end of the twentieth century, Germany had "developed into [a] de facto multicultural societ[y]," because, by the time of the "recruitment stop" of guest workers in November 1973, "German was host to some 2.6 million foreigners" (2013, 2). The second and more recent example of monocultural rhetoric comes from the AfD, the "third-largest group in the Bundestag," the German Parliament (Chase 2017). In their online *Manifesto for Germany*, the AfD explains that because "identity is primarily shaped by culture," it is the "statutory duty of federal and state governments" to "preserve German Culture, Language and Tradition" (AfD 2016, 45, 46). The AfD explains that German culture, allegedly under the threat of globalization and multiculturalism, is

> derived from three sources: firstly, the religious traditions of Christianity; secondly, the scientific and humanistic heritage, whose ancient roots were renewed during the period of Renaissance and the Age of Enlightenment; and thirdly, Roman law, upon which our constitutional state is founded. Together, these traditions are the foundation of our free and democratic society, and they determine daily patterns of social interaction in society, and shape the relationship between the sexes as well as the conduct of parents towards their children.
>
> (AfD 2016, 46)

The first and third sources, Christianity and Roman law, are euphemisms for traditional gender roles, a dog-whistle technique often employed in extreme political rhetoric. AfD's definition of Germanness is thus based on a longing for a strict Christian and heterosexual social unit that most people in German do not abide by or support, as evidenced by the diverse composition of the Bundestag in which the AfD occupied, as of January of 2019, only ninety-one out of the 709 seats (*Deutscher Bundestag* 2019).

Xenophobic responses to multiculturalism that imagine a homogenous past are not exclusive to Germany hence the global mobility of the Diasporic Coming-of-age genre. Some sectors of Great Britain, a nation that also saw a great diasporic influx in the second half of the twentieth century, responded similarly. In analyzing English immigration and multicultural policies, Paul Gilroy argues that in order to conceptualize post-World War II English identity, a xenophobic sector of the population crafted a post-imperial melancholic vision that imagines Britain as a victim of citizen-migrants, who used to be subjects of the British Empire and who now threaten the political body of Britain: an ethnical menace that destabilizes the identity of the former metropolis. This melancholic vision aims to erase the brutality and guilt of the empire in order to enshrine a conception of imperialism as a noble effort to bring civilization (Gilroy 2005, 90). In turn, it feeds racism and xenophobia. The nature of Diasporic Coming-of-age Novels is to counter these reactionary responses with nuanced representations of hybrid identities in both these European settings and elsewhere.

Turkish-German Identity in Berlin

Challenging "the clichéd idea of guest workers" sometimes characterized as unskilled young men, Hasan's parents in *Selam Berlin* "arrived in Germany at the same time as numerous guest workers, but his father came to study, and his mother came from a good family in Istanbul," thus expanding and signifying a heterogeneity in the Turkish diaspora (Vlasta 2016, 243). Hasan begins his story much like Dickens's David Copperfield, stating his name and birthplace, thus inscribing the novel in the coming-of-age genre and acknowledging its European context. As Hasan tells his name in the opening pages, however, he explains that the different settings where he lives have different appellatives; and, with a hint of sarcasm and simultaneous resistance to the Berlin context changing his name, he characterizes the full name his parents gave him as pretty: "Mein Name ist Hasan Kazan. In Berlin nennen mich einige Leute 'Hansi,' obwohl meine Eltern mir den schönen Namen Hasan Selim Khan gegeben haben. Ach ja, meine Eltern ..." [My name is Hasan Kazan. In Berlin some people call me "Hansi" although my parents gave me the pretty name Hasan Selim Khan. Oh yeah, my parents ...] (Kara 2003, 5). His discussion of name segues into his parents, who, like the Iqbals in Zadie Smith's *White Teeth*, fear the influence of European society in their children's upbringing (see Chapter 3).

Hasan explains his parents' contradictory worldview, a product of their diaspora in Germany. They admire Germany's technical ingenuity but abhor tolerant social attitudes towards drugs and sexuality. In Diasporic Coming-of-age Novels the values and mores of the protagonists' parents often clash with those of the host society. Hasan's parents "glaubten an den Westen" [believed in the West] because it represents "Fortschritt, Technik und Arbeit" [progress, technology, and work] (Kara 2003, 5). However, they are afraid that Hasan and his brother will succumb to the liberal cultural influence of Berlin, lose their traditional values, and become "Kiffer, Hippies oder Homos" [stoners, hippies, or homosexuals] (5). Hasan's father Said sends his sons to attend high school in Istanbul, while he stays back to work in the travel agency he runs with his Turkish college friend Halim.

After high school, when Hasan is nineteen and attempting to figure out his path, the Berlin Wall falls. This momentous event in German history prompts Hasan to go back to Berlin: "Ich wollte voll in die Berlin-Party mit einsteigen und alles mitmachen, ja genau, das wollte ich. Es gab nichts, was mich noch in Istanbul hielt" [I completely wanted to get in on the Berlin party and take part in all of it, exactly, that is what I wanted. There was nothing left to keep me in Istanbul] (9). Against his parents' wishes, Hasan begins his quest for self-determination as he flies self-funded to Berlin, thus illustrating the formative process's force to move the plot forward. His mother tries to stop him, arguing that there are no bourgeois accommodations for him there: "Als Ausländer wirst du höchstens Taxifahrer oder Kellner" [As a foreigner you will become at most a taxi driver or waiter] (15). Her understanding of Germany's body politic places her son in menial jobs, a fear that is realized when Hasan tries to enroll at the prestigious Humboldt University but never hears back. Unlike Charles Dicken's characters Pip and David Copperfield, supported by their families and accepted into institutions of higher education, Hasan is self-funded and ostracized. Hasan tries to become a student of archeology, but finds surprise and ridicule from the University's officials. The first he encounters, asks him with astonishment, "Sie sind Türke und wollen Archäologie studieren?" [You are Turkish and want to study archeology?] (Kara 2003, 52). The irony for the official is that this backward-looking discipline would see Hasan as an object of study and not as a researcher. The second official mispronounces his name and then reinforces his non-belonging by announcing he is the first Turkish person to ever apply: "'Sie werden von uns angeschrieben, Herr Käzzän.' 'Kazan, wiederholte ich deutlich …' Ich war es leid, ständig meinen Namen falsch betont zu hören … 'Sie sind der erste türkische Student der sich bei uns anmeldet.' Sie lächelte". ["We will be in contact, Mister Käzzän." "Kazan" I repeated clearly … I was tired of constantly hearing my names mispronounced … "You are the first Turkish student to apply." She smirked] (53). They do not contact him again. Out of necessity and an opportunity in his friend circle, Hasan accesses the world of film as an actor, the professional choice of the protagonists of Goethe's *Wilhelm Meisters Lehrjahre* and Hanif Kureishi's *The Buddha of Suburbia* (see Chapter 3), giving him the chance to experiment with his identity. Hasan's acting experience differs from that of the eponymous Wilhelm, who fittingly plays Shakespeare's *Hamlet*, because Hasan is unable to freely choose complex or interesting characters. Similarl to Karim in *The Buddha,* Hasan is type-casted in stereotypical roles such as exotic foreigners or criminals.

The most salient example of the tension between Germany's melancholic and convivial visions happens when film director Wolf asks Hasan how he understands his experience of cultural hybridity. In Wolf's movie, Hasan plays the drug-dealer Mehmet. In between takes, Wolf asks Hasan: "Sag mal, so unter uns, wie ist es denn? … so zwischen den Kulturen, Sprachen, hin- und hergerissen zu sein" [Between you and me, tell me, what is it like? … to be split between cultures, languages, here and there] (221–222). However, before Hasan can say anything, Wolf answers his own question:

"Du bist hier geboren und aufgewachsen. Du bist Deutscher … Du spielst … ein Junge aus Kreuzberg, der schnell das Messer zückt … Alle schauen und denken: Ein Araber, ein Ali, ein Türke. Schwarze Haare, braune Augen …" lachte Wolf. "Ist ja dein Hintergrund. Berliner aus dem Morgenland."

["You were born and raised here. You are German … You play … a young man from Kreuzberg who quickly pulls out his knife … Everyone looks at you and thinks: An Arab, an Ali, a Turk. Black hair, brown eyes …" he laughed. "That is your background. A Berliner from the Orient."]

(Kara 2003, 222)

Wolf does not care about what Hasan's answer because he has already reduced Hasan to his features and laughingly encapsulated him in the name Ali, which recalls the world of "Ali Baba and the Forty Thieves," one of the stories in *One Thousand and One Nights*.

This one-sided conversation prompts Hasan to ponder his own identity and realize that Wolf is wrong, therefore liberating himself, at least in his own self-conception, from such a stereotype:

> Ich glaube, Wolf hatte die irrige Idee von zwei Kulturen, die aufei-nanderprallen. Und so einer wie ich mußte ja dazwischen zerrieben werden. Eigentlich hatte ich alles von beidem. Von Ost und West, von deutsch und türkisch, von hier und da. Aber das konnten Leute wie Wolf nicht verstehen oder wollten es nicht verstehen. Sie sahen in mir immer einen Problemfall. Jemanden, der zwischen den Kulturen hin- und hergerissen war, jemanden der nicht dazugehörte. Piss off! Ich war so, wie ich war. Die anderen versuchten mir Probleme einzureden, die ich nicht hatte. Sie konnten mit so einem wie mir nicht umgehen. Ich paßte nicht in ihr Bild, und sie konnten mich nicht einordnen. Ich war wie ein Flummiball, sprang zwischen Osten und Westen hin und her, ha. [*sic*]

> [I believe, Wolf had the wrong idea of two cultures that clash. And that someone like me would be pulverized in the clash. Actually I had every-thing from both. From East and West, from German and Turkey, from here and there. But people like Wolf could not understand that or they did not want to understand. They saw in me always a problematic case. Someone who was split here and there, between cultures, someone who did not belong. Piss off! I was who I was. The others tried to encumber me with problems I did not have. The did not know what to do with me. I did not fit in their picture, and they could not classify me. I was like a bouncy ball, bounced between East and West, here and there, ha].

> (Kara 2003, 223)

To the question of whether he is one or the other, here Hasan answers that he is both. In contrast to Karim who ultimately embodies a stereotype, Hasan is able to emancipate from external and racist conceptualizations of his identity. Kara depicts his character as a multi-faceted individual whose hybridity is not a source of anxiety for the protagonist but eventually of joy and cultural wealth. This is an optimistic alternative for Diasporic Coming-of-age Novels. By the end of the novel, Hasan still has not found an accommodation or partner, and is still unsure of what occupation he wants or where to go, he expresses this uncertainty with enthusiasm: "Ich wollte weiter nach Westen, nach London, New York, San Francisco oder nach Osten? Nach Tokio, Teheran, Taschkent. Flüghafen, Bahnhöfe, Hotelzim-mer. Nicht hier, nicht da, einfach fort sein. Ja, das wollte ich hey, ho, let's go" [*sic*] [I wanted go further West, to London, New York, San Francisco, or further East? Tokyo, Tehran, Tashkent. Airports, train stations, hotel rooms. Not here, not there, simply gone away. Yes, that is what I wanted, hey, ho, let's go] (Kara 2003, 381)! At the end, his future, like that of the coming-of-age genre, is global and remains to be seen.

Maturity as Brotherhood and Joyful Queernes

tschick differs from the Diasporic Coming-of-age Novels in Chapters 3, 4, 5, and *Selam Berlin,* because it is not written by an author of a diaspora drawing from his own experience of cultural hybridity. Instead, Hamburg-born Wolfgang Herrndorf represents a German boy without any apparent migration background. However, diaspora is so important to the definition of national social bodies in contemporary globalized societies, that the novel foregrounds the theme of hybrid identity and the intersection between diaspora and coming-of-age processes. The concurrent representations of two marginalized coming-of-age processes inform and support each other. On the one hand, the autodiegetic narrator Maik Kingenberg experiences ostracism and loneliness marked by his inability to correctly read social cues and his weak sense of self, both evidenced by a school episode to be discussed in depth. On the other hand, Andrej Tschichatschow, Tschick, is marginalized experience by poverty, alcoholism, and importantly his ethnic difference. As Maik explains on their first meeting, Tschick

> war ein Russe, wie sich dann rausstellte. Er war mittelgroß, trug ein schmuddeliges weißes Hemd, an dem ein Knopf fehlte, 10-Euro-Jeans von KiK und braune, unförmige Schuhe, die aussahen wie tote Ratten. Außerdem hatte er extrem hohe Wangenknochen und statt Augen Schlitze … Sah aus wie ein Mongole. (42)

> [was Russian, it turned out. He was average height, had on a dirty white shirt that was missing a button, bargain basement jeans, and misshapen brown shoes that looked like dead rats. He also had extremely high cheek-bones and slits instead of eyes … They made him look Mongolian.]
>
> (Herrndorf 2012, 36)

A common trait of Diasporic Coming-of-age Novels, two formative processes appear in *tschick* instead of the one single process of traditional *Bildungsromane.* The concurrent processes of Maik and Tschick reflect the free floating rather than defined outcomes available in their social setting. Although Maik's process is more readily available due to the ubiquity of his voice, Tschick's is just as important. Indeed, neither could Maik strengthen his sense of self without Tschick nor could Tschick be brave enough to accept his sexual identity without Maik. Rather than marriage and ideal citizenship as markers of maturity, as studied in Chapters 1 and 2, focused on the Proto-*Bildungsromane* and traditional *Bildungsromane*, Maik reaches a stage of completeness by gaining a newfound joy for life and a sense of self that does not depend on how he is seen or nicknamed by others. Maik also stands up to his abusive father, which he had never been able to do before. In a parallel, Tschick is able to come out. Although not written by an author of a diaspora in a metropolitan host society, nor explicitly meant for diasporic readers, *tschick* is paramount to the understanding of the direction globalized societies are taking to become ever more comfortable with fluid national identities that can integrate difference without pushing for the cultural erasure that full assimilation implies. *tschick* offers a case study on the formative process of two social outcasts in a society whose political body underwent momentous changes throughout the twentieth century through to today.

The beginning of the novel is untraditional as it starts at the end of the story, with the adolescent Maik at a police station, concussed and confused from the car accident that will be described at the end of the novel and ignorant of the consequences of having stolen a car with his friend Tschick. This Diasporic Coming-of-age Novel thus subverts the classic expectation of finding the protagonist at the end in a bourgeois accommodation like that of the gentleman writer and family man David Copperfield. Maik's end is closer to Karim Amir's in *The Buddha of Suburbia* or Piri Thomas's in *Down These Mean Streets*: Arriving at a sense of contentment and optimism but still uncertain about the future. In direct opposition to the definition of *hero* for the protagonists of traditional *Buildingsromane*, Maik is sarcastically called a hero twice in this first chapter. First he does it himself, when he realizes that he is old enough to be criminally accountable, a legal marker for maturity: "hab ich mir vor Angst in die Hose gepisst. Maik Klingenberg, der Held" (7) [got so scared I pissed myself. Mike Klingberg, hero (Herrndorf 2012, 1)]. Second, a police officer mockingly calls him hero after Maik asks if he needs a lawyer, "Unser Held hier will wissen, ob er einen Anwalt braucht! Blutet den ganzen Boden voll, pisst sich in die Hosen wie ein Weltmeister und – will *seinen Anwalt* sprechen!" (10) [Our hero here wants to know if he needs a lawyer! Bleeding all over the floor, pissing himself like a champ, and wants to talk to *his lawyer*! (Herrndorf 2012, 4)]. The novel introduces Maik as an unsuccessful man, unworthy of praise or admiration either in self-appraisal or by near-strangers, whose physical response to fear is humiliatingly portrayed as unfit for his age. Maik's ultimate outcome in the novel is therefore not to reach a final accommodation or to be an Enlightened man. Rather, as the end of the novel attests, Maik's particular marker of maturity, his heroism, is to find belonging and comradery, not with his native German peers, but among the social outcasts available to him in the globalized context, others undergoing the similar experiences of alienation and flux. The globalized setting enables a possibility that did not exist in traditional *Bildungsromane*, to build relationships of mutual support with people who are ethnically and culturally different and thus find belonging in global—rather than regional or national—networks.

The novel then returns in Chapter 4 of forty-nine to the beginning of the story, where Maik outlines the obstacles to his belonging in his social setting. He understands he is lonely, which he ascribes to being boring, but readers can quickly figure out that Maik's troubles are actually due to his inability to read and follow social ques, as well as his hostility towards strangers. Maik displays a desire to belong among his native German peers, but his evaluation of the causes of his marginalization is incorrect. Readers begin to understand why Maik is not invited to the birthday party of his beautiful classmate Tatiana Cosic, the social event of the year. Maik's marginalization becomes clear in an episode that earns him the short-lived nickname "Psycho." This episode begins with a word prompt story assignment in "Mr. Schuermann's German class, sixth grade" where the students create a short story that includes "Urlaub, Wasser, Rettung und Gott" (24) [vacation, water, rescue, and God (Herrndorf 2012, 18)]. "Die meisten haben sich erst mal an dem Wort Urlaub festgehalten. Da rudert die Kleinfamilie an der Côte d'Azur rum, und dann geraten sie vollkommen überraschend in einen höllischen Sturm und rufen 'o Gott,' und werden gerettet und so" (25) [Most of the students grabbed on the word "vacation." A little family is paddling around off the Côte d'Azur and are taken totally by surprise by a terrible storm and yell "oh, God" and are then rescued or whatever (19)]— Maik explains. Unaware that the other students are following an unspoken social rule to keep the stories superficial, Maik tells the story of his mother going on "vacations" to a "Beauty Farm" that is, in reality, an alcoholic rehabilitation clinic. In front of the whole class Maik reads,

> Sie ist ja Alkoholikerin. Sie hat Alkohol getrunken, solange ich denken kann, aber der Unterschied ist, dass es früher lustiger war. Normal wird vom Alkohol jeder lustig, aber wenn das eine bestimmte Grenze überschreitet, werden die Leute müde oder aggressiv, und als meine Mutter dann wieder mit dem Küchenmesser durch die Wohnung lief, stand ich mit meinem Vater oben auf der Treppe, und mein Vater hat gefragt: "Wie wär's mal wieder mit der Beautyfarm?" (27)

> [She's an alcoholic. She's drunk booze for as long as I can remember but the difference is that it used to be funnier. Everyone is normally funny when they drink, but when a certain line is crossed people get tired or aggressive. And when my mother started walking around our place with a kitchen knife again, I was standing upstairs with my father as he called down, "How about another trip to the beauty farm?"]

> (Herrndorf 2012, 21)

Maik thinks he has done a good job and expects praise from Mr. Schummermann who, surprisingly to Maik, reacts with anger: "'Was grinst du denn so blöd?

Findest du das auch noch lustig?' … 'Maik,' hat er gesagt, und dann hat er sich wider zu mir umgedreht. 'Das ist deine *Mutter*. Hast du da mal drüber nachgedacht?'" (33) ["Why are you grinning like an idiot? Do you think this is funny?" … "Maik" he said, turning around again to face me. "That's your *mother*. Did you ever stop to think about that?" (25)]. At this point readers know that, although Maik wants to belong, as evidenced by his desire to attend Tatiana's party and complete his school assignment, he does not and indeed cannot fit in with his classmates. Formal schooling, a hegemonic institution that teaches the young protagonists of *David Copperfield*, *Great Expectations*, or *Maurice* how to become citizens and workers and the social mores, often becomes an obstacle to the protagonists' formative processes in Diasporic Coming-of-age Novels. In *The House on Mango Street*, *The Buddha of Suburbia*, and *White Teeth*, formal schooling is the setting where Esperanza Cordero, Karim Amir, and Irie Jones learn about their racial differences and outcast status. Maik's inability to understand his social setting in school is part and parcel of the Diasporic Coming-of-age Novel: many protagonists are simply no longer mirrors of the hegemonic mores and ideal values of their social settings.

Maik does not stand a chance: In addition to his mother's alcoholism, his father switches between neglect and physical violence, and, although his father was once a successful real estate developer, the family has fallen into financial ruin. Similar to the failure of formal schooling to impart social mores, family institutions in Diasporic Coming-of-age Novels often lack role models for the protagonists. Maik explains of his own social skills, "Solange die Leute undfreundlich sind, kann ich vor Aufregung kaum laufen. Aber wenn sie auch nur ein bisschen freundlich werden, fang ich immer gleich an, sie zu beleidigen" (63) [When somebody is hostile to me, I'm so nervous that I can barely keep my knees from buckling. But if they are even the slightest bit friendly, I immediately start insulting them (Herrndorf 2012, 57)]. Maik's communicative abilities are decidedly unserviceable, in contrast to those of the heroes of traditional *Bildungsromane*, great artists, philosophers, correctly masculine, eventually married and accommodated.

In addition to the presence of Tatiana, whose parents are "aus Serbien oder Kroatien" (23) [from Serbia or Croatia (17)], *Migrationshintergrund* colors many of Maik interactions—most often in the service industry. For example, Maik's "Liebenskrankenschwester kommt aus Libanon und heißt Hanna" (15) [favorite nurse is from Lebanon and is named Hanna (9)]. However, as with every other social interaction, Maik has trouble understanding the social rules. When his family was more financially stable, they "hatten auch mal einen Inder für den Garten" (75) [had an Indian working as a gardener for a while (69)], and an old Vietnamese woman who "mit dem Reden hat sie's nicht so" (74) [can't really speak German (68)] comes to clean his house. Maik is always embarrassed by these interactions:

Ich will diese Leute immer ganz normal behandeln, aber sie beneh-
men sich wie Angestellte, die den Drech für einen wegmachen ...
allein mit der Vietnamesin in einem Raum fühle ich mich wie Hitler.
Ich will ihr immer sofort das Staubtuch aus der Hand reißen und
selber putzen. (75)

[I want to treat them like regular people, but they act like they're ser-
vants who clean the dirt out of your way ... when I'm alone in a room
with the Vietnamese woman I feel like Hitler. I always want to grab the
rags out of her hand and clean everything up.]

(Herrndorf 2012, 69)

His inability to understand how to treat the immigrants working in his
house is a synecdoche for the national house, also unable to make sense of
difference and riddled with historic guilt. Because Maik makes a reference to
Hitler, his wanting to "clean everything up," takes on the meaning of the
historic *dirtiness* of Nazi Germany.

It is this complicated young person whom Tschick chooses to befriend. It
is not wholly unsurprising, as Tschick is a complicated young person as
well. Much like Maik in the school's social hierarchy, "Tschick war ein Asi,
und genau so sah er auch aus" (41) [Tschick is trash, and that's exactly what
he looked like (35)].[4] When the teacher first introduces Tschick to the class,
he highlights Tschick's social and historical difference, pronouncing his
name incorrectly as if Tschick's name hurt the teacher's tongue, an issue
that Esperanza faces in the Anglo Chicago context in *The House on Mango
Street*, discussed in Chapter 4:

Andrej Tschicha ... schoff heißt unser neuer Mitschüller, und wie wir
an seinem Namen bereits unschwer erkennen, kommt unser Gast von
weit her, genau genommen aus den unendlichen russischen Weiten, die
Napoleon in der letzten Stunde vor Ostern erboten hat – und aus denen
er heute, wie wir sehen werden, auch wieder vertrieben werden wird.
Wie vor ihm Karl XII. Und nach ihm Hitler. (44)

[Andrej Tschicha ... schoff is the name of our new classmate, and as
you can no doubt discern from his name, our guest has come from far
away. The boundless Russian expanses, which Napoleon conquered in
1812 and, as we'll see, was soon expelled from again. Just as Charles
XII had been before him and Hitler would be after him] [ellipsis in the
original.]

(Herrndorf 2012, 38)

The teacher, the representative voice of an institution tasked with forming
good citizens and skilled workers, defines Germanness, and indeed
Europeanness, in imperialistic terms: Others are known only insofar as
they are conquered and colonized. This first introduction irreparably

cements Tschick's marginalization. The phrase "our guest" here inter-pellates Tschick as a visitor, and thus someone with no plausible claim to Germanness. The possessive "*our* guest" implies a relationship of owner-ship. The last line in the quotation historicizes Tschick within a genealogy of unwanted intruders who sought to impose themselves (and were just as unwelcome) and failed.

The unlikely pair first become friends in the beginning of summer, when Tschick steals an old Lada, a Russian car manufactured in the 1970s amid the remnant of East Berlin, and convinces Maik to break with the boredom of his lonely summer.[5] Like the "good relationships" in traditional *Bildungsromane*, Tschick offers Maik the opportunity to grow and jumpstart his formative process. Unlike traditional *Bildungsromane*, however, where often the "good partner" is less a character and more a device through which the protagonist can transform, this friendship simultaneously jumpstarts Tschick's own coming-of-age as well. Tschick's key marker of maturity will be to come out, which his friend-ship enables. But throughout the novel his homosexuality is already implied, when Tschick asks Maik whether he is gay on three different occasions, and when he describes his uncle in Russia: "Ich habe einen Onkel in Moskau, der läuft den ganzen Tag in einer Lederhose mit hinten Arsch offen rum. Ist aber völlig okay sonst, mein Onkel. Arbeitet für die Regierung. Und er kann ja nichts dafür, dass er schwul ist. Ich find's wirklich nicht schlimm" (85) [I have an uncle in Moscow who runs around in leather pants with the ass cut out of them. He's totally cool otherwise. Works for the government. And he can't do anything about the fact that he's gay. There's really nothing wrong with it] (Herrndorf 2012, 80). Tschick thus lays the groundwork for his eventual coming out, made possible only by his trust in Maik. For both of them, it is the dis-covery of friendship and belonging, not to the social whole, but with each other, that enables them to grow, become braver, and eventually assert themselves in the face of adversity and violence.

A key moment for the conceptualization of nationality takes place when the pair talk about Tschick's origin and he has the chance to ponder his family's identity in his own voice. The conversation concludes by highlighting the senselessness of trying to pinpoint a single and homogeneous ancestry. The pair is deciding where to go in the stolen car and Tschick suggests *Wallachia*, a made-up place where his grandfather supposedly lives. That their journey is to a utopia—a place that does not exist—is very suggestive as the formative process in Diasporic Coming-of-age Novels often does not have a clear objective. Maik then asks Tschick where *he* is from, to which he replies "Deutscher. Ich hab'n Pass" (98) [German. I have a passport] (92). Tschick responds not with his origin but with his nationality, which are different. This legal marker of belonging might be sufficient explanation for Tschick, but Maik presses on:

"Aber wo du herkommst?"

"Aus Rostov. Das ist Russland. Aber die Familie ist von überall. Wolgadeutsche. Volkdeutsche. Und Banater Schwaben, Walachen, jüdische Zigeuner —"

"Was?"

"Was, was?"

"Jüdische Zigeuner?"

"Ja, Mann. Und Schwaben und Walachen —"

"Gibt's nicht."

"Was gibt's nicht?"

"*Jüdische Zigeuner*. Du erzählst einen Scheiß. Du erzählst die ganze Zeit Scheiß."

"Überhaupt nicht."

"Jüdische Zigeuner, das ist wie englische Franzosen! Das gibt's nicht."
...

"Aber Zigeuner ist keine Religion, Mann. Jude ist Religion. Zigeuner ist einer ohne Wohnung."

"Die ohne Wohnung sind zufällig Berber."

"Berber sind Teppiche," sagte Tschick.

Ich dachte lange nach, und als ich Tschick schließich fragte, ob er *wirklich* jüdischer Zigeuner wäre, und er ganz ernst er nickte, da glaubte ich es ihm. (98–99)

["Yeah, but where are you from?"

"A city called Rostov. It's in Russia. But my family is from all over — Volga Germans, ethnic Germans. Danube Swabians, Wallachians, Jewish Gypsies ..."

"What?"

"What what?"

"Jewish Gypsies?" .

"Yeah, man. And Swabian and Wallachian ..."

"No such thing."

"As what?"

"Jewish Gypsies. You're talking shit. You're talking nothing but shit."

"Not at all."

"A Jewish Gypsy would be like an English French. There's no such thing." ...

"Gypsy isn't a religion, man. Jewish is a religion. A Gypsy is just someone without a home."

"People without homes are Berbers."

"Berbers are carpets," said Tschick.

I thought about it for a while longer and when I asked Tschick one last time whether he was *really* Jewish Gypsy and he nodded solemnly, I believed him.]

(Herrndorf 2012, 92–93)

Although it appears to start with some sense of truth, the conversation quickly turns to humor and nonsense. For Maik there appear to be clear taxonomies of identity, which is why he expects his friend to explain clearly where he is from and *what* he is. Tschick surprises Maik by providing mixes and combinations that Maik thought impossible, thus showing that thinking of identity in terms of purity and clear definitions is impossible not only in his family, but also in society at large. Like Irie Jones does by the end of her formative process in Zadie Smith's *White Teeth*, Maik and Tschick dismiss the whole oppositional project of critiquing nationalist discourses. They just dismiss ideas of nationalism and identity rather than seriously engage them. Those ideas just are not relevant to them; they are not part of their lived experience.

Many adventures through the summer prompt Maik and Tschick to bond, but two decisive moments serve to illustrate their reciprocal formative processes. The first occurs after Maik and Tschick get separated in a small village. Found out by the police, their Lada identified as stolen, Maik and Tschick run in opposite directions, Tshick with the Lada, Maik with a stolen bike, without cellphones or any way to contact each other. Maik makes his way to the woods "allein, keuchend und aufgeregt" (138) [alone, wheezing and anxious] (Herrndorf 2012, 132), and tries to think of the place where they could meet again. Without ever having discussed it, Maik comes up with the plan of meeting "an den *letzten* sicheren Ort zurück, wo man vorher war" (139) [in the last *safe* place [where they had] been together] (133), which leaves three possible spots. He chooses the one that feels more likely: "je länger ich darüber nachdachte, desto überzeugter war ich, dass Tschick da auch draufkommen würde. Weil ich ja auch daraufgekommen war" (139) [the more I thought about it the more convinced I was that it would occur to Tschick too. Because it occurred to me (133)]. After two days of hardship, Maik makes it to the observation platform where he literally finds a message in a bottle: "Graf Lada arbeitet im Sägwerk. Bleib hier, ich hol dich bei Sonnenuntergang" (141) [Count Tschickula is working at the sawmill. Stay here and I'll pick you up at sunset (135)]. There, Tschick arrives in the stolen Lada, now painted black with different plates. "Ich umarmte Tschick, und dann boxte ich ihn, und dann umarmte ich ihn wieder. Ich konnte mich überhaput nicht beruhigen. 'Mann!', schrie ich. 'Mann!'" (142) [I hugged Tschick, then punched him, then hugged him again. I couldn't calm down. "Man!" I shouted. "Man, oh, man!" (136)]. It is the first time in Maik's life that he has achieved such a level of intimacy. He is excited to see his friend but perhaps even more by how meaningful it is to him, for the first time, to develop a deep connection.

The second decisive moment comes when they meet the mysterious girl Isa, living in a landfill. She wants to reach her sister in Prague, but it is unclear if she is returning there or not. Her unknown origin attests to the little importance that national origin has in this friend group, a microcosm that represents a convivial vision of German identity. Isa starts following them and Tschick becomes jealous at first, telling Isa to stay away from them on account of her terrible smell. But as they spend more time together and Isa helps them steal gasoline for the Lada, they become closer and Isa even proposes sex to Maik. They end up only kissing, but the possibility of sexual intimacy is entirely new. Before Isa leaves on a bus to Prague, the three climb on top of a hill, write their initials on a rock, and promise to come back fifty years later. Maik experiences joy as he says, "Ich finde es toll, dass wir jetzt hier sind, und ich bin froh, dass ich mit euch hier bin. Und dass wir befreundet sind" (175) [I want you to know that I'm happy here with you. And that we're friends (168)]. Rather than through marriage or a professional accommodation, in this Diasporic Coming-of-age Novel Maik finds access to belonging into a social whole by means of friendship with other outcasts who can only be there because Germany has become a globalized setting.

In the last few chapters of the novel, the two heroes reach various conclusions for their formative processes that are made possible only by the strong sense of self-knowledge they achieve individually and by their trust in each other. Tschick is finally able to come out to his friend: "er meinte, dass [er Mädchen] beruteilen könnte, weil es ihn nicht interessieren würde ... Das hätter er noch niemanden gesagt, und jetzt hätte er es mir gesagt" (214) [he said he could judge [girls] because he wasn't interested in them ... He had never told anyone, he said, and now he had told me (207)]. And Maik breaks with his own self-definition of coward when he faces his fear of the Autobahn and is overcome with "ein euphorisches Gefühl, ein Gefühl der Unzerstörbarkeit" (215) [a feeling of bliss, a feeling of invincibility (209)]. Weeks later, after their adventure has ended in a car accident, Maik's father tries to coerce Maik to blame it all on Tschick. Maik's father considers it easy to shift the blame to a marginalized person, unable to defend himself. When Maik bravely refuses, his father beats him until he is lying on the floor:

Die Schläge trafen mich überall, ich fiel vom Stuhl und ruschte auf dem Fußboden rum, die Unterarme vorm Gesicht... . Zuletzt lag ich so, dass ich zwischen meinen Armen heraus durchs Terrassenfenster sah. Ich spürte die Fußtritte immer noch, aber es wurdem langsam weniger" (230)

[The blows struck me everywhere, and I fell of my chair and squirmed around on the floor with my forearms in from of my face... . By the end I was lying on the floor in such a way that between my arms I could see out the window to the backyard. I felt the kicks, but they were coming more slowly.]

(Herrndorf 2012, 222)

Despite the severity of violence, Maik tells the judge it was his fault, while Tschick tries to take all the blame, thus bringing their comings-of-age to a close. Unlike the sarcastic use of the word "hero" that Maik uses to self-deprecate in the opening chapters, Maik and Tschick have now become brave heroes for each other.

Maik and Tschick do not define the predominant mores and values of the contemporary German society because there is no clear definition of what these mores could be. Evoking the wild and unconventional life that Wilhelm Meister led more than 200 years before, full of artistry, social critique, and unconventional family structures, Maik and Tschick explore their inner selves and how they fit into their own German society. Maik and Tschick are certainly not ideal citizens, Tschick finishing his formative process in a detention center, Maik vandalizing his own house with the help of his mother. But Maik and Tschick do reach a stage of completeness, of maturity, bravery, and companionship that neither had known before. Diasporic Coming-of-age Novels in particular, but also most variations of the contemporary genre in general, have the amazing power to show the complex formation of social outcasts not so that they may become prescriptive of the ideal male bourgeois social body, as is the case in *David Copperfield*—a difficult enough endeavor—but rather to render complex images of globalized and cosmopolitan societies, and to enable marginalized people to experience bliss, love, and fulfilment—whatever that may mean for them.

Notes

1 Translations from *Selam Berlin* from German to English are mine. All translations from *tschick* are from Tim Mohr's commendable, albeit sometimes over-permissive, translation, *Why We Took the Car*. Whenever I cite the novel *tschick*, two sets of page numbers will appear: the first refers to Herrndorf's original German text, the second refers to the page number in Tim Mohr's English translation.
2 In the original German, the title of the novel *tschick* is purposefully not capitalized. Because all German nouns must be capitalized, the lowercase "t" signifies a clearly aesthetic, but also linguistic, departure from traditional German norms.

3 To clarify, B. Venkat Mani is referring to the *Polinationaler Literatur und Kunstverein (Polikunst)* in the context of his analysis of Aras Ören's literary work. It is relevant to note that Luise von Flotow describes *PoLiKunst* not as a publishing house, as does Mani, but as "an association founded primarily as a movement of foreign artists yet also designed to represent their interests [...] which in an attempt to avoid the usual patronizing treatment *(Bevormundung)* accorded foreigners, restricted its membership to foreign writers/artists" (8). Further, Rita Chin explains that *PoLiKunst* "aimed to use literature to build a grassroots movement of laborers brought together by the shared sociohistorical experiences embedded in the very language *(gastarbeiterdeutsch)* that guest workers used" (Mani 2002, 115).

4 Tim Mohr's translation of "Asi" as "trash" is accurate, but the reasoning behind this translation bears an explanation. Asi is the colloquial contraction of Asozialer, which, at first glance, seems to be closer to the English *antisocial*. However, *antisocial* does not carry in English the connotations that it does in German. *Trash* is a better translation than *antisocial* as it communicates both the derogatory intention of the word and the socioeconomic distinction that Maik is trying to convey. Asozialer also has an implicit association with Nazi Germans, who famously persecuted Asoziale, broadly defined as criminals in general and as Aryans who had intimate relationships with Jewish people, identifying them with the schwarzem Winkel [black triangle] in concentration camps, similarly to how Jewish people were forced to wear a yellow triangle and homosexuals a pink one. Some readers might misinterpret Asi as a short slang term for Asian. This would be an incorrect translation, as evidenced by the fact that both Maik and Isa are called Asi in other parts of the novel.

5 The normalized rather than exotic Lada functions like Tschick's sneakers and other global commodities to signify accurately the globalized setting in which these two characters undergo the enduring process of maturation.

7   The Future of Diasporic Coming-of-age Novels

Ocean Vuong and Gabby Rivera

To delimit what the coming-of-age genre can be and what it can become is an exercise in futility. The literary representation of the internal process by which young people negotiate their independence and interdependence with their social settings has developed in unexpected ways over time and shows no signs of slowing down in variegated geographies. The coming-of-age genre will remain a site for the ever-complex task of handling maturation. In our globalized world, formative processes will continue to serve diasporic individuals as a laboratory for identity, a tool for young people everywhere to process and puzzle over the models of adulthood that globalized media and their local environments offer them. Young readers, theater-goers, and YouTube users are more exposed to conflicting expectations of adulthood than ever before. The COVID-19 pandemic attests to the interconnectedness of humankind in terms of economy, media, or cultural consumption, as well as on our very bodies. In such a context, the Diasporic Coming-of-age Novel continues to develop, written by and about people whose bodies are displaced and whose minds are nurtured by globalized cultural and artistic products.

In order to bring this study to a close this final chapter will discuss the possible futures of the Diasporic Coming-of-age Novel, rather than attempting to narrowly define what the coming-of-age genre is currently or has been in the past. Further, in taking a retrospective view of the study as a whole, with its focus on specific sets of diasporas, this chapter enumerates the essential characteristics of the coming-of-age genre in general and of Diasporic Coming-of-age Novels in particular, since their extensions are so broad. Finally, to make an informed prediction of the incipient branches growing out of the core works analyzed in previous chapters—all works already well established in literary national and global canons—I analyze two recent Diasporic Coming-of-age Novels to parse the possibilities the genre can enable in years to come, set in ever-changing and globally interconnected cities in the U.S.: Ocean Vuong's *On Earth We're Briefly Gorgeous* (2019) and Gabby Rivera's *Juliet Takes a Breath* (2019).

These novels further deepen several analytical opportunities touched upon in previous chapters. First, both novels establish a productive and intersectional dialogue between queerness and diasporic subjectivity. The characters' sexualities, self-identified as gay and lesbian respectively, beg the question of what queerness can symbolize in a diasporic context as protagonists proceed in becoming adults. Queerness within a diasporic community often means a rejection from it due to traditional hetero-normativity, grounded at times in religion, as is the case of the Muslim parents of the protagonist, Hasan, in Yadé Kara's Selam Berlin (see Chapter 6) and patriarchal cultural values, as in the case of Gloria Anzaldúa's account of coming out as a lesbian in *Borderlands / La frontera* (foundational to Chapter 3). As Eithne Luibhéid explains, in the general context of migration, "queer is used to mark the fact that many standard sexuality categories and social relations upheld colonialist, xenophobic, racist, and sexist regimes" (Luibhéid 2005, xi). Unsurprisingly, any sexuality that falls outside of heteronormative and patriarchal rules has also been a cause of migration, as is the case in E.M. Forster's novel Maurice (see Chapter 2) and a reason for host societies to reject migrants: "For example, … lesbians and gays were barred for decades from entering the United States as legal immigrants. Some scholars date lesbian and gay exclusion from 1917, when people labeled as 'constitutional psychopathic inferiors' were first barred from entering the United States…. This category included "persons with abnormal sexual instincts" (xii).

Secondly, these novels take place mostly outside of the usual cities that have been associated with large diasporic groups, and are thus less concerned with the representation of insular communities that band together. In *On Earth We're Briefly Gorgeous*, the Vietnamese protagonist and narrator Little Dog undergoes his formative process mainly in the urban scape of Hartford, Connecticut and a nearby rural space: a tobacco farm. Unlike the home of Esperanza Cordero in Sandra Cisneros's *The House on Mango Street* (studied in Chapter 4), Little Dog's apartment, which he shares with his mother and grandmother, is not located within a singularly Vietnamese diasporic community. Instead, the diasporic community is comprised of people of different national origins, and dwell both in his urban space of "the predominantly Latinx neighborhood of Franklin Avenue" where "no one made a double take at the yellow-white woman speaking her own tongue" and the rural space of the farm, where "undocumented migrants from Mexico and Central America," as well as from "the Dominican Republic" and even "a white guy […] from Colchester" work together (Vuong 2019, 51, 59, 88). Similarly, the eponymous protagonist and narrator in *Juliet Takes a Breath* undergoes her formative process in Portland, Oregon, where she "had no one, just me" (Rivera 2019, 102), rather than in her native Bronx where her Puerto Rican community is so tight and insular, she explains, "there isn't enough air to breathe" (14). Because Little Dog is not part of an exclusively Vietnamese diasporic enclave, and Juliet undergoes her short, summer-long, formative process away from home, these novels enable the re-evaluation of the notion of diaspora, to consider whether a diaspora needs to be defined by a geographically-bound community and, further, to ponder whether the category of Diasporic Coming-of-age Novel can encompass such experiences of individual (rather than communitarian) alterity.

Thirdly, these novels enable the analysis of one possible future for readers who are diasporic individuals who, although still part of a diaspora rather than lone migrants, are not necessarily geographically bound to a linguistically or culturally distinct neighborhood or area, and other readers who want to gain some insights into these experiences. In this sense, the immediacy of social interactions in a single-diasporic community is minimized. The novels are still diasporic, however, because the protagonists frame their experiences of alterity, and the expectations of their parents, as dependent on Vietnamese and Puerto Rican ancestries respectively. As Ricardo Ortíz explains in his definition of diaspora, the term "necessarily suggests identification with a group, *however scattered*, committed to the same work of cultural retention, reproduction, and revival of a home culture in an alien, foreign, 'host' setting" (Ortíz 2017, no page number). Little Dog and Juliet are certainly scattered in smaller urban centers than the ones in the previous chapters of this study (such as New York, Chicago, London, and Berlin) and, yet, they retain their connection to their national ancestry, and thus their diasporic community, as an important anchor for the development and negotiation of their identities. As well, in profoundly reflecting on their relationship with their mothers, they underscore the multi-generational nature of diaspora, another key category for the definition of the concept according to Ortíz (2017, no page number).

Finally, it is important to mention in the context of this final chapter that coming-of-age narratives, in general, do not constitute necessarily a genre of resistance. Because coming-of-age narratives do not flourish only in the context of marginalized and diasporic literature, they can be conservative and hegemonic. Storytelling corporations like *Disney* and *DreamWorks*, continue to rely on the appeal of the coming-of-age genre to fill theaters worldwide with simple stories that largely adhere to the archetypal plot of traditional *Bildungsromane*, studied in depth in Chapters 1 and 2. These corporations use the genre to tell and retell formative processes with characters who resemble each other even in their physical traits. From Jasmine in *Aladdin* (1992), to Mulan in *Mulan* (1998), to Rapunzel in *Tangled* (2010), and Elsa in *Frozen* (2013), thin, wide-eyed, dainty-nosed heroes and princesses, all resembling each other regardless of their origin, nationality, or ethnic heritage, find successful accommodations, becoming citizens, workers, and often spouses. The further industrialization of the production of coming-of-age novels is certainly a possible future of the genre, which can nonetheless coexist with more nuanced variations of the genre, as are the novels studied in this chapter.

Three Categories: Coming-of-age Novels, Traditional *Bildungsromane*, and Diasporic Coming-of-age Novels

Industrialized versions of coming-of-age narratives level the plots as much as they level the physical features of the protagonists in order to provide an often-inaccurate, but perhaps well-intentioned, display of the globalized world that more and more of their audience is in fact experiencing. The coming-of-age genre, in its bare essentials, encompasses novels about a young person who, through a formative process, becomes an adult. Youth may take on several meanings, as some novels begin with infancy and even birth (such as Charles Dickens's *David Copperfield* and Zadie Smith's *White Teeth*) while others begin when the protagonist is already an adolescent or a young adult (as in the case of Hanif Kureishi's *The Buddha of Suburbia* and Wolfgang Herrndorf's *tschick*). Just as varied as the notion of youth can be, adulthood is defined in very different ways, especially in Diasporic Coming-of-age Novels, where the characters are frequently unable to access legal markers of maturity, such as citizenship, despite undergoing a formative process. Instead of these legal markers, the characters are able to define adulthood in their own terms, sometimes with markers of self-love, friendship, and resistance to systems of oppression. In addition to this simplest of plots, the coming-of-age genre as a whole foregrounds the formative process as a main theme and driver of plot. Throughout this formative process, readers become familiar with the internal life of the protagonist because the forces that drive the formative process are internal rather than external.

The originating iteration of the coming-of-age genre is the traditional *Bildungsroman*, which, in addition to the formative process and the internal focus on the narration, also forefronts the struggles of the middle class. Traditional *Bildungsromane* (studied in depth in Chapters 1 and 2) necessarily have clear mentors who are idyllic role models with few, or no, reprehensible defects. They end in marriage, as a symbolic bind with the social whole, and when the protagonists achieve an accommodation as citizens and workers that the readers are meant to imitate. While there are contemporary examples that fit these characteristics, usually mass-produced by corporate broadcasters in the media of film and television, traditional *Bildungsromane* represent only a small part of the capacious coming-of-age genre.

Diasporic Coming-of-age Novels disregard many of the conventions of traditional *Bildungsromane*. Instead, framed in diasporas, they present characters who lack clear models of adulthood. Their parents are often models of disidentification, especially when they are first generation migrants, because they frequently uphold old-fashioned worldviews that do not match the values and mores of the host society. This disidentification is particularly clear in *The Buddha of Suburbia* and *White Teeth* (studied in Chapter 3) where the protagonists characterize their parents as strict, narrow-minded, and sometimes even embarrassingly antiquated, frequently because of their religious practices. Because neither their parents nor the adults in their community function as idyllic role models, the characters are forced to piecemeal their models from the people around them, including their peers. For the same reason, they must negotiate contradictory expectations from their diasporic community and the host society, and then decide which values and mores they adopt and internalize, and which are contradictory to their own notion of identity. As reflected by the wide variety of novels in this book, the outcomes of these formative processes are varied. It is most often hopeful, as the characters understand their identity in nuanced terms, but it can end in the heterotopias of prison and the streets, or death. In the particular cases of novels such as the ones in this chapter, the characters must also address their intersectionality; that is, the combined systems of power that marginalize them simultaneously in terms of class, gender, sexuality, and race.

Commingling, Scattered Diasporas

Ocean Vuong's novel displays an urgent need to parse the recent migration element of the Vietnamese diaspora in the U.S. as central to the lived experience of the protagonist Little Dog and his family. Migration is central to Little Dog's identity. As Chih-ming Wang explains, the fall of Saigon in 1975, part of the "infamous war in Vietnam," and subsequent diasporas from Vietnam, Cambodia, and Laos, are an ever-present trauma for refugee families who were "violently disrupted, dislocated, and even irreparably destroyed" (Wang 2013, 161). In this context, Renny Cristopher explains that Vietnamese-U.S. literature aims to "bridge the gap between their pasts, their current lives as exiles, and the English-language readers of their countries of refuge" (Christopher 1995, 32). And, indeed, memory and the consequences of an "unspeakable and irrepressible" violent past are central themes of Little Dog's formative process (Wang 2013, 162). Although the Vietnamese diaspora has a shorter literary history than some of the ones studied previously, it is extremely wealthy in memoirs and fictionalized accounts of migration and formative processes split between nations: to name a few, Le Ly Hayslip's *When Heaven and Earth Changed Places* (1989), Lê Thị Diễm Thúy's *The Gangster We Are All Looking For* (2003), Viet Thanh Nguyen's Pulitzer-Prize-winning *The Sympathizer* (2015) and, more recently, Thi Bui's graphic novel *The Best We Could Do* (2017). Viet Thanh Nguyen's work on migration is particularly and profoundly analytical of the colonialism and war that intersect the stories of Vietnamese diasporic communities in the U.S. In his essay "I Love America. That's Why I Have to Tell the Truth About It," he explains that being "American but born in Vietnam [his] origins are inseparable from three wars: the one the Vietnamese fought against the French; the one the Vietnamese fought against each other; and the one the U.S. fought in Vietnam" (Nguyen 2018, no page number). Further, although he identifies the U.S. nationalistic discourse on the war to justify it as a "a noble, if possibly flawed, example of

American good intentions," he asserts the war was "just one manifestation of a centuries-long expansion of the American empire that began from its own colonial birth and ran through the frontier, the American West, Mexico, Hawaii, Guam, Puerto Rico, the Philippines, Japan, Korea, Vietnam and now the Middle East" (no page number). The diasporas described in this chapter are thus a direct consequence of the American imperialist project. But, unlike Diasporic Coming-of-age Novels of the past, the authors of these novels are acutely aware of this colonialist history, a theme both Little Dog and Juliet address and parse overtly.

I analyze some of the characteristics of the Puerto Rican diaspora in Chapter 5 in a reading of Piri Thomas's *Down These Mean Streets* (1967). In this problematic and homophobic novel, the main dilemma the protagonist Piri faces is how to reconcile his Puerto Rican ancestry with the fact that the larger New York City context regards him as Black-American and the impossibility of intersectionality in his experience. Like Piri, the titular character Juliet explored in this chapter travels outside New York in order to explore her identity in other U.S. settings. Unlike Piri, however, she ponders her place in the social whole as a "citizen yet foreigner" (González 2011, 81). Importantly, Piri does not reflect on the diasporic dimension of his community. He does not discuss the migration of his ancestors, perhaps because migration is not a part of his lived experience. Conversely, Juliet and her queer "no-labels" cousin Ava discuss the history of Puerto Rico and of "banana republics" at length (89). Even though migration is not a part of Juliet's lived experience, she recognizes the importance that it has on her present. As Juan González explains, only Puerto Ricans

> among all Latin Americans arrive here [in the U.S.] as U.S. citizens, without the need of a visa or resident alien card. But this unique advantage, a direct result of Puerto Rico's colonial status, has also led to unexpected obstacles. Despite our de jure citizenship, the average North American, whether white or black, continues to regard Puerto Ricans as de facto foreigners.
>
> (González 2011, 81)

Juliet knows the tension of belonging and not, as she is integrated in the U.S. body politic but her latinidad, race, and alterity are fetishized by her white mentor, Portland feminist writer, Harlowe Brisbane.

In *On Earth*, Little Dog's autodiegetic narrative neither opens with his infancy nor closes with a level of accommodation corresponding to his adulthood. Instead, rather than a linear and chronologic narrative, the book follows a cyclical timeline, which, like history, "moves in a spiral, not the line we have come to expect" (Vuong 2019, 27). The author implies a cultural and personal conception of time that doubles as an explanation of the generic manipulation essential to the coming-of-age genre. The narrator explains that, in his conception of time, memory plays a crucial role for the development of the self not only as important events happen, but as he remembers them, his present path affected by the presence of the past: "We travel through time in a circular trajectory, our distance increasing from an epicenter only to return again" (27). Consequent to this circular conception of time, the novel as a whole jumps back and forth, as the narrator describes short vignettes of his inner life with his mother, the primary addressee of the novel. The string that connects the vignettes comes not in chronology but in a free and freeing association of ideas. For example, when Little Dog comes out as gay to his mother in part two of three, the narrative of this conversation is constantly interrupted (and thus intersected) by the narrative of his realization of his sexual identity.

However circular and anti-chronologic the story (or fabula, to use the terms of Russian formalism and so often invoked in coming-of-age novels), the plot (or *syuzhet*) begins in Vietnam, develops in Hartford, and ends when the protagonist becomes a writer in New York City, an ending reminiscent of both Charles Dickens's traditional *Bildungsroman, David Copperfield*, and, more closely, Cisneros's *The House on Mango Street*, where the protagonists become writers at the end of their formative processes. Because my aim is to analyze the formative process, I opt to piece Little Dog's coming-of-age chronologically. Little Dog's plot does not only narrate his own story, but also that of his grandmother Lan and his mother Hong, or Rose. Like the knights of Proto-*Bildungsromane* of medieval Europe (studied in Chapter 1), Little Dog finds crucial parts of the puzzle of his identity in the stories of not just his parents, which remain highly significant mentors, but also his ancestors. His grandmother's life is importantly intersected by the U.S. military presence in Vietnam. We learn that Lan, a name meaning Lily that she gives herself, "having been born nameless," after escaping from an arranged marriage "to a man three times her age," becomes a "sex worker for American GIs on R&R" (Vuong 2019, 39, 46). The history of U.S. soldiers' perpetuation of sexual violence in Vietnam leaves a mark on Little Dog's racial heritage because the result of his grandmother Lan's unvolitional sex work with U.S. soldiers, itself a product of the systemic and intersectional oppression of poor Asian women before and during the Vietnam war, is a mixed-race daughter, Rose, whose father is a nameless soldier.

In a similar way to his grandmother Lan, Little Dog also choses his name. However, unlike Lan, he had "another name—the name I was born with" (20). This original name, given by a shaman, "means Patriotic Leader of the Nation" (20). Little Dog's father, a physically abusive drunk who almost beats Rose to death once they move to the U.S., beams at the thought of his son becoming "the leader of Vietnam" (21). In the U.S. the name acquires a mocking irony, a reminder of the devastation of Vietnam and his father's violence. Instead, Little Dog is a sweet name that protects him. The narrator explains in a long section that warrants full quotation, that the name is given by his female ancestors, and represents their protective love:

I have and have had many names. Little Dog was what Lan called me. What made a woman who named herself and her daughter after flowers call her grandson a dog? A woman who watches out for her own, that's who. As you know, in the village where Lan grew up, a child, often the smallest or weakest of the flock, as I was, is named after the most despicable things: demon, ghost child, pig snout, monkey-born, buffalo head, bastard—little dog being the more tender one. Because evil spirits, roaming the land for healthy, beautiful children, would hear the name of something hideous and ghastly being called in for supper and pass over the house, sparing the child. To love something, then, is to name it after something so worthless it might be left untouched—and alive. A name, thin as air, can also be a shield. A Little Dog shield.

(Vuong 2019, 18)

Interlaced in his own story, Little Dog shows that his identity is intersected by the memory of violence of the Vietnamese war, a fact that connects his experience of that of the larger Vietnamese diaspora in the U.S., regardless of how geographically scattered it might be. He does so primarily through his mother's history, especially in relation to her light skin color and trauma. Because Rose has lighter skin, she undergoes violent racist acts at the hands of her Vietnamese peers: "When you were a girl in Vietnam, the neighborhood kids would take a spoon to your arms, shouting, 'Get the white off her, get the white off her!'" (Vuong 2019, 64) Little Dog inherits Rose's experiences of discrimination and war not only in genetic terms, but also because her Post-Traumatic Stress Disorder (PTSD) manifests in nightmares and physical abuse. As Little Dog explains, "The first time you hit me, I must have been four" (13). He associates the repeated home violence with PTSD: "I read that parents suffering from PTSD are more likely to hit their children. Perhaps there is a monstrous origin to it, after all. Perhaps to lay hands on your child is to prepare him for war" (13). In this way, the trauma of the past is an ingredient of the future. Although the war is over, Little Dog feels its violence in his own skin. Rose's work in a nail salon, where she must constantly apologize to wealthier white women customers, contributes to the deterioration of her mental health.

Three salient events in Little Dog's own formative process serve to parse his negotiation with identity and mark important moments of maturity in his formation: the first time he stands up to his mother's physical violence, his relationship to Trevor, and when he comes out to his mother. Vuong contextualizes the first event situated at home within violent class struggle in the U.S. In school, Little Dog is relentlessly bullied because of his race, short stature, and apparent femininity. He explains that the kids "would call me *freak, fairy, fag*" and physically assault him, slapping him in groups and telling him to "speak English" (14, 24). It is significant that these experiences of alterity happen at school, since they show that this hegemonic institution, where children ideally receive a formal education not only in knowledge but also in morality, marginalizes rather than educates Little Dog. The school site is a staple of racist and homophobic harassment present in other Diasporic Coming-of-age Novels such as *The Buddha of Suburbia* (see Chapter 3), *White Teeth* (see Chapter 3), *The House on Mango Street* (see Chapter 4), and *tschick* (see Chapter 6).

Beyond the context of school, Little Dog experiences the embarrassment of his broken English when, in a butcher shop, he is unable to translate the word "oxtail" for his mother. The linguistic barrier so common to many diasporic communities moves her to uncomfortably act like a cow in an attempt to communicate with the butcher, much to Little Dog's embarrassment and the butcher's amusement. It is because of these joint experiences of marginalization that Little Dog begins his "career as our family's official interpreter [… in order to] fill in our blanks, our silences, stutters, whenever I could" (32). Simultaneously as Little Dog finds his voice as the family's translator, he finds the voice to stand up to both his mother and bullies at school: "The time, when I finally said stop. Your hand in the air, my cheek bone stinging from the first blow. 'Stop, Ma. Quit it. Please.' I looked at you hard, the way I had learned, by then, to look into the eyes of my *bullies*" [my emphasis] (11). Stopping the violence inflicted on his body is an important marker of maturity that is intimately related to his mastery of the English language. It thus comes as no surprise that his selected path into adulthood is in the study of letters. The older narrator, a Little Dog who is already "twenty-eight years old, 5ft 4 in tall, 112lbs" (10), explains to his mother about his career path:

> I told you how I came to be a writer. How I, the first in our family to go to college, squandered it on a degree in English. How I fled my shitty high school to spend my days in New York lost in library stacks, reading obscure texts by dead people, most of whom never dreamed a face like mine floating over their sentences—and least of all that those sentences would save me.
>
> (Vuong 2019, 15)

The sentences he reads save his life in very material terms, since they enable him to find a voice that can stop violence, but also in a metaphorical sense, they give him the language to understand his emotions and puzzle over his process of formation.

Love is another key event of coming-of-age. Little Dog's relationship with Trevor enables him to explore his sexual desire and, importantly, to come to the realization that his sexuality is an integral part of who he is. Little Dog first meets Trevor when, in the summer after his fourteenth birthday, Little Dog finds a job in the farm that belongs to Trevor's grandfather, Mr. Buford. The year is 2003, marked in Little Dog's memory because "Bush had already declared war on Iraq" (Vuong 2019, 86). In the farm, most of the workers are "undocumented migrants from Mexico and Central America, save for one, Nico, who was from the Dominican Republic [and] Rick, a white guy in his twenties from Colchester, who, it was said, was on the sex offender list" (88). The workers in the farm are paid "under the table, in cash," a fact that is merely convenient for Little Dog but necessary for his co-workers (86). Most of the workers in the farm are criminalized by the mere fact of their existence. In particular, the undocumented migrants are experiencing what Lisa Marie Cacho describes as "social death," that is, the ineligibility of certain people for personhood due to their "(il)legal statuses within U.S. law" that render them "legally ineligible ... not just racialized but rightless, living nonbeings, or, in Judith Butler's words, as 'something living that is other than life'" (6). Among them, Little Dog is labeled a "Chinito," a label that he does not resist even though he is aware it means little Chinese person in Spanish (87). Little Dog does not correct Manny, the Salvadorian man who misidentifies him, because it is his first day and wants to get along with the other workers, even though that means a flattening of his identity that is not necessarily hostile but just ignorant. This name leveling corresponds with the similarity these characters representative of diverse diasporic communities have with each other insofar as they want to help their families and must fend for themselves.

It is in this widely diasporic setting that Little Dog meets Trevor, a high school junior two years older than himself, grey-eyed and tall. The first time Little Dog sees him, Trevor is wearing a "metal army helmet" that reminds him of the soldiers his grandmother once had to work for (Vuong 2019, 94). Trevor shares with Little Dog a common hatred of their abusive and violent fathers. As Little Dog explains, Trevor was "working the farm to get away from his vodka-soaked old man," another violent drunk father, something Little Dog and Trevor have in common. This initial connection sparks a friendship that enables Little Dog to understand Trevor as a complex person and see past his prejudice against white men:

> Up until then I didn't think a white boy could hate anything about his life. I wanted to know him through and through by that very hate. Because that's what you give anyone who sees you, I thought. You take their hatred head-on and cross it, like a bridge, to face them, to enter them. 'I hate my dad, too,' I said to my hands, now still and dark with chain grease.
>
> (Vuong 2019, 94)

The longer they know each other, "for two more summers after that first one," the more Little Dog's feelings start to deepen, until he reveals in synesthetic beauty that it was color, not words, that he feels for Trevor (106). The first time they have sex, they "didn't fuck at all" since there is no penetration (113). Instead, high on "weed and cocaine," Trevor "penetrates" Little Dog's cupped hands, an experience that, although a "mock attempt," "was *real*" [emphasis in original] (114). The attention to colors and the sensations they spark or can symbolize is a common motif in Diasporic Coming-of-age Novels; Toni

Morrison's *The Bluest Eye* (1970) and Zadie Smith's *White Teeth* foreground the necessity of color as symbol in their titles.

Importantly for the concurrent formative process that Trevor is undergoing, when they "switch roles" so that Trevor is the one who makes the fist around Little Dog's penis, Trevor reacts with fright: "'I can't. I just—I mean …' He spoke into the wall. 'I dunno. I don't wanna feel like a girl. Like a bitch. I can't, man. I'm sorry, it's not for me—' He paused, wiped his nose. 'It's for you. Right?'" (120). This initial dread in performing an act that Trevor sees as feminine foreshadows his incapacity to accept his sexual identity and his eventual tragic end in a drug overdose: "Trevor was alone in his room when he died, surrounded by posters of Led Zeppelin. Trevor was twenty-two. Trevor was" (Vuong 2019, 178). As Little Dog poignantly explains of Trevor immediately after he tries but fails to bottom with his hands, "This was also called dying" (121).

However important these first attempts at sex are, the most life-changing moment in their relationship comes a little after that, when they have penetrative sex for the first time, the climactic moment of the novel. Little Dog feels utterly vulnerable, "more naked than I was with my clothes off—I was inside out" (203). The coming-of-age novel always relies on the inner life of the character as the drive of plot and main theme. Here, the metaphorical most inner and guarded parts of the character come to the outside, truly a stunning metaphor of what Diasporic Coming-of-age Novels enable their protagonists to achieve: a profound knowledge of their inner selves. This experience of sex is particularly vulnerable for Little Dog because, not knowing "how to prepare myself," he has a bowel movement during intercourse (203). At this, Little Dog immediately feels like he has tainted Trevor "with his faggotry, the filthiness of our act exposed by my body's failure to contain itself" (203). However, contrary to Little Dog's expectation that Trevor would react angry and cruel, Trevor takes him to the river and, in a "wordless act … of mercy" cleans Little Dog's body with his tongue, while reassuring Little Dog that he was "good as always" (205–206). The image of his clean body in the river recalls but subverts Rose's earlier story or cruel harassment when children in Vietnam would take spoons to her arms, shouting, "Get the white off her, get the white off her!" (63). In Little Dog's case, however, the cleaning is a moment of enormous tenderness. Little Dog experiences a cleanliness until then unknown: it is okay to be who he is and to have accidents. In this moment, he knows himself to deserve warmth and kindness.

Years later, in one of their final conversation before Trevor's death, the following exchange happens. Little Dog is able to accept his sexuality while Trevor characterizes it as a phase:

> "Is it true though?" His swing kept creaking. "You think you'll be really gay, like, forever? I mean," the swing stopped, "I think me … I'll be good in a few years, you know?"

I couldn't tell if by "really" he meant very gay or truly gay.

"I think so," I said, not knowing what I meant.

(Vuong 2019, 188)

This exchange functions much as does the very significant addition of nuancing the best characteristics of marriage that *Pride and Prejudice* brought to the coming-of-age genre. Their relationship and this moment both show that one is not just gay, but can choose the traditional male, traditional female, taking turns, or undifferentiated gay and that gay can be stubbornly understood as temporary or permanent. The phrase "not knowing what I meant" leaves future possibilities of the expression open rather than capitulating to some culture's drive for closed definitions of sexual identity. While Little Dog's transitions into a more fulfilled adulthood and becomes a writer when he moves to New York, Trevor's dream of going to school to become a physical therapist are crushed by an overdose of heroine laced with fentanyl.

The third salient moment that marks Little Dog's maturity, at the age of seventeen, is when he comes out to his mother in the "bright Dunkin' Donuts, two cups of black coffee" steaming between them (Vuong 2019, 129). *Dunkin' Donuts* seems an odd public place for such a private conversation. Yet it is purposefully humdrum, like all fast food chains, an easily recognizable simulacrum of a copy. Its ordinary nature contrasts with the extraordinary news—at least for Rose—that Little Dog is about to reveal. Rose knows he would not have met her there if it was not a momentous occasion. When Little Dogs starts rambling about doughnuts and croissants, Rose asks him to get to the point: "Say what you have to say, Little Dog" (129).

His process of coming out is an important conclusion to the confusing realization of his queer identity. However confusing, unlike the painful wrestling with homosexuality that characters undergo in other coming-of-age novels cited in this study (see Chapter 2, E.M. Forster's *Maurice* and Chapter 5, Piri Thomas's *Down These Mean Streets*), Little Dog accepts his queerness with a certain ease more frequent in recent novels such as *Juliet Takes a Breath*. Instead of using the Vietnamese word for gay, which, Little Dog explains is "pê-dê—from the French pédé, short for pedophile," he simply explains, "I don't like girls" (130). Rose reacts at first with fear: "'They'll kill you,' you shook your head, 'you know that'" (130). Even if she is unaware of the terminology, she is keenly aware of social violence and knows that identity is a social construct. She then shares a secret of her own that conveys her vulnerability, that she was once forced to abort a boy that would have been Little Dog's older brother. Rose draws a parallel between the social violence that Little Dog could experience and her own story of forced abortion, a violation of her reproductive rights made possible by the disenfranchisement of her class and gender. After throwing up and a quiet ride home, Rose quietly accepts her son, not with words, but with a gesture of love: "I'll pull my chair and, taking off my hood, a sprig of hay caught there from the barn weeks before will stick out from my black hair. You will reach over, brush it off, and shake your head as you take in the son you decided to keep" (140). At the very end of the novel, much like Karim Amir in *The Buddha of Suburbia*, Little Dog explains that his family is the thing he wants to run toward.

This novel, the narrator's letter to his mother, at times a collection of poems and short aphorisms, unlocks what the coming-of-age genre can be. It underscores the hybridity of language while it breaks open the definition of alterity in general and re-signifies diaspora in particular. Little Dog's cyclical self-history of himself portrays a scattered diaspora unified not by geographic proximity, but rather by the memory of war, their common language, and experiences of class marginalization. However, his real and lived experience of diasporic communities is not only that of a Vietnamese community in the nail salon or televised U.S. Vietnamese communities that include Tiger Woods, but also of his Latinx community in Hartford and the criminalized workers in the tobacco farm. This points to an experience where distinct diasporas intermingle with each other, in ways that defy the national distinctions of diasporic communities. As such, Little Dog is participating in a cultural exchange largely absent in previous chapters: not only of the host society with the diasporic community, but between diasporic communities. Little Dog as a farm worker and his mother in the nail shop have more in common with the undocumented workers in the farm than with the wealthy clients at the nail salon. Further, Little Dog's experience of love happens with a white American boy, reminiscent of the soldiers in Vietnam, who also finds refuge in the farm from his abusive father. Alterity in this novel is thus a set of experiences that bring people together despite their variegated backgrounds and national origins, a new anti-national possibility of Diasporic Coming-of-age Novels.

As much as Little Dog focuses on the past, Juliet Milagros Palante looks to the future. Instead of starting her story in her parents or grandparents' migrations, she focuses on her own process of becoming, not grounded primarily in memory, but rather on what is to come, her hope of self-realization. Even though she eventually discusses the history of Puerto Rico and the term "banana republics," neither she nor her immediate family experience migration from Puerto Rico to the mainland U.S., so migration is thus not at all key to her formative process. She does not look to her parents primarily as mentors or models, especially not their migratory past, but instead to the writings of Harlowe Brisbane, the fictional and famous white feminist author of the second-wave feminist spoof *Raging Flower: Empowering Your Pussy by Empowering Your Mind*.[1] Juliet's focus on what is to come is even inscribed in her last name: Palante (from Pa'lante), which, the novel glosses as a "Puerto Rican slang, also used in Latin America and other parts of the Caribbean. Contraction of *para Adelante*, meaning to move forward. A call out into the world for our people to always keep it moving" (Rivera 2019, v).

In focusing on the construction of the future self as a driver of the formative process, author Gabby Rivera invites a possibility of the coming-of-age genre that has been largely disregarded in other Diasporic Coming-of-age Novels: the possibility of an overtly didactic text. Juliet represents the possibility of Diasporic Coming-of-age Novels to focus on emerging and intersectional identities that only partially regard a/the diasporic past as the metaphorical site to question and ponder multigenerational and communitarian identities. Juliet's naïveté throughout the novel makes her a relatable protagonist to young readers who, like her, are in the process of learning what concepts such as feminism, gender, and intersectionality mean and how they can assist them in their own formative processes. The reader thus learns alongside her. Her naïveté, however, does not make her a dumb or simple character. On the contrary, Juliet has a profound inner life as she tries to understand her place in her family and the U.S. as a queer woman of color. She is brave in leaving her background behind in order to find new mentors and ideas across the country, thus reminiscent of the heroic dimension of the coming-of-age genre.

Much like Little Dog, there are three defining events that serve to analyze her formative process and the new possibilities she opens for the genre. First is her restlessness and decision to do an internship with Harlowe in Portland. The second is her realization of Harlowe's flaws, her subsequent search for multiple mentors, and her final reconciliation with Harlowe. The third is, like Little Dog, her coming out to her mother Mariana and the possibility this implies for her to understand her sexuality. The formative processes of queer characters involve, more often than not, a form of coming out as a marker of maturity and a signifier of adulthood since it is an important moment of self-affirmation, frequently after a confusing process of experimentation, misunderstandings, and a resistance to heteronormative violence (whether it be more subtly systemic and ideologic as is the case of Wolfgang Herrndorf's *tschick*, or more obvert and criminalized, as are the cases of Forster's *Maurice* and Reinaldo Arenas's *Antes que anochezca* [*Before Night Falls*]).

Unlike Little Dog's decade-long coming-of-age, Juliet's is short, spanning only the summer of 2003. Juliet is nineteen years old (born in September 6, 1983). The novel begins chronologically with the letter that Juliet writes to Harlowe in order to explain her desire for an internship. In it, she recognizes that diasporic communities such as her own are oppressed by systemic poverty and marginalization: "my neighborhood is stuck in a sanctioned and fully funded cycle of poverty" (Rivera 2019, 4–5). It is important to mention that although her neighborhood is characterized as poor, her own family seems to be middle-class. Although Juliet does not explain her class background in detail, we are made aware that her parents have college degrees, that one of her aunts, Titi Wepa, is a police officer and the other, Titi Penny (the mother of Juliet's queer cousin Ava), married into a wealthy family in Miami (89). Juliet herself is no stranger to higher education. However, she wants to leave the Bronx, where most people never leave, in order to trade "pancakes for peace," that is, the suffocating contentment of the familiar (symbolized in comfort food) for the peace implied at the far end of growth. At this moment, Juliet defines herself as a "closeted Puerto Rican baby-dyke from the Bronx" in need of a hand, wanting to "fight the good fight," which she understands to be the fight of feminism, a word that nevertheless sounds "too white, too structured, too foreign; something I can't claim" (3). Even in this initial letter, Juliet points to the exclusionary nature that she associates with feminism, and foreshadows her necessity to come to her own intersectional definition of the term. Importantly, Juliet announces her admiration for her own mother who is, throughout the story, only a partial mentor. Juliet explains that at the same time that her mother balances "the rhythm of an entire family on her shoulders," she is "working on a master's degree," and rhetorically asks: "That's a feminist, right? But my mom still irons my dad's socks" (3). Juliet recognizes her mother's strength and only partially rejects what she sees as a symbol of the traditional gender norms that she does not want to replicate. Her eventual nuance of her definition of feminism resolves her question, as she is able to understand it as a complex term that encompasses varied experiences of liberation and empowerment (that also include her little brother), not exclusive to a white wealthy person such as Harlowe.

Her initial restlessness and the myriad questions she asks about her identity in that initial letter set her formative process into motion. This is the curiosity inherent in all coming-of-age novels, to understand one's own identity and place in the world. It is a mostly internal process nonetheless stirred and affected by the expectations of others and their mentorship. Her formative process begins in full when she leaves the Bronx for Portland—not before tempestuously and spontaneously coming out to her family, a point I will return to later.

Juliet's first impression of Harlowe is overall positive. Harlowe seems like a perfect role model like the ones of traditional *Bildungsromane*: a moral and successful adult that the young protagonist ought to imitate. Harlowe is compassionate and kind, and immediately praises Juliet's "fresh aura" and tells her that she "must be the sun" (Rivera 2019, 45, 46). The cracks in Harlowe's foundation start to show when Juliet attends an Octavia Butler Writing Workshop with Harlowe and her primary lover Maxine: "confident, Black, and vibrating with good-ass energy" (94). During the workshop, two white women express their frustration at not receiving attention from the majority Black group. One of them explains: "It's like in my feminism we're equals. Why does any group have to have the dominant voice? I know reverse racism isn't technically real, but, like, this kinda felt like that" (111). At this, Juliet and Maxine roll their eyes, but Harlowe decides to address them:

> It's not about having a "dominant voice." It's about women of color owning their own spaces and their vices being treated with dignity and

respect... . Our entire existence is constantly being validated and yeah, we have lots of shit to deal with because of the patriarchy. But for goodness sake, check your privilege. We're the ones that need to give women of color space for their voices.

(Rivera 2019, 111)

While Harlowe's intention is clearly benign, Maxine becomes enraged at the idea that white women need to give women of color space: "Y'all don't need to give us anything," Maxine explains (113). This event shows Harlowe's misunderstanding of intersectional oppression, which creates a distance between her and Maxine, eventually leading to their breakup.

However, the brunt of Harlowe's well-intentioned but negatively-impacting misunderstanding of intersectionality comes later in the summer, when Harlowe is confronted about her racial insensibility in a reading of her new book in Portland's landmark bookstore *Powell's City of Books*. It is important to mention that, at this moment, Juliet has recently gone through a breakup with her white girlfriend Lainie, who has found a new interest in a young woman called Sarah and violently broke up with Juliet with a harsh letter, so Juliet is particularly sensitive to the violence inflicted on her. In Harlowe's reading, Maxine's lover Zaira perniciously asks:

Harlowe, do you think that tacking on a message of unity and solidarity for queer and trans women of color at the end of Raging Flower was powerful enough to make a difference? ... Do you think that this message is enough to rally non-white women to your particular brand of feminism? To be your blood sisters?"

(Rivera 2019, 205)

Harlowe, visibly uncomfortable, responds with a statement that dishonestly stereotypes and hurtfully flattens Juliet's identity, robbing Juliet of the power to expound her own self:

Do I think that queer and trans women of color will read my work and feel like they see themselves in my words? Not necessarily, but some will and do. I mean, I know someone right now sitting in this room who is a testament to this, someone who isn't white, who grew up in the ghetto, someone who is lesbian and Latina and fought for her whole life to make it out of the Bronx alive and get an education. She grew up in poverty and without any privilege. No support from her family, especially after coming out, and that person is here today. That person is Juliet Milagros Palante, my assistant and friend, who came all the way from the Bronx to be a better feminist, and all that is because of *Raging Flower*.

(Rivera 2019, 206)

Juliet is understandably crushed. Her mentor has betrayed her. Not only does Harlowe's speech show a profound misunderstanding of who Juliet is and how intersectionality operates as a combination of systems of oppression that make Juliet's experiences fundamentally different from Harlowe's, the speech is also ridden with half-truths and flat-out lies. Juliet's family has not abandoned her, especially her aunts and cousin. As I mentioned before, her family is not as poor and uneducated as Harlowe makes it out to be. And, especially, Juliet is not there to be a better feminist in Harlowe's definition of feminism, but to grow and forge her own self, Harlowe's feminism being only a part of the immensely complex process of growing up.

Juliet continues to use the tool of geographical displacement for self-exploration as she flies to Miami to meet her aunt Titi Penny and cousin Ava. These women and role models enable Juliet to further nuance her understanding of feminism, as Ava explains that Harlowe's feminism is imperfect, characterized by "white supremacy or second-wave white feminism" (223). Titi Penny also helps, as she reveals that she, herself, is not entirely straight, having fell in love with "our super's daughter" Magdalena in the context of her past as an activist in the Young Lords (232). Having learned other, more flexible, forms of queerness from her relatives and a deeper understanding of feminism, Juliet returns to Portland to finish her internship. In a moment of catharsis and maturity, Juliet tells Harlowe that her admitting her racism and apologizing is simply not enough, that she must do better. Juliet says, "This is a moment of reckoning. I love you, but I refuse to continue loving someone who won't be real about their shit and change their actions to match" (295). In forcing Harlowe to this moment of reckoning, Juliet finds her voice and becomes a teacher to her mentor. In the final pages of the novel, Juliet returns to the medium of the letter, but this time she writes to herself, in contrast to the initial timidity of her letter to Harlowe: "You are a bruja. You are a warrior. You are a feminist" (Rivera 2019, 302).

The third defining event that I mentioned is Juliet's coming out to her mother Mariana, a crucial moment in most queer comings-of-age. Her coming out is dragged out through the novel. First, Juliet blurts it out when her family is pressuring "boy talk" on her before leaving for Portland. At first, Titi Wepa brushes Juliet's confession off as a trick to keep undesirable boys away: "Ah, the dyke-n-dodge trick. I've used it many times. It's a classic" (25). Juliet's mother then asks: "Why don't you just tell them that you have a boyfriend," to which Juliet responds: "Why lie? I don't have a boyfriend. And I think I'm a lesbian" (25). The first few weeks after that, Juliet and her mother exchange silence. A few weeks later, when they finally speak to each other, Mariana insists "it's a phase" (74). Through a process unavailable to the readers, Mariana gives an indication that through conversations with her queer sister, Titi Penny, she has achieved a more understanding stance toward her daughter's queerness. And although it is not directly said, much like Little Dog's mother, who accepts him with a gesture of love rather than words, Mariana accepts her daughter when she tells her: "Listen, nena, I don't know what you're going through, but I want to try. I don't want us to be a mom and a daughter who don't talk and all they do is fight I cannot do that with you, my Juliet" (270). Finally, in growing not only *up* but also *away* from both her mother and Harlowe, Juliet ends up finding her own voice and, much like Little Dog, expresses her intention to become a writer: "I felt bold and ready to write down my story" (203).

Conclusion

Unlike the novels in previous chapters, these novels open the possibility of connections and solidarity between diasporic communities with different national origins. In *On Earth*, the experience of diaspora underscores the similarities between diasporic peoples, a sense of unity that is echoed in *Juliet Takes A Breath*. In her final letter, Juliet writes: "Surround yourself with other beautiful brown and black and indigenous and Morena and Chicana, Native, Indian, mixed race, Asian, gringa, boriqua babes" (Rivera 2019, 302). These novels understand diaspora thus as a process that bridges peoples not only from diasporic communities and host societies, but across diasporas.

In diminishing the barriers between single-nation diaspora, the novels also introduce a new striking characteristic to the genre: They both ponder on the themes of migration and coloniality in an explicit way that shows a profound, and at times academic, understanding of the concepts. These novels cannot claim to be naïve of the diasporic literary history that came before them. They certainly are not, as Juliet discusses coloniality and "banana republics" with her cousin and Little Dog analyzes migration with the extended metaphor of monarch butterflies.

Juliet first finds the concept of banana republics in her reading of Howard Zinn's *A People's History of the United States* (1980). In it, she finds the hidden history of Latin America, ransacked by the United Fruit Company "in the name of bananas and coffee and other natural resources. Fuck, just when you thought the US couldn't be any more brutal" (Rivera 2019, 138). Juliet, disappointed that her girlfriend-at-the-time does not want to engage in the brutal parts of U.S. colonialism, turns to her cousin. Ava tells Juliet of Lolita Lebrón, "only the illest Puerto Rican freedom fighter nacionalista. She, like, tried to blow up Congress in the fifties" (149). This introduction to the history of Puerto Rico ignites in Juliet a voracious curiosity not for her own family's diasporic history, but for the history of her people. Juliet concludes her research with vital rhetorical questions that show how important history has become to her understanding of her social environment:

> How did I not know this history? How could I walk around my block with a boricua bandanna wrapped around my head or march down Fifth Avenue next to the Goya float in the Puerto Rican Day Parade but

not have even one clue that people were imprisoned and killed because they rallied against the US occupation of Puerto Rico?

(Rivera 2019, 153)

Little Dog reflects on the migration of monarch butterflies throughout the novel, finding symbolic similarities between their migration and that of his family. Little Dog explains that, in the case of the butterflies,

> Migration can be triggered by the angle of sunlight, indicating a change in season, temperature, plant life, and food supply. Female monarchs lay eggs along the route. Every history has more than one thread, each thread a story of division. The journey takes four thousand eight hundred and thirty miles, more than the length of this country. The monarchs that fly south will not make it back north. Each departure, then, is final. Only their children return; only the future revisits the past.

(Vuong 2019, 8)

For Little Dog, the lived experience of migration changes the people who undergo it irremediably. Interestingly in his metaphor, it is the children of diaspora who have the chance to revisit the past, to go back into history, either familiar or national, and understand it fully and complexly, the way Juliet does once she has started to read and explore her diaspora.

These novels show the evolution of the Diasporic Coming-of-age Novel into a narrative genre profoundly aware of itself. The characters interact and discuss, in obvert and subtle ways, their connection to the works that came before them. In doing so, they represent a marker of maturity for the genre itself, which will, nonetheless, continue to offer itself as a laboratory for identity, for children to puzzle over who they are and how they fit into their globalized societies.

As it always has, the coming-of-age genre will continue to grow and transform, to represent the formative processes of people in both the mainstream and importantly in the margins of an increasingly comingled world. Readers of the genre who are outcasts themselves, or adults who are socially marginalized due to their sexuality, race, gender, national background, ability, or any of the other numerous identity markers that intersect in a single subjectivity, will continue to find refuge from injustice and companionship in the heroes of coming-of-age novels. Because these novels do not provide one definite or perfect way to be an adult, they enable complex and intersectional understandings of identities. The coming-of-age genre is more varied than ever and, more than ever, its readership is as complex as the characters it portrays. As the genre continues to evolve to represent more liminal and varied formative processes, diverse readers will continue to find what this genre has always meant for many, including me, the best antidote to despair.

Note

1 Nancy McHugh defines second-wave feminism as "The feminist movement, sometimes called the 'Women's Movement', that began in the late 1960s. In the US it was influenced by the strategies and tactics of the Civil Rights movement and in the UK by the labour rights movement. The phrase 'the personal is the political' became a rallying cry in the movement to argue for such things as the right to an abortion and equal pay for equal work. Furthermore 'the personal is the political' made clear that domesticity, marriage and gender norms were political, reflecting social values that were made to appear to be biological givens." McHugh further explains that the critiques of second-wave feminism "have noted its largely heterosexual, middle-class and white focus. Especially in the US movement, feminists were not especially concerned with working-class labour issues. In both the US and UK feminists frequently treated the concerns of Black women and lesbians as divisive to the movement instead of an important rallying point" (McHugh 2007).

References

Abbott, Porter. *The Cambridge Introduction to Narrative*. Cambridge UP, 2008.

Achebe, Chinua. *Things Fall Apart*. Anchor Canada, 2009.

Althusser, Louis. *On the Reproduction of Capitalism: Ideology and Ideological State Apparatuses*. Trans. G. M. Goshgarian. Verso, 2014.

AfD (Alternative für Deutschland AfD). "Manifesto for Germany." AFD, 2016. https://www.afd.de/wp-content/uploads/sites/111/2017/04/2017-04-12_afd-grundsatzprogramm-englisch_web.pdf.

Alvarez, Julia. *In the Time of the Butterflies*. Penguin Group, 1994.

Anaya, Rudolfo. *Bless Me, Ultima*. Grand Central Publishing, 1972.

Anzaldúa, Gloria. *Borderlands La Frontera*. Aunt Lute, 2007.

Arenas, Reinaldo. *Antes Que Anochezca: Autobiograía*. Tusquets, 2003.

Ashcroft, Bill. *Post-Colonial Studies: The Key Concepts*. Routledge, 2007.

Austen, Jane. *Pride and Prejudice*. Wisehouse Classics, 2016.

Bakhtin, Mikhail. *Speech Genres and Other Late Essays*. Trans. Vern W. McGee. U of Texas P, 1986.

Bellamy, Richard. *Citizenship: A Very Short Introduction*. Oxford UP, 2008.

Bejel, Emilio. "'Antes Que Anochezca': Autobiografía De Un Disidente Cubano Homosexual." *Hispamérica*, vol. 25, no. 74, 1996, pp. 29–45. *JSTOR*, JSTOR, www.jstor.org/stable/20539913.

Benitez-Rojo, Antonio. *The Repeating Island: The Caribbean and Post-Modern Perspective*. Duke UP, 1992. p. 3.

Beverley, John. "Anatomía Del Testimonio." *Revista De Crítica Literaria Latinoamericana*, vol. 13, no. 25, 1987, pp. 7–16. *JSTOR*, JSTOR, www.jstor.org/stable/4530303.

Betz, Regina. "Chicana 'Belonging' in Sandra Cisneros' The House on Mango Street." *Rocky Mountain Review*, vol. 66, no. 2, 2012, pp. 18–33.

Buckley, Jerome. *Season of Youth: The Bildungsroman from Dickens to Golding*. Cambridge UP, 1974.

Bulosan, Carlos. *America Is in the Heart: A Personal History*. U of Washington P, 2014.

Cacho, Lisa Marie. *Social Death: Racialized Rightlessness and the Criminalization of the Unprotected*. New York UP, 2012. ProQuest Ebook Central, http://ebookcentral.proquest.com/lib/purdue/detail.action?docID=1051351.

Chase, Jefferson. "AfD: What you need to know about Germany's far-right party." *Deutsche Welle*, September 24, 2017, https://p.dw.com/p/2W7YF.

Cheesman, Tom. *Novels of Turkish German Settlement*. Camden House, 2007.

Chin, Rita. *The Guest Worker Question in Postwar Germany*. Cambridge UP, 2009.

Christopher, Renny. *The Viet Nam War/The American War*. U of Massachusetts P, 1995.

Cisneros, Sandra. *A House of My Own*. Alfred A. Knopf, 2015.

Cisneros, Sandra. *The House on Mango Street*. Vintage Contemporaries, 1984.

Cruz-Malavé, Arnaldo. "The antifoundational foundational fiction of Piri Thomas." *Centro Journal*, vol. 24, no. 1, 2012, pp. 4–19. https://search-proquest-com.ezp roxy.lib.purdue.edu/docview/1032973881?accountid=13360.

Dabney, Ross. *Love and Property in the Novels of Dickens*. U of California P, 1967.

Deleuze, Gilles and Felix Guattari. *Kafka: Toward a Minor Literature*. U of Minnesota P, 1986.

Deutscher Bundestag. "Sitzverteilung im 19. Deutschen Bundestag." *Parlament*. October 22, 2019, https://www.bundestag.de/parlament/plenum/sitzverteilung_19wp.

Díaz, Junot. *The Brief and Wondrous Life of Oscar Wao*. Riverhead Books, 2007.

Dickens, Charles. *Oliver Twist*. Oxford UP, 1999.

Dickens, Charles. *David Copperfield*. Oxford UP, 1981.

Dickens, Charles. *Great Expectations*. Oxford UP, 1973.

Dye, Ellis. "*Wilhelm Meister* and *Hamlet*, Identity and Difference." *Goethe Year-book*, vol. 6 no. 1, 1992, pp. 67–85. Project MUSE, doi:10.1353/gyr.2011.0254.

Eigler, Friederike. "Wer hat 'Wilhelm Schüler' zum 'Wilhelm Meister' gebildet?: Wilhelm Meisters Lehrjahre und die Aussparungen einer hermeneutischen Verstehens- und Bildungspraxis." [Who formed Wilhelm Schüler into a Wilhelm Meister?: Wilhelm Meister's Apprenticeship and the Recesses of a Hermeneutic Understanding and Educational Practice]. *Goethe Yearbook*, vol. 3, 1986, pp. 93–119.

Eschenbach, Wolfram von. *Parzival*. Ed. Karl Lachmann. Walter de Gruyter & Co., 1965.

Eurostat. "Asylum and first time asylum applicants by citizenship, age and sex Annual aggregated data." *Eurostat*. May 15, 2019, https://ec.europa.eu/eurostat/en/web/products-datasets/-/MIGR_ASYAPPCTZA.

Farley, Christopher John. "That Old Black Magic." *Time*, vol. 156, no. 22, November 2000, p. 14. *EBSCOhost*,search.ebscohost.com/login.aspx?direct=true&db=f5h &AN=3787418&site=ehost-live.

Feng, Pin-chia. *The Female Bildungsroman*. Peter Lang, 2000.

Fernández Vázquez, José Santiago. *Reescrituras postcoloniales del Bildungsroman*. Verbum, 2003.

Fernández, Johanna. *The Young Lords: A Radical History*. U of North Carolina P, 2020. Project MUSE, muse.jhu.edu/book/72262.

Fielding, Heather. "Assimilation After Empire: Marina Lewycka, Paul Gilroy, and the Ethnic *Bildungsroman* in Contemporary Britain." *Studies in the Novel*, vol. 43, no. 2, 2011, pp. 200–217.

Flaubert, Gustave. *L'Éducation sentimentale*. Gallimard, 2005.

Flotow, Louise von. "Preface." *Fremde Discourse on the Foreign*. Ed. Gino Chiellino. Guernica, 1995.

Forster, E. M. *Maurice*. Norton, 1987.

Forster, John. *The Life of Charles Dickens*. James R. Osgood & Company, 1875.

Garland Mahler, Anne. "The 'Colored and Oppressed' in Amerikkka: Trans-Affective Solidarity in Writing by Young Lords and Nuyoricans." *From the Tricontinental to the Global South: Race, Radicalism, and Transsnational Solidarity.* Duke UP, 2018, pp. 106–159.

Gilroy, Paul. *Postcolonial Melancholia.* Columbia UP, 2005.

Goethe, Johann Wolfgang von. *Wilhelm Meisters Lehrjahre. Goethes Werke,* Müncher Ausgabe, vol. 5, Carl Hanser Verlag GmbH & Co., 1985a.

Goethe, Johann Wolfgang von. *Wilhelm Meisters Wanderjahre. Goethes Werke,* Müncher Ausgabe, vol. 17, Carl Hanser Verlag GmbH & Co., 1985b.

Gold, Joseph. *Charles Dickens: Radical Moralist.* U of Minnesota P, 1972.

Gonzalez, Juan. *Harvest of Empire.* Penguin Books, 2011.

Guidotti-Hernández, Nicole. *Unspeakable Violence.* Duke UP, 2011.

Gustafson, Susan E. *Goethe's Families of the Heart.* Bloomsbury, 2016.

Hall, Stuart. "Cultural Identity and Cinematic Representation." *Framework: The Journal of Cinema and Media,* no. 36, 1989, pp. 68–81. *JSTOR,* www.jstor.org/stable/44111666.

Hamid, Mohsin. *The Reluctant Fundamentalist.* Harcourt, 2008.

Hansen, Randall. *Citizenship and Immigration in Postwar Britain.* Oxford UP, 2000.

Herder, Johann Gottfried von. *Herder: Philosophical Writings,* edited by Michael N. Forster, Cambridge UP, 2002. ProQuest Ebook Central, https://ebookcentral.pro quest.com/lib/purdue/detail.action?docID=201704.

Herrera, Yuri. *Señales que precederán al fin del mundo.* Periférica, 2010.

Herrndorf, Wolfgang. *tschick.* Rowohlt, 2012.

Herrndorf, Wolfgang. *Why We Took the Car.* Trans. Tim Mohr. Arthur A. Levine Books, 2014.

Hesse, Herman. *Demian: Die Geschichte von Emil Sinclairs Jugend.* S. Fischer, Verlag, 1921.

Hosseini, Khaled. *The Kite Runner.* Riverhead Books, 2003.

Houston, Gail Turley. *Consuming Fictions: Gender, Class, and Hunger in Dickens's Novels.* Southern Illinois UP, 1994.

Howe, Susanne. *Wilhelm Meister and His English Kinsmen: Apprentices to Life.* Columbia UP, 1930.

Irvine, Robert. *Jane Austen.* Routledge, 2005.

Iversen, Anniken Telnes. *Change and Continuity: The Bildungsroman in English.* Dissertation, University of Tromsø, 2009.

Jeffers, Thomas L. *Apprenticeships: The Bildungsroman from Goethe to Santayana.* Palgrave Macmillan, 2005.

Johnson, Claudia. *Jane Austen: Women Politics and the Novel.* U of Chicago P, 1988.

Jost, François. "Variations of a Species: The *Bildungsroman.*" *Symposium: A Quarterly Journal in Modern Literatures,* vol. 37, no. 2, 1983, pp. 125–146.

Joyce, James. *A Portrait of the Artist as a Young Man.* Penguin Modern Classics, 1975.

Kalra, Virinder, et al. *Diaspora and Hybridity.* Theory, Culture & Society Series. Sage, 2005.

Kant, Immanuel. "Beantwortung der Frage: Was ist Aufklärung?" *Spiegel.* 1784. https://gutenberg.spiegel.de/buch/beantwortung-der-frage-was-ist-aufklarung-3505/1.

Kara, Yade. *Selam Berlin.* Diogenes Verlag, 2003.

Katzenstein, Peter J. *Policy and Politics in West Germany: The Growth of a Semi-sovereign State.* Temple UP, 1987.

Kipling, Rudyard. "The White Man's Burden, 1899." *Modern History Sourcebook.* Fordham University, 2019. http://www.fordham.edu/halsall/mod/Kipling.html.

Klusmeyer, Douglas B. and Demetrios G.Papademetriou. "Immigration Policy in the Federal Republic of Germany: Negotiating Membership and Remaking the Nation." NED – New edition, 1st ed., Berghahn Books, 2009. *JSTOR*, www.jstor.org/stable/j.ctt9qcrnk.

Kureishi, Hanif. *The Buddha of Suburbia.* Penguin Books, 1991.

Kushigian, Julia Alexis. *Reconstructing Childhood: Strategies of Reading for Culture and Gender in the Spanish American Bildungsroman.* Bucknell UP, 2003.

La Jaula de Oro. Directed by Diego-Quemada Díez. Animal de Luz Films, Kinemascope Films, Machete Producciones, 2013.

Lazarus, Emma. "The New Colossus." Poetry Foundation. https://www.poetryfoundation.org/poems/46550/the-new-colossus.

LeClair, Thomas. "The Language Must Not Sweat." *New Republic.* March 21, 1981. https://newrepublic.com/article/95923/the-language-must-not-sweat.

Lee, Chang-Rae. *Native Speaker.* Riverhead Books, 1995.

Leibniz, G. W. *The Principles of Philosophy known as Monadology. Early Modern Texts.* Ed. Jonathan Bennett. www.earlymoderntexts.com,2007.

Luibhéid, Eithne. "Introduction: Queering Migration and Citizenship." *Queer Migrations: Sexuality, U.S. Citizenship, and Border Crossings.* U of Minnesota P, 2005.

Luiselli, Valeria. *Tell Me How It Ends: An Essay in Forty Questions.* Coffee House Press, 2017.

Mani, B. Venkat. "Phantom of the 'Gastarbeiterliteratur.'" *Migration und Interkulturalität in neueren literarischen Texten.* Ed. Aglaia Blioumi. Ludicium, 2002. pp. 112–129.

McHugh, Nancy. "Second Wave Feminism." *Feminist Philosophies A-Z,* Edinburgh UP, 2007.

Medalie, David. "The Line of *Maurice*: Forster, Hollinghurst and the 'Social Fabric.'" *English Studies in Africa.* vol. 60, no. 1, 2017, pp. 46–59.

Meisel, Martin. "The Ending of Great Expectations." *Essays in Criticism,* vol. XV, no. 3, 1965, pp. 326–331.

Mignolo, Walter. *The Darker Side of Western Modernity.* Duke UP, 2011.

Mileck, Joseph. "Names and the Creative Process: A Study of the Names in Hermann Hesse's 'Lauscher," 'Demian," 'Steppenwolf," and 'Glasperlenspiel.'" *Monatshefte,* vol. 53, no. 4, 1961, pp. 167–180. JSTOR, www.jstor.org/stable/30161813.

Mora, Vicente Luis. "La identidad migrante y su reflejo literario en libros sobre inmigración en los Estados Unidos." *Impossibilia,* no. 2,2011, pp. 48–62.

Morarasu, Nadia Nicoleta. "Challenges in Translating Proper Names from Dickensian Novels." *Translation Studies: Retrospective and Prospective Views,* Editura Fundaţiei Universitare, 2007, pp. 97–110.

Moretti, Franco. *The Way of the World: The Bildungsroman in European Culture.* Verso, 2000.

Morgenstern, Karl. *Über das Wesen des Bildungsromans.* [On the Nature of the Bildungsroman] Inländisches Museum. Hrgs. v. C. E. Raupach. Bd. 1, H. 2. Dorpat, 1820.

Morrison, Toni. *The Bluest Eye.* Pan Books, 1990.

Nguyen, Viet Thanh. "I Love America. That's Why I Have to Tell the Truth About It." *Time*. November 25, 2018. https://time.com/5455490/american-like-me/.

Novalis. *Heinrich von Ofterdingen*. Goldmanns Gelbe Taschenbücher, 1964.

Olsen, Tillie. *Yonnondio: From the Thirties*. Delta/Seymour Lawrence, 1979.

Ortíz, Ricardo L. "Diaspora." *Keywords for latina/o studies*. Eds. D. R. Vargas, L. La Fountain-Stokes, & N. R. Mirabal. New York UP, 2017.

Pacheco, José Emilio. *Las Batallas en el Desierto*. Era, 1981.

Pimentel, Luz Aurora. *El espacio en la ficción*. Siglo XXI, 2001.

Pirholt, Mattias. "Imitation and Simulation: Novalis's Heinrich Von Ofterdingen." *Metamimesis: Imitation in Goethe's "Wilhelm Meisters Lehrjahre" and Early German Romanticism*, vol. 124, Boydell and Brewer, 2012, pp. 114–154. JSTOR, www.jstor.org/stable/10.7722/j.ctt1x730r.9.

Pirholt, Mattias. "A Symbolic-Mystic Monstrosity: Ideology and Representation in Goethe's *Wilhelm Meisters Lehrjahre*." *Goethe Yearbook*, vol. 16, 2009, pp. 69–100.

Powell, Enoch. "Enoch Powell's 'Rivers of Blood' speech." *The Telegraph*, 2007, http://www.telegraph.co.uk/comment/3643823/Enoch-Powells-Rivers-of-Blood-speech.html.

Pratt, Mary Louise. "Arts of the Contact Zone." *Profession*, 1991, pp. 33–40. *JSTOR*, JSTOR, www.jstor.org/stable/25595469.

Rigoni, Isabelle. "Intersectionality and Mediated Cultural Production in a Globalized Post-Colonial World." *Ethnic and Racial Studies*, vol. 35, no. 5, 2012, pp. 834–849.

Rivera, Gabby. *Juliet Takes a Breath*. Dial Books, 2019.

Rowling, J. K. *Harry Potter and the Sorcerer's Stone*. Scholastic, 1998.

Sagel, Jim. "Sandra Cisneros: Conveying the Riches of the Latin American Culture Is the Author's Literary Goal." *Publishers Weekly*, vol. 238, no. 15, 1991, p. 74.

Saldívar, José David. *Border Matters: Remapping American Cultural Studies*. U of California P, 1997.

Saldívar-Hull, Sonia. *Feminism on the Border: Chicana Gender Politics and Literature*. U of California P, 2000.

Salmerón, Miguel. *La novela de formación y peripecia*. A. Machado Libros, 2002.

Sánchez Becerril Ivonne. "México nómada: Señales que precederán al fin del mundo de Yuri Herrera, y Efectos secundarios de Rosa Beltrán." *Escrituras Plurales: Migraciones en espacios y tiempos literarios*. Ed. Silvana Serafin. La Toletta Edizioni, 2014. pp. 107–121.

Sánchez González, Lisa. *Boricua Literature: A Literary History of the Puerto Rican Diaspora*. New York UP, 2001.

Satrapi, Marjane. *The Complete Persepolis*. Pantheon Books, 2007.

Scott, Sir Walter. "Emma." *Quarterly Review*, vol. 14, 1815.

Sedgwick, Eve Kosofsky. *Epistemology of the Closet*. U of California P, 1990.

Shakespeare, William. *Hamlet*. Edited by Martin Puchner et al., The Norton Anthology of World Literature, vol. 3, Norton, 2012.

Shaw, George Bernard, *Introduction to Bloom's Modern Critical Views: Charles Dickens*. Ed. Harold Bloom. Chelsea House, 2006, pp. 59–70.

Sin Nombre. Directed by Cary Joji Fukunaga. Primary Productions, Canana Films, Creando Films, 2009.

Sinclair, Upton. *The Jungle*. W.W. Norton & Company, 2003.

Smith, Zadie. *White Teeth*. Vintage International, 2001.

Straßburg, Gottfried von. *Die Geschichte der Liebe von Tristan und Isolde*. Ed. Gottfried Weber. Wissenschaftliche Buchgesellschaft Darmstadt, 1983.

Sutherland, Kathryn. "Chronology of composition and publication". *Jane Austen in Context*. Ed. Janet Todd. Cambridge UP, 2005.

Swaine, Jon. "Margaret Thatcher complained about Asian Immigration to Britain." *The Telegraph*. December 30, 2009, http://www.telegraph.co.uk/news/politics/margaret-thatcher/6906503/Margaret-Thatcher-complained-about-Asian-immigration-to-Britain.html.

Thomas, Piri. *Down These Mean Streets*. New American Library, 1968.

Tieck, Ludwig. *Der Runenberg: Eine Erzählung*. *Frühromantische Erzählungen*, Zweiter Band. Ed. Paul Kluckhohn. Phillip Reclam, 1933.

Triadafilopoulos, Triadafilos. *Becoming Multicultural: Immigration and the Politics of Membership in Canada and Germany*. UBC Press, 2013.

Triadafilopoulos, Triadafilos, and Karen Schönwälder. "How the Federal Republic Became an Immigration Country: Norms, Politics and the Failure of West Germany's Guest Worker System." *German Politics & Society*, vol. 24, no. 3 (80), 2006, pp. 1–19, www.jstor.org/stable/23742736.

Trump, Donald. "Presidential Announcement Speech." *TIME*, June 16, 2015. http://time.com/3923128/donald-trump-announcement-speech/.

United Nations. "United Nations Department of Economic and Social Affairs, Population Division." *UN*. December 2015, https://www.un.org/en/development/desa/population/migration/publications/populationfacts/docs/MigrationPopFacts 20154.pdf.

Vlasta, Sandra. *Contemporary Migration in Literature in German and English: A Comparative Study*. Internationale Forschungen zur Allgemeinen und Vergleichenden Literaturwissenschaft Series. Brill Rodopi, 2016.

Vuong, Ocean. *On Earth We're Briefly Gorgeous*. Penguin Press, 2019.

Wang, Chih-ming, "Politics of Return: Homecoming Stories of the Vietnamese Diaspora." *Positions: Asia Critique*, vol. 21, no. 1, winter 2013, pp. 161–187.

Watt, Ian. *The Rise of the Novel*. U of California P, 2001.

Weedon, Chris. *Identity and Culture: Narratives of Difference and Belonging*. Open UP, 2004.

Whalen, Carmen Teresa and Víctor Vázquez-Hernández. *The Puerto Rican Diaspora: Historical Perspectives*. Temple UP, 2005.

Yúdice, George. "Testimonio y Concientización." *Revista De Crítica Literaria Latinoamericana*, vol. 18, no. 36, 1992, pp. 211–232. *JSTOR*, JSTOR, www.jstor.org/stable/4530631.

Zarka, Yves Charles. "First Philosophy and the Foundation of Knowledge." *The Cambridge Companion to Hobbes*. Ed. Tom Sorell. Cambridge UP, 1996.

Zinn, Howard. *A People's History of the United States*. Harper Perennial, 1999.

Index

Printed in the United States
By Bookmasters